S0-AVH-829

THE DEVILS AND EVIL SPIRITS OF BABYLONIA.

VOL. I

AMS PRESS
NEW YORK

PLATE I.

Part of the tablet supposed to contain a mention of the Babylonian Garden of Eden (K. 111).

THE

DEVILS AND EVIL SPIRITS

OF

BABYLONIA,

BEING BABYLONIAN AND ASSYRIAN INCANTATIONS AGAINST THE DEMONS, GHOULS, VAMPIRES, HOBGOBLINS, GHOSTS, AND KINDRED EVIL SPIRITS, WHICH ATTACK MANKIND.

TRANSLATED FROM THE ORIGINAL CUNEIFORM TEXTS, WITH TRANSLITERATIONS, VOCABULARY, NOTES, ETC.

BY

R. CAMPBELL THOMPSON, M.A.

ASSISTANT IN THE DEPARTMENT OF EGYPTIAN AND ASSYRIAN ANTIQUITIES, BRITISH MUSEUM.

VOL. I.

"*EVIL SPIRITS.*"

London:

LUZAC AND CO

1903.

Library of Congress Cataloging in Publication Data

Thompson, Reginald Campbell, 1876-1941, tr.
The devils and evil spirits of Babylonia.

Reprint of the 1903-04 ed. published by Luzac, London, which was issued as v. 14-15 of Luzac's Semitic text and translation series.
CONTENTS: v. 1. Evil spirits.—v. 2. Fever sickness and headache.
1. Incantations, Assyro-Babylonian. 2. Assyro-Babylonian language—Texts. 3. Demonology, Assyro-Babylonian. I. Title. II. Series: Luzac's Semitic text and translation series; v. 14-15.
PJ3791.T5 1976 133.4'27 73-18855
ISBN 0-404-11353-2

Reprinted from an original copy in the collections of the Cleveland Public Library

From the edition of 1903, London
First AMS edition published in 1976
Manufactured in the United States of America

International Standard Book Number:
Complete Set: 0-404-11353-2
Volume I: 0-404-11354-0

AMS PRESS INC.
NEW YORK, N. Y. 10003

133,427
T377d
v.1

L.I.F.E. College Library
1100 Glendale Blvd.
Los Angeles, Calif. 90026

TO MY FATHER,

REGINALD E. THOMPSON, M.D.

030800

Preface.

The object of the two volumes which form the present work is to supply the student of Assyrian Demonology with English transliterations and translations, with the necessary notes, etc., of the documents printed in the Sixteenth and Seventeenth Parts of *Cuneiform Texts from Babylonian Tablets, etc.*, which have been recently issued by the Trustees of the British Museum. An examination of these two Parts will show that they contain copies of all the Tablets belonging to the Series Utukki Limnûti, Asakki Marsûti, and Ṭi'i, i.e., "Evil Spirits," "Fever Sickness," and "Headache," which have now been identified, together with the texts of a considerable number of compositions of a similar character.

These collections of Evil Spirit Texts form large and important sections of the native literature concerning Babylonian and Assyrian Demonology, and there is reason to believe that the material now published represents about one-half of that belonging to the three Series mentioned above which was known to the scribes of Aššurbanipal. Of the condition of the archetypes in pre-Babylonian times we have no information whatever, but there is no reason to doubt that the versions which were adopted as standard texts in the reign of Aššurbanipal represented substantially the readings of the primitive documents. We are, in short, justified in assuming that we have in our hands at the present time tolerably accurate copies of the exorcisms and spells which the Sumerian and his Babylonian successor employed, some six or seven thousand years ago, to avert the attacks of devils, and to ward off malign influences of every kind.

The first to make known to the world the character of the Evil Spirit Texts was the late General H. C. Rawlinson, Bart., G.C.B., who published in the Fourth Volume of the *Cuneiform Inscriptions of Western Asia*, London, 1875, as much of the text of the Fifth and Sixteenth Tablets as had then been identified. During the period of the preparation of the seventy plates which form the Fourth Volume printed copies of many of them were supplied to M. François Lenormant, and to various other scholars, and M. Lenormant issued some months before the appearance of the British Museum publication his *La Magie chez les Chaldéennes et les Origines Accadiennes*, in which he gave renderings of several of the texts relating to Evil Spirits. In the year 1887 Professor Sayce, in his *Hibbert Lectures*, gave English translations of the greater number of the texts with which M. Lenormant had already dealt, as well as of others. The translations, however, of both these scholars were necessarily incomplete, for the simple reason that only a portion of the available material had been published by the late Sir Henry Rawlinson, who made no pretence of publishing in his immortal Corpus of cuneiform texts more than specimens of the various classes of literature which were known to the Babylonians and Assyrians. Subsequently several of the texts of this class have been studied and referred to in the publications of various Assyriologists, but the present work represents the first attempt which has been made to deal with any of the groups of the Evil Spirit Texts as a whole, and of course no connected translations of them have before appeared.

In this and the following volume of Messrs. Luzac's "Semitic Text and Translation Series" transliterations and translations of about two hundred and forty tablets and fragments belonging to various collections in the British Museum are given, and it is believed that about one hundred and sixty of these are published in *Cuneiform Texts from Babylonian Tablets, etc.*, Parts XVI and XVII, for the first time. The present publication is intended to do for the "Evil Spirit" Series, and the Series relating to Fevers and Headaches, what Professor Zimmern has done for the *Shurpu* Series, and Professor Tallqvist for the *Maḳlu* Series.

The reader's attention is called to the fact that where it has been impossible to assign to Tablets their correct position in their Series, they have been indicated by the letters "A," "B," "C," etc. In translating the texts the renderings into English have been made as literal as possible, and wherever possible the Assyrian word has been translated by the same English equivalent.

The material given in the following pages will be found to afford abundant proof of the fact that a considerable proportion of the magical practices which are in use in the East to the present day were well known to the inhabitants of Mesopotamia several thousands of years ago, and that many of them were borrowed by the Hebrews and other dwellers in Syria and Persia from their neighbours on the Tigris and Euphrates.

As was to be expected, a number of misconceptions have arisen during the last few years as to the purport of certain magical texts, and as an example of this may be specially mentioned the views which have been promulgated concerning Tablet "K," (ll. 183 ff.), for it has been confidently asserted that this document contains an allusion to the Biblical Garden of Eden. The text of this tablet mentions a place called Eridu, and a plant or tree named *kiškanû*, of dense growth and shining appearance, which grew beside the abyss, i.e. the Ocean or Sea; the place where the plant grew was said to be the couch of a god. Immediately following these statements is a reference to Shamash and Tammuz, who are said to dwell "in its interior," and mention is next made of the "mouths of the rivers." Such are the statements of the tablet, but basing their opinion on certain interpretations of the above text, some Assyriologists have asserted that the Babylonian Garden of Eden was in the immediate vicinity of Eridu, and they have identified the tree or plant with the Tree of the Knowledge of Good and Evil, which was believed to grow in the Hebrew Paradise. Quite recently, however, the missing portion of this text has been identified, and it is now clear that the text is an incantation and nothing more. This document, the opening lines of which have been so strangely misunderstood, indicated to the magician, who was about to treat his afflicted patient, that a certain kind of plant or tree, the original of which, according to tradition, grew in Eridu, and afforded a dwelling to Shamash and Tammuz, contained magical properties; and acting on this information the magician was directed to make use of a portion of the *kiškanû* plant or tree on behalf of the said patient. The text actually states that the gods themselves made use of this plant to work a miracle of healing, and the implication is that as the *kiškanû* plant was on this occasion of great benefit, it may again be made to perform the healing of a sufferer, always provided that suitable Words of Power were recited by a duly qualified person, and appropriate ceremonies were performed, before the plant itself was used as a remedy. Thus there is no reason for believing that the text of Tablet "K" contains any allusion to the Garden of Eden, or that the plant *kiškanû* is anything more than a herb or shrub which was used in working magic. Further, the identification of the *kiškanû* plant with the "vine" has nothing to rest upon, and still less does it in any way represent the Babylonian equivalent of the Tree of Life. "The mouths of the rivers" have nothing to do with the four rivers of the Hebrew Paradise, and the new fragment leaves no room for doubt that the line in which they are mentioned merely explains the locality from which the gods obtained the plant, namely, from the confluence of two streams or rivers.

To Mr. L. W. King I owe many thanks for his friendly help in this work, and especially his assistance in reading doubtful signs on the clay tablets.

In conclusion, my thanks are due to Dr. E. A. Wallis Budge for much kind help, and for his numerous suggestions in such parts of the volume as deal with comparative magic.

R. Campbell Thompson.

London, June 1st, 1903.

NOTE.

Page 137, l. 75. The meaning of the word *itti*, here translated "Wheatears," is doubtful. By an oversight the Sumerian equivalent was incorrectly given as "wheat" in the note.

LIST OF TABLETS.

SERIES UTUKKI LIMNÛTI.

TABLET III.—K. 224 + 2,378 : K. 8,262 : K. 9,314 : S. 715 and Rm. 541 (probably parts of the same tablet) : D.T. 271 : No. 35,611 : No. 38,594 (Part XVI, Plates 1–8) : S. 996 (Part XVI, Plate 50).

TABLET IV.—K. 2,355 + 3,212 and K. 4,892 + 4,938 and K. 4,857 + 4,887 and K. 5,123 (fragments of the same tablet): K. 5,020 + 5,129 + 81–7–27, 249 : K. 2,578 + 4,641 + 5,166 + 5,256 and K. 4,632 + 4,889 + 5,038 + 5,130 + D.T. 287 (fragments of the same tablet); K. 2,410 + 5,442 : K. 5,082 (Part XVI, Plates 9–11) : No. 45,744 (Part XVI, Plate 50) : No. 36,589 (Part XVII, Plate 46).

TABLET V.—K. 2,507 + 3,255 + S. 1,425 : K. 2,528 + D.T. 7 : K. 2,954 : K. 3,121 : K. 3,218 : K. 4,658 + 9,367 : K. 4,943 + 6,043 : K. 5,096 + 5,725 + 13,547 : K. 8,508 : K. 9,405 + 10,534 : K. 10,175 : K. 12,000, *k* : K. 12,000, *n* : K. 13,536 : No. 38,798 : No. 45,539 : No. 46,296 + 46,374 + 46,408 (Part XVI, Plates 12–16) : K. 12,921 : K. 14,219 (Part XVI, Plate 41).

TABLET X.—K. 4,947 (Part XVI, Plate 17) + K. 4,988 (Part XVII, Plate 49).

TABLET XV.—No. 47,736 (Part XVI, Plate 18).

TABLET XVI.—K. 2,406 and K. 9,390 (probably parts of the same tablet) : K. 2,968 : K. 2,977 + 3,116 : K. 3,122 : K. 4,627 + 8,810 : K. 4,870 : K. 4,904 + 5,294 + 5,363 : K. 5,156 + 5,220 : K. 5,238 : S. 1,448 : 81–2–4, 410, *b* : No. 33,712 : No. 34,106 : No. 36,690 (Part XVI, Plates 19–23) : No. 47,852 (Part XVII, Plates 47–48).

TABLET "A."—No. 55,473 : K. 4,965 (Part XVI, Plates 24–26) : No. 46,288 : K. 4,856 (Part XVII, Plate 3). This tablet precedes Tablet "B."

Tablet "B."—K. 5,009 + 5,060 and K. 3,152 + 5,244, *a* + 83-1-18, 769 (parts of the same tablet) : K. 4,661 + 4,821 + 4,939 + 5,086 + 5,164 + 5,697 + 11,576 : K. 5,143 and K. 5,292 (parts of the same tablet) : K. 5,330 : No. 35,056 + 35,191 + 35,193 (Part XVI, Plates 27–29).

Tablet "C."—K. 2,435 : K. 2,470 and K. 5,290 + 8,059 (probably parts of the same tablet) : K. 4,863 + 13,311 and S. 69 (probably parts of the same tablet) : K. 4,955 + 11,116 + Rm. 269 : K. 4,970 : K. 5,079 + 12,030 : K. 5,251 : K. 8,475 + 12,040 : S. 793 (Part XVI, Plates 30–34) : K. 4,911 (+ 4,955, etc.) : K. 6,602 : K. 11,903 (Part XVI, Plate 41) : K. 4,917 : K. 8,476 : 81-2-4, 332 : No. 60,886 (Part XVII, Plate 46).

Tablet "D."—K. 4,871 : K. 5,005 (Part XVI, Plates 35–36).

Tablet "E."—K. 2,337 + 4,971 + 6,022 : K. 5,100 and Rm. 314 (probably parts of the same tablet) (Part XVI, Plate 37).

Tablet "F."—K. 3,054 (Part XVI, Plate 38).

Tablet "G."—K. 5,179 (Part XVI, Plate 39).

Tablets "H," "I," "J."—No. 52,456 : No. 38,447 : K. 4,825 (Part XVI, Plates 40–41) and small fragment K. 10,185 (Part XVI, Plate 41).

TABLET OF A SIMILAR SERIES.

Tablet "K."—K. 111 + 2,754 + 5,227 + 5,295 + 7,525 + 7,632 + 7,633 : K. 3,235 + 4,959 + 5,178 and K. 4,626 + 5,115 + 12,000, *aa* (probably parts of the same tablet) : K. 4,867 and K. 12,000, *bb* (probably parts of the same tablet) : K. 4,886 : K. 4,905 + D.T. 150 + Rm. 243 : K. 5,120 : K. 5,133 + 5,336 + 9,391 and K. 5,183 (parts of the same tablet) : K. 11,543 : No. 36,690 (reverse) : No. 55,479 + 55,548 and No. 55,608 (parts of the same tablet) (Plates 42–49).

Introduction.

Introduction.

FROM the earliest times Eastern races, in common with the rest of mankind, have always held a firm belief in the existence of evil spirits, ghosts, and all kindred powers. The phenomena of death, the mystery of disease and sickness, and all the other events of common occurrence in daily life gave rise to speculations about the unseen world, which gradually led to a distinction, although slight at all times, between good and evil spirits. The early Semitic people of Babylonia, whoever they may have been or wherever they may have migrated from, found a theology ready to their hands in their adopted country, which they took over from its primitive inhabitants the Sumerians, doubtless grafting to it many of the beliefs of their forefathers. To the latest times, down to a century or two before the Christian era, they retained the doctrines in their original language, making interlinear translations of them for use in the temples and among the doctors, and it is owing to this that we can speak with tolerable certainty on many points of the early religion of Babylonia.

There is little comparatively that shows traces of original Semitic composition in the books and documents relating to spirits, for by far the greater part of the enormous mass of material of this class is written in the Sumerian language, either with or without a Babylonian or Assyrian translation, and the numerous Sumerian words for the various forms of spirits and demons were either incorporated bodily in the newcomers' language, with, of course, the necessary phonetic changes, or were translated either exactly or paraphrastically. Indeed, it is a remarkable thing that that portion of the Semitic stock which entered Babylonia, although receptive on all points, seems to have been very limited in original ideas regarding the ghost world; and this is not unnatural, since at that early period the Semite can hardly have been much more than a nomad possessing only the beginnings of a civilization. He recognized "gods" (singular, ILU; plural, ILÂNI[1]) in common with the rest of his stock; he seems to have had some idea that the soul or EKIMMU, literally "the thing which is snatched away,"[2] possessed supernatural powers, or at least an existence; but beyond this it is exceedingly difficult to say how much of his later psychology and eschatology was original, and how much was borrowed. This much seems certain,

[1] The original meaning of ILU, like the Hebrew אֵל, is of course unknown. The Sumerians indicated the word "god" by a star (✳), and we are therefore justified in assuming that the Sumerians believed that their gods inhabited the sky.

[2] The form *ekimmu* is distinctly against the view that it means "the snatcher," which would probably be *ikkimu*.

however, that words like UTUKKU "spirit," ALÛ "demon," LILÛ some form of ghost with feminine counterparts LILÎTU and ARDAT LILÎ, and probably GALLÛ "devil," were all borrowed from the Sumerians, and the names of two others, RABIṢU "lurker" and AḪḪAZU "seizer," are probably free renderings of Sumerian words for which the Babylonian had no exact equivalents. All these words occur in set phrases constantly in the incantations, and of the other names for spirits we find the following list: ILU, EKIMMU, ŠÊDU, LABARTU, LABAṢU, and LAMASSU; of these the first two have already been explained, but of the linguistic origin of the remainder very little is known. Indeed, among the other Semitic tribes, with the exception of the Arabs, the comparative paucity of words signifying demons is very marked, and most of the few which they employ are borrowed directly from Babylonia, the Hebrews using שֵׁאדִים (i.e., ŠÊDU) and לִילִית (i.e., LILÎTU), and in Rabbinic times שאדין and לילין (i.e., LILÛ). רוח, which is another word used by the Rabbis to mean "spirit," is the ordinary word in Hebrew for this, and corresponds to EKIMMU.

It is therefore evident that when the Semitic Babylonian took over the learning of his Sumerian predecessors, he seems also to have unconsciously adapted and enlarged his ideas to fit their beliefs, receiving their doctrines in their entirety as worthy of implicit trust, and in the belief that his teachers must necessarily understand the supernatural powers peculiar to their own country.

(1) The various Classes of Evil Spirits.

The primitive Sumerian recognized three distinct classes of evil spirit, all ready to torment the hapless wanderer.[1] First came the disembodied human soul which could find no rest, and so wandered up and down the face of the earth; secondly, the gruesome spirits which were half human and half demon; and thirdly, the fiends and devils who were of the same nature as the gods, who rode on the noxious winds, or brought storms and pestilence. Each of these three kinds was divided up into classes according to the several characteristics of the evil spirits which composed them, and the six chief of these are enumerated in the constantly recurring line UTUKKU LIMNU ALÛ LIMNU EKIMMU LIMNU GALLÛ LIMNU ILU LIMNU RABIṢU LIMNU, "Evil Spirit, evil Demon, evil Ghost, evil Devil, evil God, evil Fiend," but this by no means includes all the powers of evil, for this list is frequently amplified by the additions LABARTU LABAṢU AḪḪAZU LILÛ LILÎTU ARDAT LILÎ, all various forms of malignant spirits.

The first evil spirit, UTUKKU, was originally a spirit, spectre, or ghost, since it is once at least used of the

[1] For the special meaning of this word in magical texts, see *infra*, p. xxviii.

spectre of a dead man raised from the Underworld. This form of magic—necromancy—was a favourite method employed for looking into the future in the East in ancient times, and a remarkable instance of it occurs in the Epic of Gilgamish. The story runs that the hero Gilgamish appeals to the god Nergal to restore his friend Ea-bani to him, and his prayer is answered, for the god opens the earth and the UTUKKU of Ea-bani rises up "like the wind," that is, probably a transparent spectre in the human shape of Ea-bani, who converses with Gilgamish.[1] The same ideas and beliefs were current among the Hebrews, for when Saul goes to visit the "woman with a familiar spirit" at En-dor she brings up Samuel out of the earth, and he answers the questions which Saul wishes to ask.[2] Among the Assyrians "Raiser of the Departed Spirit"[3] was a recognized title of the sorcerer, and from this and the story in the Gilgamish Epic it is evident that such practices as necromancy were not uncommon. How far the UTUKKU differed from the EKIMMU (which is the proper word for a departed spirit) is difficult to say; it was a ghost or spectre that either lurked in the desert lying in wait for man,[4] or it might have its home

[1] L. W. King, *Babylonian Religion*, p. 75.

[2] 1 Sam., xxviii, 7.

[3] *W.A.I.*, ii, 51, 2, r. 20, 21.

[4] Tablet III, l. 28, p. 5.

in the mountains, sea, or graveyard,[1] and evil would befall him on whom it merely cast its eye.[2]

The second of the six, the ALÛ, is a demon that hides itself in dark corners and caverns in the rock, haunting ruins and deserted buildings and slinking through the streets at night like a pariah dog. It lies in wait for the unwary, ready to rush out from its hiding-place to "envelop him as with a garment," or, coming into the bedchamber by night, it steals sleep away from weary mortals by standing over their beds and threatening to pounce upon them should they dare to close their eyes.[3] It is a horrible apparition, at times without mouth, limbs, or ears, a half-human, half-devilish creation borne probably by the ghoulish LILÎTU or ARDAT LILÎ to some man to whom she has attached herself.[4] This latter tradition remained current long after Babylon had fallen, and it reappears in the Rabbinic stories which relate how Lilith bore to Adam demons and spirits.[5] The Rabbis were of opinion that a man might have children by allying himself with a demon,[6] and although they would naturally not be visible to human beings, yet when that man

[1] *W.A.I.*, ii, 17, i, 3, and Haupt, *Akkad. u. Sumer. Keilschr.*, p. 82, i, 3.

[2] Tablet "C," l. 179, p. 152.

[3] For these see Tablet "B."

[4] See Tablet "B," l. 18.

[5] Eisenmenger, *Entdecktes Judentum*, ii, 413.

[6] Ibid., p. 421.

was dying they would hover round his bed, and after his death would hail him as their father.[1] There seems to be an allusion to this monstrous connection in the following extract from an Assyrian hymn to the Sun-god :—[2]

"He on whom an evil Spirit hath rushed,
"He whom an evil Demon hath enveloped in his bed,
"He whom an evil Ghost hath cast down in the night,
"He whom a great Devil hath smitten,
"He whose limbs an evil God hath racked (?),
"He—the hair of whose body an evil Fiend hath set on end,[3]
"He whom . . . [a Hag-demon] hath seized,
"He whom [a Ghoul] hath cast down,
"He whom a Robber-sprite hath afflicted,
"He whom the Handmaid[4] of the Night-Phantom hath wedded,
"The man[4] with whom the Handmaid of the Night-Phantom hath had union[5]."

The third is the EKIMMU or Departed Spirit, the soul of the dead person which for some reason

[1] Ibid., p. 425.

[2] *W.A.I.*, v, 50, i, 41.

[3] Cf. Job, iv, 15, "Then a spirit passed before my face; the hair of my flesh stood up."

[4] "Handmaid" and "man" are translations of the Assyrian words which have special reference to persons of marriageable age.

[5] *iḳrimu*, Syriac ܥܪܘܡ.

cannot rest, and wanders as a spectre over the earth. After death, the souls of men and women who died in the ordinary course of nature entered into the Underworld, "the House of Darkness, the seat of the god Irkalla, the House from which none that enter come forth again," where they remained trying to eke out a wretched existence by feeding on dust and mud, and receiving the offerings and libations paid to them by their descendants and relations on earth. If for any reason these attentions should cease, and the spirit of the dead man be forgotten, then it was forced by hunger and thirst to come forth from its abode in Hades to seek on earth the food and water which no longer filtered through to satisfy its wants, and, roaming up and down, it sought what it might devour. If it found a luckless man who had wandered far from his fellows into haunted places,[1] it fastened upon him, plaguing and tormenting him until such time as a priest should drive it away with exorcisms. This is expressly stated on a tablet of this class which runs :—

" The gods which seize (upon man)
    Have come forth from the grave ;
" The evil wind-gusts
    Have come forth from the grave ;

[1] This is the interpretation of the word *muttaliku*, "wanderer," which occurs so often in the magical texts to indicate the patient.

"To demand the payment of rites and the pouring
out of libations,
They have come forth from the grave;
"All that is evil in their hosts, like a whirlwind
Hath come forth from the grave."[1]

Or again:—

"The evil Spirit, the evil Demon, the evil Ghost,
the evil Devil,
"From the earth have come forth;
"From the Underworld unto the land they have
come forth;
"In heaven they are unknown,
"On earth they are not understood,
"They neither stand nor sit,
"Nor eat nor drink."[2]

In making offerings to the dead lies the base of the principle of ancestor-worship; the descendants give food and drink to the *manes* of their forefathers that they may not need to return to earth to demand from the living the care and attention that is their due. Even in the enlightened period of the later Assyrian empire, about B.C. 650, this belief was prevalent among the

[1] Tablet "Y," vol. ii. Among the ancient Egyptians, if offerings were not paid to the deceased, he was obliged to wander into unclean places to eat such filth and drink such dirty water as he might find in the course of his wretched wanderings (Budge, *Book of the Dead*, chapters 52–53).

[2] Tablet "CC," vol. ii.

highest in the land, for we find Aššurbanipal desecrating the ancient tombs of the Kings of Elam and carrying away their bones and causing the rites paid to them to cease, so that their spirits might have no rest.[1] In the Epic of Gilgamish, when the wraith of Ea-bani has been raised from the dead by Nergal, it describes the Underworld :—[2]

" The man whose corpse lieth in the desert—
" Thou and I have oft seen such an one—
" His spirit resteth not in the earth ;
" The man whose spirit hath none to care for it—
" Thou and I have oft seen such an one—
" The dregs of the vessel, the leavings of the feast,
" And that which is cast out into the street are his food."

But under certain circumstances the soul of a dead man never entered the Underworld, as is clear from the poem quoted above. The *ekimmu*-spirit of an unburied corpse could find no rest and remained prowling about the earth so long as its body was above ground. In the Fourth Tablet of the Series " Evil Spirits " various disembodied ghosts are exorcised and addressed individually :—[3]

" Whether thou art a ghost unburied,
" Or a ghost that none careth for,
" Or a ghost with none to make offerings to it."

[1] *W.A.I.*, v, 6, 70 ff.
[2] King, *Babylonian Religion*, p. 176 ; Gilgamish Epic, Tablet xii.
[3] Tablet IV, col. v, 5.

"Or a ghost that hath none to pour libations to it,
"Or a ghost that hath no posterity."

This last line shows that the duty of making oblations to the dead devolved, as was natural, on the eldest son and direct descendants, and this is one of the reasons for the overwhelming desire of the Semite for children to perpetuate the family name. There are other instances in which souls which cannot obtain rest are mentioned, e.g. :—

"He that lieth in a ditch . . . .
"He that no grave covereth . . . .
"He that lieth uncovered,
"Whose head is uncovered with dust,
"The king's son that lieth in the desert,
"Or in the ruins,
"The hero whom they have slain with the sword."[1]

But in addition to the ghosts of the unburied or uncared-for dead, the souls of men and women who died violent or unnatural deaths or who departed this life before fulfilling or completing certain duties could obtain no rest, and were compelled to remain as disembodied spirits to haunt mankind, until they were laid to rest by exorcism. Among these may be mentioned the following :—

"He that hath died of hunger in prison,
"He that hath died of thirst in prison,

[1] K. 156, col. ii, l. 6 ff., *W.A.I.*, ii, 17, and Haupt, *Akkad. u. Sumer. Keilschr.*, p. 86.

"The hungry man who in his hunger hath not smelt the smell of food,
"He whom the bank of a river hath made to perish,
"He that hath died in the desert or marshes,
"He that a storm hath overwhelmed in the desert,
"The Night-wraith that hath no husband,
"The Night-fiend[1] that hath no wife,
"He that hath posterity[1] and he that hath none."[2]

Many of these ghosts are merely elaborations of the preceding class, being the souls of those who were lost or forgotten. The "Night-wraith that hath no husband," who has the same characteristics as the Lilith of Rabbinic tradition, will be referred to again later on. The words "He that hath no posterity" of course refer to the man who has no descendants to pay him due rites.

Other ghosts are the women who die in childbirth or while nursing their babes. The idea is that they will return in some form to seek their child.[3]

[1] I very much doubt the existence of a "Night-fiend (literally Man of the Night Spirit) that hath no wife." The LILÛ, LILÎTU, and ARDAT LILÎ ("Night-wraith, Woman of the Night Spirit") occur constantly in the incantations, but I am not aware of any occurrence of IDLU LILÎ ("Man of the Night Spirit"), and it seems most probable that this line is only a scribe's parallel to the previous one, the text being entirely a grammatical composition for the use of students. "He that hath posterity" is quite similar: see p. xxxi.

[2] K. 156, col. ii, l. 22 ff., *W.A.I.*, ii, 17, and Haupt, *Akkad. u. Sumer. Keilschr.*, p. 88.

[3] See pp. 41, 55.

This is a common form of ghost in Oriental countries. Doughty relates [1] how in Arabia he "heard scritching owls sometimes in the night; then "the nomad wives and children answered them with "mocking again, *Ymgebâs! Ymgebâs!* The hareem "said, It is a wailful woman, seeking her lost child "through the wilderness, which was turned into this "forlorn bird." Among the Malays, if a woman dies in childbirth, she is supposed to become a *langsuyar* or flying demon, a female familiar. To prevent this glass beads are put in the mouth of the corpse, a hen's egg is put under the armpits, and needles in the palms of the hands. This stops the dead woman shrieking, waving her arms, or opening her hands.[2] The original Langsuyar was supposed to be a kind of night owl,[3] like the Lilith of Rabbinic tradition,[4] and is similar therefore to the ghost of which Doughty speaks. In India the ghost of a woman who dies in childbed is a very terrible demon indeed.[5]

The souls of the devoted temple-women who die of disease, and of men or maidens who have reached a marriageable age and yet die unmarried, are also included in the category of ghosts.[6]

---

[1] *Arabia Deserta*, vol. i, p. 305.

[2] Skeat, *Malay Magic*, p. 325 (quoting Sir William Maxwell).

[3] Ibid., p. 325.

[4] Isaiah, xxxiv, 14.

[5] Crooke, *Popular Religion and Folklore of Northern India*, vol. i, p. 269.

[6] Tablet IV, ibid., col. iv, l. 45 ff., p. 38; col. v, l. 21, p. 40.

If an *ekimmu* which could find no rest came back to earth he might fasten himself on anyone who had been in some way connected with him in this world. The chance sharing of food, oil, or clothes during life constituted an act which gave the spirit after death a claim to return to its friend or even casual acquaintance to demand the rites which would give it peace. Even the mere act of eating, drinking, or anointing or dressing oneself in company with another person without receiving or giving anything was enough. Such ghosts are denounced individually in three paragraphs of four lines each at the end of a long incantation where all possible kinds of spectres are exorcised :—

"Whether thou be one with whom on a day I have eaten,
"Or with whom on a day I have drunk,
"Or with whom on a day I have anointed myself,
"Or with whom on a day I have put on apparel."

The other paragraphs are similar—"Whether thou be one with whom I have entered and eaten," and "whether thou be one with whom I have eaten food when I was hungry," and so on.[1] Moreover, if a man only looked upon a corpse he rendered himself liable to be attacked by the departed spirit.[2]

[1] Tablet IV, col. v, l. 35 ff., and Tablet V, col. i, l. 58.

[2] On this and the ceremonies prescribed to free the man from the ghost, see Zimmern, *Ritualtafeln*, p. 164.

The belief in the EKIMMU-spirit had obtained such a hold over the Assyrians, that they even went the length of deducing omens from the appearance of such a ghost in a house. As a rule it was held to be an evil omen, whether it was merely a silent apparition or whether it gibbered or uttered some words and awaited some response; it foretold certainly the destruction of the house, and in the latter case the owner of the house would die in addition. The same omen-text[1] bears witness to the prevalence of the universal belief in apparitions which come during the night to the bedside where the man lies, and describes their actions over or under the bed.

The threat that is held over the heads of all spectres of this class is that no rites shall be paid to them until they have departed. Whether they are to be rewarded with their due after they have left the possessed man is not stated.

The fourth spirit is the GALLÛ, a devil which perhaps sometimes assumes the form of a bull, since it is once described as "the *gallû*, the headstrong bull, the great ghost."[2] Like the *alû* it prowls about the streets of the city, and apparently it is neither male nor female;[3] in fact, it is sexless. The word is used in classical Assyrian as a term of abuse, for we find Sennacherib describing the hostile Babylonians as *gallû limnûti*, "evil devils."[4]

[1] K. 8,693.
[2] Tablet V, col. iii, l. 14.
[3] Ibid., l. 17.
[4] G. Smith, *Hist. of Senn.*, p. 114, l. 6.

The fifth supernatural being is ILU LIMNU, or "evil god," presumably a more general term, for it is left indefinite, and there are few, if any, descriptions of it like the other spirits.

The sixth spirit, the RABIṢU, as its name implies, is a lurking demon which, as the text quoted above shows,[1] sets the hair of the body on end, but little is known of its other characteristics.

Of the three next, the LABARTU, LABAṢU, and AḪḪAZU, the LABARTU has a whole series of texts written against her. It is a female demon, the daughter of Anu, the trusted and accepted of Irnina, and she makes her home in the mountains, or cane-brakes of the marshes. Especially were children exposed to her attacks, and in the Series called by her name, which gives directions for driving her away, there are special ceremonies to be performed in connection with certain mystic words which are to be written on a stone and hung round the neck of a child.[2]

The AḪḪAZU or "Seizer" was a demon of some kind, but we know nothing of its attributes, and the same may be said of the LABAṢU, which is here translated "ghoul"; the meaning, however, is quite uncertain.

Another triad of demons bore the interesting names of LÎLÛ, LILÎTU, and ARDAT LILÎ. The second is

[1] p. xxvii.
[2] Myhrman, *Z.A.*, xvi, p. 147.

obviously the feminine counterpart of the first, but it is difficult to discriminate between LILÎTU and the third, ARDAT LILÎ. LILÎTU is undoubtedly the word from which the Hebrew Lilith was borrowed, which occurs in Isaiah, xxxiv, 14, "The wild beasts of the desert shall also meet with the wild beasts of the island, and the satyr shall cry to his fellow; the screech owl (לִילִית) also shall rest there, and find for herself a place of rest." The Rabbinic literature also is full of legends of her doings. According to tradition she bore to Adam devils, spirits, and *lîlîn* (i.e. the same word as the Assyrian LILÛ).[1] But although there is no doubt that the LILÎTU was a night spirit, it is improbable that the Lilith should have any real connection with the Hebrew *laîlah*, "night." The Rabbis naturally assumed that there was such a connection, and on the face of it such a comparison was plausible; but the evidence of the Assyrian word LILÛ shows that we can no longer accept what would otherwise be a reasonable derivation. If we are to find a Semitic derivation for it at all, and if it has not been taken over from the Sumerian, which seems most probable, it may be connected with *lalû*, "to be abundant," *lalû*, "luxuriousness" and *lulû*, "lasciviousness, wantonness."[2]

The ARDAT LILÎ differs from the LILÎTU in that her

[1] Eisenmenger, ii, p. 413.
[2] This is the view held by Martin, *Textes Religieux*, p. 25.

relations with human beings are much closer, and she thus takes over the functions of the Hebrew Lilith. The word ARDATU, as has been explained above, always implies a marriageable woman, and this use bears further testimony to this. In one of the magical texts the sick man is described as one whom the ARDAT LILÎ has wedded.[1] In the explanatory text K. 156,[2] mention is made of the ARDAT LILÎ "that has no husband," a restless ghost that wanders up and down, forced by her desire to roam abroad, unable to rest quietly until she is satisfied. She therefore appears to have been the spirit of a woman, such as that which came to tempt St. Antony, and it is probably she who gives birth to the ALÛ or devil half-human, half-spectre, while the LILÎTU, although the female counterpart of the LILÛ, was less human in its characteristics.

These were the principal spirits, but they formed only a single class of the powers of evil which might attack man. Witchcraft, sorcery, the Evil Eye, which cast a baneful glance, the Evil Tongue, which let fall a minatory word, and the evil man, were all foes which the exorcist had to meet. The Evil Eye is a very real terror to the Oriental, and it is even personified as a demon in a Syriac charm:—"The Evil Eye went forth from the stone of the rock,

[1] See p. xxvii.

[2] See p. xxxii.

and the angel Gabriel met her."[1] There is a similar text in Assyrian about it :—

" It hath looked on the traveller,
" And like wood cut for poles
" It hath bent his neck.
" Ea hath seen this man and
" Hath placed food at his head,
" Hath brought food for his body,
" Hath shown favour for his life."[2]

The "evil man" may possibly have an echo in the old Rabbinic tradition, that the souls of the wicked when they die are the devils which are in this world.[3]

The Underworld EKURRA, the dwelling of the god Bel, was the abode of demons, whence they went forth to seize upon men.[4] This was a tradition which descended to the Arabs concerning the Jinn, of which half are malignant and half good demons, and they inhabit the seven stages which form the edifice of the Underworld :[5] in passing it is worth noting that the Arabic for a madman is *majnûn*, or one possessed by Jinn. The Babylonian devils also dwelt in Eridu as the servants of Ea and Damkina, ready to pounce on the hapless "wanderer."[6] The lonely mountains, too,

[1] H. Gollancz, *Selection of Charms*, p. 93.
[2] Tablet " U," Vol. II.
[3] Eisenmenger, ii, p. 427.
[4] Tablet " P," Vol. II.
[5] Doughty, *Arabia Deserta*, vol. i, p. 259.
[6] Tablet XV, p. 87.

were the home of many spectres, and from a recently identified text we learn that :—

" Headache hath come forth from the Underworld,
" It hath come forth from the Dwelling of Bel,
" From amid the mountains it hath descended upon the land,
" From the ends of the mountains it hath descended upon the land,
" From the fields not to return it hath descended,
" With the mountain-goat unto the fold it hath descended,
" With the ibex unto the Open-horned flocks it hath descended,
" With the Open-horned unto the Big-horned it hath descended." [1]

There is certainly an echo of this in the Syriac magic lore, in one of the charms against lunacy which ends :— . . . "[O Evil Spirit of Lunacy,] you "will needs go forth from the bones, from the sinews, "from the flesh, from the skin, and from the hair unto "the ground, and from the ground (passing) to iron, "and from iron to stone, and from stone (you will "pass on) to the mountain. This writing must be "sealed. Amen! Amen!" [2]

The deserts and ruins were also favourite haunts of

[1] Tablet III, Series *Ṭi'i*, Vol. II.

[2] H. Gollancz, *Selection of Charms*, p. 91.

ghosts and goblins.[1] The ghoul of the Arabs dwells in the desert and appears to travellers in a friendly guise in order to make them lose their way,[2] and in the same way in the Assyrian belief it is the traveller who is most liable to attacks.

The occupation of ruins by spectres is a universal superstition, and one to be explained by the belief that the spirit prefers a house if it can obtain it, and that it selects a deserted habitation because there are no longer in it any amulets or charms, or tutelary gods to keep it out. An inhabited house they may attack and force a way in temporarily, but on their presence there becoming known, the owner will at once take steps to render it untenable by them and drive them forth with the help of the exorcist. For this reason also the desert and inaccessible mountains, as affording dwellings far remote from mankind, were assigned as the probable locality for all malignant powers. A Syriac story of the ninth century testifies to this belief concerning ruins, for we read: "And while "a certain man was passing at night along the road "by the side of a fire temple of the Magians which "had been a ruin for some time, devils sprang out "upon him in the form of black ravens, and they "entered into him and convulsed him."[3] In an

[1] See Tablet "B," l. 98, p. 139.

[2] Mas'ûdî, *Prairies d'Or*, iii, p. 318.

[3] Budge, *Thomas of Marga*, vol. ii, p. 599.

Ethiopic magical prayer written for 'Ahita Mîkâêl the same belief appears, for it prescribes certain glorious names, probably to be recited, "at the front and at the "doors if thou wouldst enter into a house which is old "or in ruins or unclean."[1]

In the New Testament the Saviour goes into the wilderness and there meets the devil.[2]

(2) THE SEVEN EVIL SPIRITS.

There are certain spirits described as "the Seven" around whom a great many poems were composed and welded into the incantations and spells. The best known is the Invocation against the Seven :—

"Seven are they! Seven are they!
"In the Ocean Deep seven are they!
"Battening in Heaven seven are they,
"Bred in the depths of Ocean.
"Nor male nor female are they,
"But are as the roaming windblast,
"No wife have they, no son can they beget ;
"Knowing neither mercy nor pity,
"They hearken not to prayer or supplication.
"They are as horses reared among the hills . . ."[3]

"Of these seven [the first] is the South Wind . . .
"The second is a dragon with mouth agape
"That none can [withstand];

[1] Budge, *Lady Meux MSS.*, Nos. 2–5, p. 216.
[2] Matt., iv, 1.
[3] Tablet V, col. v, l. 28.

"The third is a grim leopard
"That carrieth off children . . . .
"The fourth is a terrible serpent . . . .
"The fifth is a furious beast (?)
"After which no restraint . . . .
"The sixth is a rampant . . .
"Which against god and king . . .
"The seventh is an evil windstorm
"Which . . . .
"These seven are the Messengers of Anu, the king,
"Bearing gloom from city to city,
"Tempests that furiously scour the heavens,
"Dense clouds that over the sky bring gloom,
"Rushing windgusts, casting darkness o'er the brightest day,
"Forcing their way with baneful windstorms.
"Mighty destroyers, the deluge of the Storm-God,
"Stalking at the right hand of the Storm-God."[1]

These Seven Spirits constantly reappear in various shapes and forms in the legends of other Semitic nations. The old Palestinian tradition of the Unclean Spirit undoubtedly owes something of its origin to them:—"The unclean spirit, when he is gone out of "the man, passeth through waterless places, seeking "rest; and finding none, he saith, I will turn back

[1] Tablet XVI, l. 13.

" unto my house whence I came out. And when he " is come, he findeth it swept and garnished. Then " goeth he and taketh to him seven other spirits more " evil than himself . . ."[1] But a still more striking evidence of the conservatism of Eastern tradition is shown in a Syriac charm which is worth quoting in full.

" [For] the fold of cattle.

" 'Seven accursed brothers, accursed sons! de- " 'structive ones, sons of men of destruction! Why " 'do you creep along on your knees and move upon " 'your hands?' And they replied, 'We go on our " 'hands, so that we may eat flesh, and we crawl along " 'upon our hands, so that we may drink blood.' As " soon as I saw it, I prevented them from devouring, " and I cursed and bound them in the name of the " Father, the Son, and the Holy Ghost, saying, 'May " 'you not proceed on your way, nor finish your " 'journey, and may God break your teeth, and cut " 'the veins of your neck, and the sinews thereof, that " 'you approach not the sheep nor the oxen of the " 'person who carries [sc. these writs]! I bind you " 'in the name of Gabriel and Michael. I bind you " 'by that angel who judged the woman that combed " '(the hair of) her head on the eve of Holy Sunday. " 'May they vanish as smoke from before the wind " 'for ever and ever, Amen!' "[2]

[1] Luke, xi, 24.

[2] H. Gollancz, *Selection of Charms*.

As will be seen from the following excerpts from the Assyrian poems, the Seven Spirits altered but little as time went on :—

" They creep like a snake on their bellies,
" They make the chamber to stink like mice,
" They give tongue like a pack of hounds." [1]

" Over the highest wall and through the thickest wall,
" Like a stormflood they can pass,
" Breaking through from house to house ;
" No door can shut them out,
" No bolt can turn them back,
" For through the portal like a snake they creep,
" And through the hinges like the wind they blow." [2]

It is they who rush over a city on the storm clouds, bringing devastation in their train, and from them come all hurricanes and tempests. They unsettle everyone that they may meet, bringing unrest, disorder, and confusion into the world, and to them is due the restlessness and desire for wandering which come upon men.

" They scour from land to land,
" Driving the maid from her chamber,
" And the man from his home,
" And the son from his father's house.

[1] Tablet " C," l. 213.
[2] Tablet V, col. i, l. 25.

"They hunt the doves from their cotes,
"And drive the bird from its nest,
"And chase the martin from its hole."[1]

The Syriac belief described above in their assailing the byres and stables, was primitive Sumerian and not a late development.

"Through the gloomy street by night they roam,
"[Smiting] sheepfold and cattle-pen;
"Shutting up the land [as with door and] bolt."[2]

"Rending in pieces on high, bringing destruction below,
"They are the Children of the Underworld.
"Loudly roaring above, gibbering below,
"They are the bitter venom of the gods.
"They are the great storms directed from Heaven,
"They are the owls which hoot over a city."[3]

They feed on mankind like vampires.

"Knowing no care, they grind the land like corn,
"Knowing no mercy, they rage against mankind,
"They spill their blood like rain
"Devouring their flesh and sucking their veins.

* * * * * *

"They are demons full of violence
"Ceaselessly devouring blood."[4]

---

[1] Tablet IV, l. 26.
[2] Ibid., Tablet IV, col. ii, l. 14.
[3] Tablet V, col. i, l. 10.
[4] Tablet V, col. iv, l. 18.

The power of spreading particular diseases was attributed to certain demons such as Ura, the plague-spirit, and Ashakku, the fever-spirit. There is a legend about Ura, the plague-spirit, which gives the vainglorious speech he made to Ishum :—

" Ura was angry, and determined
" To ravage the whole world,
" But Ishum, his counsellor, appeased him
" That he abandoned [his wrath] . . . .
" And thus spake the hero Ura :—
" 'Whosoever shall praise this song,
" 'In his shrine may plenty abound . . . .
" 'Whosoever shall magnify my name,
" 'May he rule the four quarters of the world ;
" 'Whosoever shall proclaim the glory of my valour
" 'Shall have none to oppose him ;
" 'The singer who chants it shall not die in pestilence,
" 'But unto king and noble his speech shall be well-pleasing ;
" 'The scribe who learns it shall escape from the foe . . . .
" 'In the shrine of the peoples where he cries my name continually
" 'His understanding will I increase.
" 'In the house where this tablet is set,
" 'Tho' I, Ura, be angry or the Imina-bi gods bring havoc,
" 'Yet the dagger of pestilence shall not approach it,
" 'Immunity shall rest upon it.' "[1]

[1] L. W. King, *First Steps in Assyrian*, p. 219.

(3) Charms and Magical Preparations.

As auxiliaries to the spells which he chanted, the magician would use various substances, animal, vegetable, or mineral, which had a ceremonial importance and were probably endued with magical power. In many instances these are of the same nature as amulets, and it is often easy to see how they have acquired their potency. Of these the simplest was pure water, which was sprinkled over the possessed person at the conclusion of an incantation, and this had a double meaning, symbolizing as it did the cleansing of the man from the spell and the presence of the great god Ea, whose emanation always remained in water and whose aid was invoked by these means. In order to drive out a Headache Demon, Marduk, according to the legend, came to Ea for advice, and he was told to take water at the confluence of two streams and sprinkle it over the man, performing as he did so certain ceremonies.[1]

Meteoric iron or aerolites[2] seem to have been used as charms or amulets, and this is quite as intelligible as the use of water, since from the nature of them both they are obtained from the habitations of the gods. But when we come to tamarisks, reeds, and other plants, or flour, or hair from beasts, it is not so easy to see why such materials should have been

[1] See p. lx.

[2] See note to p. 105.

adopted for magical purposes. A branch of tamarisk or the date-spathe[1] were held aloft in the hand during the exorcism which was to repel the attacks of demons and lay them under a ban, and this shows that they were possessed of magical power. Here we can see an idea similar to that of the use of water in magic, for just as water contains the power of the god Ea, so will any piece of tamarisk contain the emanation of the tree-spirit which lives in the sacred tamarisk-shrub.[2] This use of branches in magic shows that the early inhabitants of Babylonia were in no wise different from other nations in believing that trees were inhabited by spirits or gods, and it is on this principle of giving a sentient or perhaps divine nature to inanimate objects that so many of the amulets can be explained. There is a curious confirmation of this use of branches in Babylonian magic on a bowl from Niffer, in the centre of which is the figure of a man, rudely drawn, holding up a branch of some tree in his hand. The rest of the bowl is inscribed with a Hebrew incantation to be recited.[3]

---

[1] See p. 23.

[2] Manna is obtained from the tamarisk, and it is very probable that while a branch of the tree itself was brandished aloft as a visible sign, its medicinal products were used internally to cure the patient. "Manna is a laxative, and a suitable expectorant in febrile affections of the lungs" (Stillé, Maisch, etc., *The National Dispensatory*, p. 1019).

[3] Hilprecht, *Explorations in Bible Lands*, p. 447. The bowl is, of course, much later than these cuneiform texts.

Certain birds possessed supernatural powers, notably the raven and the hawk :—

"A raven, the bird that helpeth the gods,
"In my right hand I hold;
"A hawk, to flutter in thine evil face,
"In my left hand I thrust forward."[1]

Among the Semites the raven was always associated with the supernatural. It was one of the birds sent forth by Noah from the Ark. The Arabs consider it a bird of ill-omen which foretells death and disaster,[2] and it is unlawful food according to the Moslem law.[3] In the Syriac *History of the Blessed Virgin Mary*[4] a certain young man is possessed by devils, but they are driven forth by exorcism and take the form of ravens; and in *Thomas of Marga* the same belief is testified to.[5]

One of the stories of Bar-Hebræus relates how in a certain village "a troop of devils appeared in the "form of men, and they said to the villagers, 'Behold, "'a camel hath strayed away from us: give us a man "'that he may search for him.' And when they "brought out a man to them to look for the camel, "he saw ravens flying about, and he made his escape,

[1] Tablet "B," l. 65.
[2] G. E. Post in *Dictionary of the Bible* (ed. Hastings), *sub voce.*
[3] Hughes, *Dictionary of Islam*, p. 535*b*.
[4] Ed. E. A. Wallis Budge, p. 47.
[5] Ed. E. A. Wallis Budge, vol. ii, p. 599. For the quotation see p. xli.

" and went into the village and said, 'In very truth, " 'these are devils and not men; furthermore, they " 'have lost no camel.' "[1]

Devils assailed Rabban-bar-'idta in the form of "black stinking ravens" which flew up and tried to force themselves into his cell to destroy him, but were driven back to the sorcerer who sent them, by reason of his night-long prayers.[2]

The hawk is another of the magic birds of the East. It was the emblem of Horus in Egypt,[3] which at once shows in how great a respect it was held. In the Syriac stories of Alexander, Nectanebus sends a drug to Philip of Macedon by means of an enchanted hawk, and it showed him a dream.[4]

On the other hand, the owl was a bird of ill-omen among the Assyrians, as it is among the more modern Semites. Dr. Budge informs me that in many villages in the Soudan this same view is held of the *bûma* or owl. If an owl hooted over an Assyrian city it was supposed to be the work of the Seven Devils.[5] The Arabs of the present day consider the owl to be the wraith of a woman seeking her child.[6] In Syria "an owl heard hooting by a sick man is an omen of his death."[7]

---

[1] *The Laughable Stories of Bar-Hebræus*, ed. E. A. Wallis Budge, No. cccxci, p. 96.

[2] Budge, *Stories of Rabban Hormizd*, p. 245.

[3] Budge, *Egyptian Religion*, p. 107.

[4] Budge, *Alexander*, p. 8.

[5] See p. 51.

[6] See p. xxxiii.

[7] Frederick Sessions, *Folklore Notes*, Folklore, vol. ix, p. 18.

It is regarded by the Malagasy as a bird of ill-omen, and is called by them the "spirit bird," for they think it to be an embodiment of spirits, and its hoot in the night is a presage of evil.[1] All three birds were unclean to the Hebrews, according to the Levitical law.[2] Aelian also bears witness to these traditions by saying that it is considered by men to be a bird that presages evil.[3]

Animals and their hair were largely used in ceremonies, and great stress was laid on the beasts being virgin. A young pig, a virgin kid, or its hair are frequently mentioned, and this condition of ceremonial cleanness was imposed on the use of such beasts even down to the Middle Ages. The "virgin kid" was largely used by the wizards of a few hundred years ago in making parchment to be inscribed with magical spells.[4]

In order to prevent the entrance of demons into the house the Assyrians hung up various plants near the door.

"The Fleabane (?) on the lintel of the door I have hung,
"St. John's wort (?), caper (?), and wheatears on the latch I have hung,
"With a halter as a roving ass thy body I restrain."[5]

---

1 James Sibree, jun., Folklore, vol. ii, p. 34.
2 Leviticus, xi. 15–16.
3 *De Natura Animalium*, X, xxxvii.
4 Waite, *The Book of Black Magic*, p. 209.
5 Tablet "B," p. 137, ll. 72 ff.

This custom has survived among the Jews of the present day, who hang aloes or cacti from the arch of the doorway as amulets.[1]

Spittle had great power in Babylonian sorcery, particularly in bewitching men or casting spells upon them. In the Third Tablet of the series "Evil Spirits," the priest claims that Ea has added his spittle to his, and although what it refers to is not quite clear, it is evident that considerable importance is attached to it.[2] Presumably the spittle took some part in the ceremonial, just as it was used in Palestine a few centuries later. In the New Testament it is said of Christ that He "spat on the ground, and made clay of the spittle, and He anointed the eyes of the blind man with the clay."[3]

(4) Traditional Forms of Exorcisms.

The Sumerians were very fond of repeating in their magical prescriptions long traditional stories of the gods, their doings, and how they were the first to discover the beneficent properties of the charms which were in daily use. Such a story is found in the text which begins "In Eridu groweth the dark *kiškanû*," which is worth giving in full here, because of certain interpretations which have been suggested for it:—

[1] G. M. Mackie, article "Amulets," *Dictionary of the Bible*, ed. Hastings, 1898.

[2] See p. 13, l. 110.

[3] John, ix, 6.

" In Eridu groweth the dark *kiškanû*
" That springeth forth in a place undefiled,
" Whereof the brilliance is shining lapis
" Which reacheth unto Ocean ;
" From Ea its way in Eridu
" Is bountiful in luxuriance,
" Where earth is, there is its place,
" And the Couch of the Goddess Id its home.
" In an undefiled dwelling like a forest grove
" Its shade spreadeth abroad, and none may enter in.
" In its depths (are) Shamash and Tammuz.
" At the confluence of two streams
" The gods Ka-Hegal, Shi-Dugal, (and) . . . of Eridu
" [Have gathered] this *kiškanû*, [and over the man]
" Have performed the Incantation of the Deep,
" (And) at the head of the wanderer have set (it).
" That a kindly Guardian, a kindly Spirit
" May stand at the side of the man, the son of his god.
" The . . . which seizeth on the hand
" Of him whose face hath not been turned towards it
" [From where] he lieth, may it retard its foot.
" May an evil . . . stand aside therefrom,
" May . . . from the mouth of the king restrain it on the way.
" May Ishtar, [the Lady] mighty, wise, and pure,
" From the dwelling-place cut it off."

The explanation of this text which has hitherto found credence among certain Assyriologists is that it contains nothing less than a reference to the Garden of Eden as it was known to the Babylonians. This view was originated by Professor Sayce in his *Hibbert Lectures* (1887, p. 237), who draws a comparison between this and the Biblical descriptions, and this is still maintained by him and Mr. Pinches in their respective books, *The Religions of Ancient Egypt and Babylonia* (*Gifford Lectures*, 1902, p. 385) and *The Old Testament in the light of the Historical Records of Assyria and Babylonia* (1902, p. 71). As it is an important point to consider, it will be as well to examine the evidence in detail; but first it must be remarked that since the last publication of this text considerable additions have been made to it, as has been mentioned in the preface. Mr. Pinches bases his translation on that of Professor Sayce's rendering in 1887 :—[1]

---

[1] Professor Sayce's latest translation (*Gifford Lectures*, 1902, p. 386) differs somewhat from that in the *Hibbert Lectures* :—

> " In Eridu a vine grew overshadowing; in a holy place was it brought forth ;
> " its root was of bright lapis, set in the world beneath.
> " The path of Ea was in Eridu, teeming with fertility.
> " His seat (there) is the centre of the earth ;
> " his couch is the bed of the primeval mother.
> " Into the heart of its holy house, which spreads its shade like a forest, hath no man entered.
> " In its midst is Tammuz,
> " between the mouths of the rivers on both sides."

Professor Sayce considers that Hommel may be right in translating *kiškanû* " palm " instead of " vine."

"Incantation: '(In) Êridu a dark vine grew, it was made in a glorious place,
"'Its appearance (aṣ) lapis-lazuli, planted beside the Abyss,
"'Which is Ae's path, filling Êridu with fertility.
"'Its seat is the (central) point of the earth,
"'Its dwelling is the couch of Nammu.
"'To the glorious house, which is like a forest, its shadow extends,
"'No man enters its midst.
"'In its inferior is the Sun-god, and the peerless mother of Tammuz.
"'Between the mouths of the rivers (which are) on both sides.'"

"Here the text breaks off, and where it again "becomes legible, the phrases are those of an ordinary "incantation, whose connecting link with the above "poetical lines is lost." Mr. Pinches draws the following conclusions from this text:—(*a*) That Eridu "was, to the Babylonians, as a garden of Eden, "wherein grew a glorious tree, to all appearance "a vine, for the adjective 'dark' may very reasonably "be regarded as referring to its fruit. Strange must "have been its appearance, for it is described as "resembling 'white lapis-lazuli,' that is, the beautiful "stone of that kind mottled blue and white." (*b*) "The "probability that it was conceived by the Babylonians "as a garden is strengthened by the fact that the "god Aê, and his path, *i.e.* the rivers, filled the place "with fertility, and it was, moreover, the abode of the "river-god Nammu, whose streams, the Tigris and "Euphrates, flowed on both sides." (*c*) "There, too, "dwelt the Sun, making the garden fruitful with his "ever-vivifying beams, whilst 'the peerless mother "of Tammuz,' probably a name of Damkina, added, "by her fructifying showers, to the fertility that the "two great rivers brought down from the mountains "from which they flowed." (*d*) "To complete still "further the parallel with the Biblical Eden, it was "represented as a place to which access was forbidden, "for 'no man entered its midst,' as in the case of the "Garden of Eden after the fall."

But I very much doubt whether the words in the text will bear the interpretation which has been put upon them, or that the points of similarity are sufficiently marked to justify the comparison. First, as to the meaning of *kiškanû*, which is supposed to be the Tree of Life, and has been identified with the vine. The *kiškanû* is a plant or tree divided in the Assyrian syllabaries into three classes,[1] *piṣû* "white," *ṣalmi* "dark," and *sâmi* "brown." Mr. Pinches, who translates *sami* "grey or blue,"[2] considers that these colours refer to the fruit of the tree, and brings forward in support of his theory that the vine is the only plant growing in the country with these

[1] *W.A.I.*, ii, 45, 4, ll. 53 ff.

[2] The exact meaning is uncertain. The word, however, is used as an epithet of gold (see Delitzsch, *H.W.B.*, *sub voce*).

three colours of fruit, and that the *kiškanû* is mentioned in the bilingual lists among plants of the vine species. But the colours may refer equally well to the flowers of the tree or plant, and no inference can be drawn from its position on the tablet on which the word occurs, for it is separated from the eight species of vine by two words, one of which is *iṣ-ṣi ṣal-mi* ("black wood"). Indeed, if any inference at all is to be drawn from its connection on this tablet (*W.A.I.*, ii, No. 4) it is distinctly improbable that *kiškanû* means a vine, since each of the eight species mentioned is marked in Sumerian with a special sign for "vine," and the Sumerian for *kiškanû* has no such specification attached.

It is, however, unnecessary to imagine a mythological meaning for *kiškanû*. The text in question is for a sick man, and the *kiškanû* is to afford the remedy for his disease. We have seen that it is a vegetable, plant or shrub, identified by the three colours white, and probably blue and brown, which grows thickly like a grove by the river-side near Eridu in Southern Babylonia, and it now remains to identify this shrub. Mr. H. H. W. Pearson, of the Royal Gardens at Kew, informs me that the description coincides with that of the *Astragalus*, of which there are many varieties. From the *Astragalus gummifer*[1] is obtained

[1] "The source of Tragacanth had been known for centuries to "be some of the spiny species of *Astragalus* growing in Asia

Tragacanth, which possesses emollient and demulcent properties, and it was used by the Greek physicians as far back as the fourth or fifth centuries, to allay cough and hoarseness and to promote expectoration.[1] It is still to be obtained in the bazaars of Bagdad, whither it comes from Persia.[2] It seems, therefore, very probable that the *kiškanû* is one of the varieties of astragalus from which Tragacanth is procured.

Again, *ana apsi tarṣu* (l. 2) cannot mean "planted beside the Abyss," but is more probably "stretcheth out unto the Ocean Deep," i.e., the water. The fourth line has been given a remarkable meaning by the totally unwarranted insertion which Professor Sayce was the first to make, of the word "(central)," the whole line thus running, "Its seat is the (central) point of the earth," or, in Professor Sayce's later translation, "His seat (there) is the centre of the earth." But the line is nothing more than "its seat is the earth," i.e., its roots go deep into the earth, and it has nothing

"Minor." All the principal species from which Tragacanth is obtained are natives of the mountainous districts in the East; Asia Minor, Armenia, Persia and Kurdistan, Syria, and Greece. The *Astragalus gummifer* is "a small shrub, about 2 feet in "height . . . . leaves very numerous, closely placed, spreading "in all directions about 1¼ inch long, pinnate, the rachis very "hard, stiff, smooth, yellow, terminating in a very sharp point, "and persistent for some years as a woody spine" (Bentley and Trimen, *Medicinal Plants*, No. 73).

[1] Stillé, Maisch, etc., *The National Dispensatory*, pp. 1642–1643.

[2] Felix Jones, *Memoirs* (1857), p. 402.

whatever to do with the ὀμφαλὸς γῆς, as Professor Sayce originally suggested (*Hibbert Lectures*, p. 238). Further, there are no grounds for Mr. Pinches' translation "the peerless mother of Tammuz," in the line "In its midst are Shamash and Tammuz."

Mr. Pinches' arguments may thus be met one by one :—

(*a*) That Eridu was as a Garden of Eden there is absolutely no reason to believe. There is no reference at all to any garden in the text, and the natural interpretation is the one to follow, namely, that the *kiškanû* grew wild.

(*b*) The presence of a river does not presuppose the presence of a garden, as Mr. Pinches would have us believe. Besides, the rivers which are mentioned have nothing to do with the River with Four Heads of Genesis, but have a purely ceremonial meaning, of which the explanation is this. The gods plucked the plant near to where two streams ran into one another, this being always a place with a magical significance. For instance, the magician is elsewhere directed to "take water at the confluence of two streams, and with this water perform a purifying incantation,"[1] or, again, he is to "take an earthen vessel which hath come from a great kiln, and at the confluence of two streams to bale up (?) water."[2]

[1] Tablet "P" (Vol. II), l. 66.

[2] Tablet VIII of the series LUḪ-KA (Vol. II), "AA," l. 31.

Inasmuch as the locality is the same in all three instances, and the texts are all of the same class, it follows that if the first are the Rivers of Eden, so also must be the second and third, which is obviously absurd. In the two last cases it is clear that a place attainable by mortals is intended, and so also is it in the Eridu text. The magician is intended to imitate the gods and pluck the *kiškanû* from an earthly spot in order to heal his patient therewith, just as the gods, whose example he follows, did in times long past.

(*c*) The mention of the presence of the Sun-god and Tammuz "in its midst" does not by any means imply the existence of a divine garden for their habitation. Three explanations of this line are possible, first, that it has an entirely mythological reference, in which case the gods mentioned are some form of tree-spirit. If this be the case, there is still no proof that the *kiškanû* was the Tree of Knowledge, since the belief in tree-spirits is general in early communities, and it would be straining the whole idea to narrow one ill-defined and vague instance down to such a very special case as the Biblical tree. Secondly, if the explanation be purely physical, and is merely the description of the ordinary characteristics of the plant wrapped up in theological language, implying that it thrives in the Sun, just as its path is that of Ea, that is, that it lives near water, still less can it be referred to the Tree in Genesis. Probably, however, the explanation is a twofold combination of the above, pointing to its divine connection by reason of its peculiar habitat and position. The case with all magical plants used as charms in these incantations is the same, that they should have some divine association and connection whence their power should emanate.[1]

(*d*) The last point, "that no man enters its midst," is the one point of similarity which this text bears with the Biblical Eden. It has been shown above that there is no mention whatever of a garden and no reason to suppose that any is referred to; that the *kiškanû* is certainly not a vine, being probably nothing more than a flowering and perhaps thorny shrub, and that its association with the gods is similar to other plants used in incantations, since it is merely intended to explain the origin of its power in magic. So that the last point mentioned above is the only remaining support for the Eden-theory. Now, it is obvious that the phrase cannot refer to Eridu, since this was a city of human habitation, and therefore it can only refer to the *kiškanû*, which "grows like a forest" or "grove," as the text itself says, and herein lies the interpretation. Either by reason of its thick growth or from its thorny character, or both, it is difficult to force a passage through, and no man can push his way into the depths of its thickets except with extreme trouble.

[1] As parallels, compare the description of the "Heart-plant" (Küchler, *Beiträge zur Kenntnis der Assyrischen Medizin*, p. 9) and the Legend of the Worm (quoted below).

In all this text there is no mention of any of the following characteristics of the Biblical Garden of Eden: the planting of a garden by a god, the existence of every tree therein, the tree of life, the tree of knowledge of good and evil or its fruit, the four-headed river, the presence of the serpent, and the Cherubim and the flaming sword.

The real explanation of the text is perfectly simple without straining after Biblical comparisons. The *kiškanû*-plant, according to tradition, grew in Eridu when the gods were nearer to mankind than in after days, and it was they who originally plucked it for medicinal use from the place where it grew where two streams met, and performed with it certain ceremonies. Their actions stamped the prescription as infallible, and sanctioned the repetition of the ceremonies in later days, so that any more modern magician or priest, in treating his patient, might have a divine model to imitate. This is all that is meant, and there is absolutely no reference to any Garden of Eden.

As another instance of the fondness of the Babylonians for going back to the most primitive periods for their models in such matters, I may cite the *Legend of the Worm*,[1] which has been hitherto unknown :—

"After Anu [had created the Heavens],
"The Heavens created [the Earth],

[1] *Legend of the Worm*, vol. ii. The text is published in *Cun. Texts*, part xvii, pl. 50.

" The Earth created the Rivers,
" The Rivers created the Canals,
" The Canals created the Marshes,
" The Marshes created the Worm.
" Came the Worm and wept before Shamash,
" Before Ea came her tears :—
" ' What wilt thou give me for my food,
" ' What wilt thou give me to devour ? '
" ' I will give thee dried bones,
" ' And scented . . . -wood.'
" ' Nay, what these dried bones of thine to me,
" ' And thy scented . . . -wood ?
" ' Let me drink among the teeth,
" ' And set me on the gums ;
" ' That I may devour the blood of the teeth,
" ' And of their gums destroy their strength
" ' Then shall I hold the bolt of the door.' "[1]

The incantation is really one which was written for people with toothache, which was believed to be due to the gnawing of small worms. By repeating the story of the creation and subsequent action of the original Worm, the magician shows that he clearly has knowledge of the name of his enemy and his methods, always a fundamental principle in magic, and he may then proceed with his instructions :

" So must thou say this : O Worm !
" May Ea smite thee with the might of his fist ! "

[1] Compare Ecclesiastes, xii, 4.

and after chanting the incantation three times, he must rub a mixture of beer, a certain plant probably of a pungent nature, and oil on the tooth of his patient.

From the facts stated in the above pages, the reader will be able to glean an idea of the scope and contents of one group of Sumerian magical texts, and it is hoped that the information therein given will induce the student of comparative folklore to investigate this important subject. It will, of course, be understood that the exact meanings of certain words are still obscure, but with the publication of new texts and further study, there is every reason for believing that we may shortly attain to a tolerably accurate knowledge of the ceremonies, enchantments, and spells which the Sumerian sorcerer employed in dealing with credulous clients some six thousand years ago.

PLATE II.

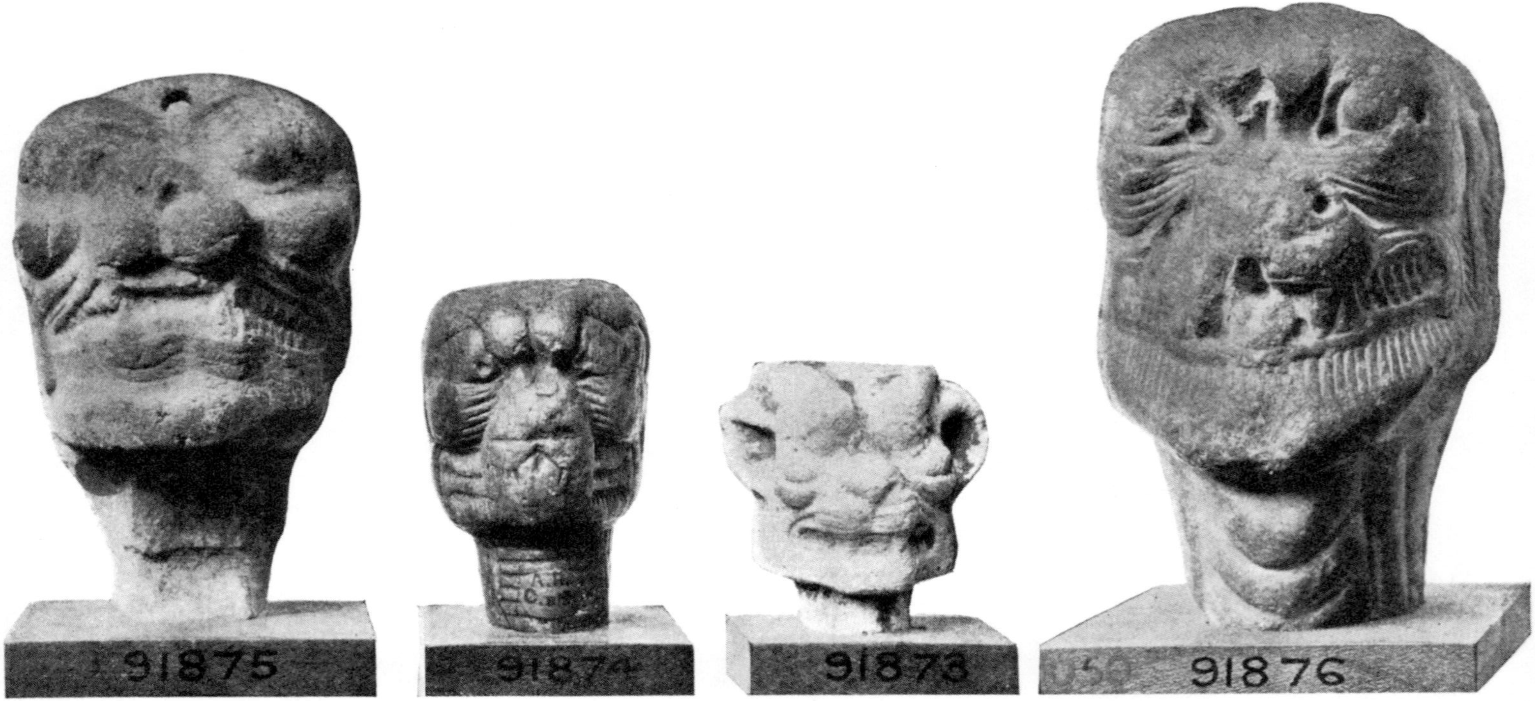

BABYLONIAN DEMONS.

Transliterations

and

Translations.

Series Utukki limnûti.

The Third Tablet.

(Plate I.)

. . . .
. . . . [1]
. . . . *-bat-ma*
. . . . [MU]-UN-ZU-ZU-NE
. . . . *al-mad-ma*
. . . . MU-UN-ŠI-IN-GAL-LA-NA
. . . . . *alu Eridu ina na-di-e-a*
. . . . NAM-ŠUB MU-UN-ŠI-IN-SUM-MA-TA
. . . . *šip-tu ina na-di-e-a*
ALAD-*ŠIG-GA ID-MU KAN-GUB
la-mas-si dum-ḳi i-da-a-a li-iz-ziz
DINGIR-NIN-GIR-SU LUGAL GIŠ-KU-GE KAN-PA
ilu „ be-el kak-ku lu-u-ta-ma-a[2]*-ta*
UTUG-ḪUL A-LA-ḪUL GIDIM-ḪUL MULLA-ḪUL DINGIR-ḪUL MAŠKIM-ḪUL
E-NE-NE-NE *šu-nu lim-nu-tum* ḪUL-A-MEŠ
SU-MU *ana zu-um-ri-ia a-a iṭ-ḫu-ni* NAM-BA-TE-MAL-E-NE
IGI-MU *ana pa-ni-ia a-a u-lam-mi-nu-ni* NAM-BA-ḪUL-E-NE
EGIR-MU *ana ar-ki-ia a-a il-li-ku-ni* NAM-BA-GIN-GIN-NE
E-MU *ana bîti*[3]*-ia [a-a i-ru-bu-ni]* NAM-BA-TU-TU-NE
*UR-MU *ana u-ri-ia a-a [ib-bal-ki-tu]-ni* NAM-BAL-BAL-E-NE
E-KI-TUŠ-A-MU *ana bît šub-ti-[ia a-a i-ru-bu-ni]* NAM-BA-TU-TU-NE

Series "The Evil Spirits."

The Third Tablet.

(Plate I.)

. . . .
. . . . I learn and
When I perform [the Incantation] of Eridu,
When I perform the Incantation . . . .
May a kindly Guardian stand at my side.
By Ningirsu, master of the sword, mayest thou be exorcised!
Evil Spirit, evil Demon, evil Ghost, evil Devil, evil God, evil Fiend,
Evil are they!
Unto my body may they not draw nigh,
Before me may they wreak no evil.
Nor follow behind me,
Into my house may they not enter,
My fence may they not break through,
Into my chamber may they not enter.

---

[1] Traces of preceding lines on 35,611: (*a*) . . . EN (*b*) . . . EN (*c*) . . . *ana-ku* (*d*) . . . [DINGIR-SILIG]-MULU-ŠAR ME-EN (*e*) . . . *ana-ku* (*f*) . . . TE-MAL (*g*) . . . *e-a* (*h*) . . . IN-TUR-RA-NE (*i*) . . . *ub*(?)-*ma*(?) (*j*) . . . IN-GAR-RA.

[2] 35,611 omits.

[3] K. 9,314, *bi-ti*.

ZI AN - NA KAN - PA [ZI] KI - A KAN - PA
niš [*šamê*(*e*)] *lu-u-ta-ma-a-ta niš irṣitim*(*tim*)
[*lu - u - ta - ma - a*] *- ta*

INIM - INIM - MA UTUG - ḪUL - A - KAN

EN E - NE - NE - NE MAŠKIM - ḪUL - A - MEŠ
šu - nu ra - bi - ṣu lim - nu - ti šu - nu

E-A E-KUR-TA *iš*[1]*-tu bît*[2] *ekurri it-ta-ṣu-ni šu-nu* E-A-MEŠ

DINGIR - EN - LIL - LA LUGAL KUR - KUR - RA - GE
E - NE - NE - NE MULU - KIN - GA - A - MEŠ
ša *ilu* „ *bêl mâtâti*[3] *mâr šip - ri šu - nu*

UTUG-ḪUL EDIN-NA MULU-TIL-LA BA-AN-GAZ
u-tuk-ku lim-nu ša ina ṣi-rim[4] *amelu bal-ṭu*[5] *i-nar-ru*

A - LA - ḪUL - IK - E TU - GIM MU - UN - DUL - LA
a-lu-u lim-nu ša ki-ma ṣu-ba-a-ta[6] *i-kat-ta-mu*

GIDIM-ḪUL MULLA-ḪUL SU-NA BA-NI-IB-DIB-DIB-BI
e-kim-mu lim-nu gal-lu-u lim-nu ša zu-um-ra
i-kam-mu-u

DINGIR-RAB-KAN-ME DINGIR-RAB-KAN-ME[7]-A SU-NA
BA-NI-IN[8]-GIG-GA[9]

la-bar-tum la-ba-ṣu ša zu-um-ra u-šam-ra-ṣu

LIL - LA EDIN - NA NI - KAS - KAS - EŠ - A - AN
li-lu-u ša ina ṣi-rim it-ta-na-aš-rab-bi-ṭu

(PLATE II.)

MULU-GIŠGAL-LU PAP-ḪAL-LA BAR-KU MU-UN-NA-TE-EŠ
ana ameli mut-tal-li-ku[10] *ina a-ḫa-ti iṭ-ḫu-u*

---

[1] K. 224 and K. 9,314, *ul.*
[2] K. 9,314, *bi-ti.*
[3] K. 224, *be-el ma-ta-a-*[*ti*].
[4] K. 224, *e-ri.*
[5] K. 224, *ṭa.*
[6] K. 224, *ṣu-ba-ti.*
[7] K. 224 omits.
[8] K. 224, IB.
[9] K. 224 adds A-AN.
[10] K. 224, *ki.*

By Heaven be thou exorcised! By Earth be thou exorcised!

Prayer against the Evil Spirits.

Incantation:—
Evil fiends are they!
From the Underworld[a] they have gone forth,
They are the Messengers of Bel, Lord of the World.
The evil Spirit that in the desert smiteth the living man,
The evil Demon that like a cloak enshroudeth the man,
The evil Ghost, the evil Devil that seize upon the body,
The Hag-demon (and) Ghoul that smite the body with sickness,
The Phantom of Night that in the desert roameth abroad,[b]

(Plate II.)

Unto the side of the wanderer have drawn nigh,

[a] *Ekurru*. On the meaning "Underworld," see Jensen, *Kosmologie*, p. 185, and Jastrow, *Religion*, p. 558.

[b] *Ittanašrabbiṭu*: for the meaning of this word compare the following passages: Tablet V, v, 40, *šunu zaḳiḳu muttašrabbiṭuti šunu*, "They are the roaming stormwind"; *Devils and Evil Spirits*, vol. ii, Tablet "N," col. i, ll. 11–12, *šêdu utukku rabiṣu rabbuti ša ana niši*^{pl} *ribâti ittanašrabbiṭu*, "The great demons, spirits, and fiends that prowl about the broad places for men"; ibid., Tablet "R," l. 6, *ša ina ṣirim kima zaḳiḳi ittanašrabbiṭu*, "who roam about the desert like the wind."

AZAG - TUR - RA SU - NA MI - NI - IN - GAR - RI - EŠ
a-šak-ku [1] *mar-ṣa ina zumri* [2] *-šu iš-ḳu-nu*
ḪUL NAM - NE - SUB - BA SU - NA GAL - LA - NA
ma-mit li-mut-tum ina zumri [2] *-šu ib-šu-u*
U-MU-UN-ḪUL-A SU-NA [3] MI-NI-IN-GAR-RI-EŠ
u-mu-un-na-a lim-nu [4] *ina zumri* [2] *-šu iš-ku-nu* [5]
NAM-TAR-ḪUL-BI-TA *nam-ta-ra lim-na ina zumri* [2] *-šu*
ib-šu-u SU-NA GAL-LA-NA
UḪ (?) - ḪUL - BI - TA *im-ta li-mut-ta ina zumri* [2] *-šu*
iš-ku-ni SU-NA GAL-LA-NA
BAR-RA-NA AŠ-ḪUL *ar-rat li-mut-ta* [6] *ina zu-um-ri-šu*
ib-šu-u GAL-LA-NA
ḪUL NAM-TAG-GA *lum-na ar-na* [7] *ina zumri* [2] *-šu*
iš-ku-ni SU-NA GAL-LA-NA
UḪ (?) NAM-TAG-GA *im-ta še-ir-ta* [8] *e-li-šu ib-šu-u*
MUḪ-NA GAL-LA-NA
ḪUL - A : *li - mut - ta* [6] *iš - ku - nu* : MU - UN - GA - GA
[9] MULU - ḪUL IGI - ḪUL KA - ḪUL EME - ḪUL
[10] UḪ (?) - ḪUL UḪ (?) - SU UḪ (?) - RI - A GAR - ŠA - A
GAR - ḪUL - GIM - MA
[MULU]-TUR-RA SU-NA *ša ina zu-mur mar-ṣi* [11]
iš-šak (?)-*nu* . . . IN-GAR-RI
. . GIG DUG - SIR - GIM (?) MU - UN - DA - AB - GE - GE
. . . *u-a ki-ma kar-pat ša-ḫar-ra* [*im-tum*?] *u-ša*-[*al-la*]-*mu*
GAR - ŠA - A GAR - ḪUL - GIM - MA KA - MU - UN - DA - AB
. . MAL (?) . .
u - pi - šu lim - nu - tum ša pa - a u - kas - su - u
UḪ (?) - ZU ḪUL-BI-TA EME BA-NI-IN-DIB-DIB-BI
kiš-pi lim-[*ni*] *ša li-ša-a* [12] *-nu u-ṣab-ba-tum*
LUGAL . . . . E - A DINGIR ḪUL - IK - E
be - lu [?] *ilu lim - nu*

Casting a woeful fever upon his body.
A ban of evil hath settled on his body,
An evil disease on his body they have cast,
An evil plague hath settled on his body,
An evil venom on his body they have cast,
An evil curse hath settled on his body,
Evil (and) sin on his body they have cast,
Venom (and) wickedness have settled on him,
Evil they have cast (upon him).
The evil man, he whose face is evil, he whose mouth is evil, he whose tongue is evil,
Evil spell, witchcraft, sorcery,
Enchantment, and all evil,
Which rest on the body of the sick man
[a] . . . . . which like a clay vessel hath consumed the spittle,
The enchantment and all evil that have closed the mouth,
The baneful witchcraft which hath seized the tongue,
The lord of . . . . . , the evil god,

[1] K. 224, *ka*.
[2] 47,852, *zu-um-ri*.
[3] K. 224, BAR-KU.
[4] K. 224, *na*.
[5] 47,852, *ni*.
[6] 47,852, *tum*.
[7] 47,852, *nu*.
[8] 47,852, for this line [*im*]-*tum šir-tum*, etc.
[9] 47,852 translates this line [*amelu lim-nu*] *pa-ni lim-nu pu-u lim-nu li-ša-nu lim-nu*.
[10] 47,852 translates this line [*kiš*]-*pi ru-ḫu-u ru-su-u up-ša-še-e* [*mimma lim-nu*], and for UḪ (?)-RI-A reads UḪ (?)-A-RI-A.
[11] 47,852, *ṣa*.
[12] 47,852 omits.

[a] Line doubtful.

KASKAL-DAGAL-LA-TA-GIM MULU-GIŠGAL-LU-BI
BA-AN-SI-EŠ
ina ḫar-ra-nu[1] *ra-pa-aš-tum ana amelu*[2] *šu-a-tum*
i-ši-ru
GA-E MULU DINGIR-EN-KI-GA ME-EN
GA-E MULU DINGIR-DAM-GAL-NUN-NA ME-EN[3]
GA-E MULU-KIN-GA-A' DINGIR-SILIG-MULU-ŠAR ME-EN[3]
GAR-TUR-RA-A-NI MULU-TIL-LA-A-NI-KU
mar-ṣu ru-us-su ana bul-lu-ṭu
EN-GAL DINGIR-EN-KI-GE MU-UN-ŠI-IN-GIN-NA
belu[4] *rabu(u)* ^{ilu}*E-a iš-pur-an-ni*
TU-AZAG-GA-A-NI TU-MU GAL-LA-NA
ta-a-šu el-lu ana te-e-a iš-kun
KA-AZAG-GA-A-NI KA-MU GAL-LA-NA
pi-i-šu el-lu ana pi-ia iš-kun
UḪ (?)-AZAG-GA-A-NI UḪ (?)-MU GAL-LA-NA
i-mat-su el-[lu]ana im-ti-ia iš-kun
MU-AZAG-GA-A-NI MU-MU GAL-LA-NA
ik-rib-šu el-lu[5] *ana ik-ri-bi-ia iš-kun*

(PLATE III.)

ZAG-MEŠ ḪE-IM-MA-AN-ḪUL-A MULU-TUR-RA[6] SU-NA
GAL-LA-NA
mu šal-pit eš-ri-e-ti[7] *ša ina zu-mur mar-ṣu*[8] *ba-ša-a*
TU-DUG-GA I DINGIR-EN-KI-GA-GE
ina " -e a-mat ^{ilu}*E-a*[9]
E-NE-NE-NE ḪUL-A-MEŠ ḪE-IM-MA-AN-SIR-RI-EŠ-A-AN
šu-nu lim-nu-ti[10] *li-in-na-as-ḫu*
GIŠ-MA-NU GIŠ-KU-MAḪ AN-NA-GE ŠU-MU
MU-UN-DA-AN-GAL
e-ri kak-ku ṣi-i-ri[11] *ša* ^{ilu}*A-nim ina ḳatâ*^{II}*-ia*
na-ša-ku

On the high road have attacked this man.
65. The man of Ea am I!
The man of Damkina am I!
The messenger of Marduk am I!
To revive the ( )[a] sick man,
70. The great lord Ea hath sent me;
He hath added his pure spell to mine,
75. He hath added his pure voice to mine,
He hath added his pure spittle to mine,
He hath added his pure prayer to mine.

(PLATE III.)

Though that which resteth on the body of the sick man
80. Had power to destroy temples,[b]
Yet by the magic of the Word of Ea
85. These evil ones will be put to flight.
The tamarisk,[c] the powerful weapon of Anu,

---

[1] 35,611, *ni*.
[2] 47,852, *a-me-lu*.
[3] Translated on 47,852 . . . [*a*]-*na-ku*.
[4] K. 224, *be-lum*; 35,611, *be-* . . . ; 47,852, *be-lu*.
[5] S. 996, *ellu*.
[6] 38,594 . . . NA.
[7] S. 996, *meš-ri ti*.
[8] 47,852, *ṣa*; S. 996, *ṣi*.
[9] 47,852, *Ea*.
[10] S. 996, *tum*.
[11] S. 996, *si-ra*.

[a] *Russu*. Possibly either for *ru'ut-su* ("his spittle") or from the root *rasâsu*, which may perhaps be the Chaldee *r'sas* (Levy, *Chald. Wörterb.*, ii, 429) meaning "to smite." Neither are, however, probable.

[b] S. 996 has *mešriti*, "limbs."

[c] *Eru* (GIŠ MA-NU). From Zimmern's *Ritualtafeln*, Nos. 46–47 (p. 156, l. 15), *VII ṣalme eri*, "Seven images of *eru*-wood," it is clear that this is a wood, and not a wooden object. It occurs frequently in these texts, and the best Semitic word to compare it with is the Syriac *'ara* (Brockelmann, *Lexicon*, p. 259, *a*), "tamarisk."

DINGIR-DUB-SAG-UNUG-KI *LIGIR KUL-UNUG-KI-GE NAM-TIL-LA SILIM-MA-MU

EGIR - MU GIN - GIN - NE

90. *ilu* „ *na-gi-ri Kul-la-bi*[1] *ana ba-la-ṭi-ia u ša-la-mi-ia arki*[2]*-ia lit-tal-lak*

UTUG-*ŠIG-GA IḌ-ZI-DA-MU MU-UN-DA-AN-GIN-NA

še-e-du dum-ḳi ina im-ni-ia a-la-ku[3]

ALAD-*ŠIG-GA ID-GUB-BU-MU MU-UN-DA-AN-GIN-NA

la-mas-si dum-ḳi ina šu-me-li-ia a-la-ku[3]

95. DINGIR-NIN[4]-AN-NA DUP-SAR-MAḪ ARALI-GE SAR-AZAG

NAM-ŠUB AZAG-GA[5] MU-UN-NA-AN-ŠIT

ilu „ *dup-šar-ra-tum*[6] *ṣir-tum*[7] *ša A-ra-al-li-e*

šip-tu ellitim(tim) ina pani-ia[8] *i-man-ni*[9]

DINGIR-NIN-GIR-SU LUGAL GIŠ-KU-GE KAN-PA

100. UTUG-ḪUL A-LA-ḪUL GIDIM-ḪUL MULLA-Ḫ[UL DINGIR-ḪUL MAŠKIM-ḪUL]

E-NE-NE-NE ḪUL-A-MEŠ[10]

SU-MU NAM-BA-TE-MAL-E-NE[11] : IGI-MU-N[AM-BA-ḪUL]-E-NE

104–105. EGIR-MU NAM-BA-GIN-GIN-NE : E-MU NAM-[BA-TU-TU]-NE

*UR-MU NAM-BA-BAL-BAL-E-NE : E-KI-TUŠ-A-[MU NAM-BA-TU-TU]-NE

a. ZI AN-NA KAN-PA ZI KI-A [KAN-PA]

---

[1] K. 8,262, *ba.*

[2] K. 8,262, *ar-ki.*

[3] K. 8,262, *ki.*

[4] 47,852 inserts NA.

[5] 47,852, IGI-MU for AZAG-GA.

[6] 47,852, *rat* for *ra-tum.*

In my hands I hold.
May the god Dubsag-Unug-ki,[a] the patron of Kullabi,
For my life and health follow after me.
A kindly Guardian marcheth on my right,
A kindly Spirit marcheth on my left,
Nin-Anna,[b] the mighty Scribe of the Underworld,
Reciteth a purifying incantation before me.
By Ningirsu, master of the sword, mayest thou be exorcised!
Evil Spirit, evil Demon, evil Ghost,
Evil Devil, evil God, evil Fiend,
Evil are they,
Unto my body may they not draw nigh,
Before me may they wreak no evil,
Nor follow behind me,
Into my house may they not enter,
My fence may they not break through,
Into my chamber may they not enter.
a. By Heaven be thou exorcised! By Earth be thou exorcised!

[7] 47,852, *tu*.
[8] 47,852, *i-na pa-ni-ia*.
[9] K. 8,262, *nu*.
[10] MEŠ-MEŠ according to the text.
[11] K. 8,262, DA.

[a] *Duḫsag-Uruk:* DUB-SAG (Brünnow, *List*, Nos. 3,937–3,938) is translated *ḳudmu* and *maḫru*, i.e. "first," "chief." For Kullabi or Kullaba, see *W.A.I.*, v, 41, 14, *g*.
[b] I.e. "Lady of Heaven."

---

b. INIM - INIM - MA UTUG - ḪUL - A - GE[1]

---

c. EN DINGIR-EN-KI E-NE : *ša* ^{ilu} „ *šu-nu ša* ^{ilu} „ *šu-nu* :
DINGIR . . . . .

d. DINGIR-EN-KUR-SIG-NUN-ME-UBARA E-NE DINGIR-NIN-KUR-SIG-NUN-[ME-UBARA E-NE]

e. A - DA - PA NUN - ME NUN - KI - GA - [GE] . . .

f. GA-E MULU-TU-TU DINGIR-EN-KI-GA-[GE ME-EN]

g. GA-E MULU-KIN-GA-A DINGIR-SILIG-MULU-ŠAR [ME-EN]

h. GAR - TUR - RA - A - NI MULU - TIL - LA - A - [NI - KU]

i. EN-GAL DINGIR-EN-KI-GE MU-UN-ŠI-IN-[GIN-NA]

108. TU - AZAG - GA - A - NI TU - MU GAL - [LA - NA]

KA - AZAG - GA - A - [NI KA - MU GAL - LA - NA]

110. UḪ (?) AZAG - GA - [A - NI UḪ (?) - MU GAL - LA - NA]

MU AZAG - GA - [A - NI MU - MU GAL - LA - NA]

UTUG-ḪUL A-LA-[ḪUL GIDIM-ḪUL MULLA-ḪUL DINGIR-ḪUL MAŠKIM-ḪUL]

. . . GA MAŠKIM . . . . . .

. . . . *lu ra - bi - ṣu* . . . . .

115. ? IGI-MU-TA ZI [AN-NA KAN-PA ZI KI-A KAN-PA]

NAM-TAR AZAG GAR-GIG GAR-ŠA-[A GAR-ḪUL-GIM-MA]

nam-ta-ri[2] *a-šak-ku ma-ru uš-tu* [*up-ša-šu-u mimma*] *lim-nu*

SU MULU-GIŠGAL-LU PAP-ḪAL-LA-GE A-NA . . . . GI-EŠ . . . .

ina zumur[3] *ameli*[4] *mut-tal-li-ku*[5] *li-in-*[*na-as-ḫu*]

---

[1] 47,852, GE.

[2] K. 224, *ru*.

[3] 47,852, *zu-mur*.

[4] 47,852, *a-me-lu*.

[5] K. 224, *ki*.

b. Prayer against the Evil Spirits.

Incantation :—
c. Of Ea are they, of [Damkina] are they!
d. Of En-kur-sig-nunme-ubara[a] are they,
Of Nin-kur-sig-nunme-ubara are they,
e. Of Adapa, the ruler of Eridu, are they!
f. I am the sorcerer-priest of Ea,
g. I am the messenger of Marduk;
h. To revive the ( )[b] sick man
i. The great lord Ea hath sent me;
108. He hath added his pure spell to mine,
He hath added his pure voice to mine,
110. He hath added his pure spittle to mine,
He hath added his pure prayer to mine.
Whether thou art an evil Spirit or an evil Demon,
Or an evil Ghost or an evil Devil,
Or an evil God or an evil Fiend,
. . . fiend . . . .
115. Be thou removed from before me!
By Heaven be thou exorcised! By Earth be thou exorcised!
May the pestilence, fever, pain, sorcery, and all evil
Be removed from the body of the wanderer.

[a] According to *W.A.I.*, ii, 56, 48, *c*, [DINGIR . . .]-KUR-SIG (*i-si-mu*)-NUN-ME = ^{ilu}*Us-mu-u sukkalli* ^{ilu}EN-KI-GA-GE, i.e. the minister of Ea, and it is possible that this is the same as DINGIR-EN-KUR-SIG-NUNME-UBARA (Brünnow, *List*, No. 2,833). DINGIR-NIN-KUR-SIG-NUNME-UBARA is read Ninkum (Brünnow, No. 11,013).

[b] See note to l. 69.

SU-MU NAM-BA-TE-MAL-E[1]-NE BAR-KU ḪE-IM-[TA-GUB]
ana zumri-ia[2] *a-a iṭ-ḫu-nu ina a-ḫa-a-ti li-iz-ziz*
EGIR-MU : *a-na ar-ki-ia a-a ir-du-ni*[3] : NAM-[BA-GIN-GIN-NE]
ZI DINGIR-GAL-GAL-E-NE-GE [KAN-PA][4]
niš ilâni^{pl} *rabûti*^{pl} *lu-u-ta-mu-[u]*[5]
NA-AN-GUB-BI-EN KA-SAR-BI . . . . .
a-a ik-ka-lu ri-kis-su lip-pa-dir

(PLATE IV.)

INIM-INIM-MA UTUG-ḪUL-[A-KAN]

EN GA-E MULU-TU-TU GA-SURRU-MAḪ [DINGIR-EN-KI-GE]
a-ši-pu ša-an-gam-ma[6]*-ḫu ša* ^{ilu}[*E-a*]
NAG-DUP *ra-am-ku ša* ^{alu}*Eridi a-na-ku* . . . .
TU NE-IN . . . BA-PA KU (?) . . . .
ši-pat . . . *pa-ša-ḫu ik-*[*kal*?] . . . . . .
. . . . TUR (?) RA (?) . . . .
. . . . *mar-ṣu ina* . . . . . .
. . . . . . A-GE BA (?) GE (?) GAR . . . . .
. . . .
TAG . . . .
. . . .
I-LU . . . .
as-kup-pat . . . .
E-A-KU . . . .
ana bîti ina e-ri-bi . . . .
DINGIR-BABBAR IGI-MU-KU DINGIR-SIS-KI [EGIR-MU-KU]
^{ilu}*Šamšu ina pa-ni-ia* ^{ilu}*Sin ina ar-*[*ki-ia*]

Unto my body may they not come nigh,
May they get hence from near me,
May they not follow after me.
By the Great Gods may they be exorcised![a]
May he not be held in bondage,
May his fetters be loosened!

(PLATE IV.)

PRAYER AGAINST THE EVIL SPIRITS.

Incantation:—
I am the sorcerer-priest of [Ea],
I am the magician of Eridu,

[Lines 131–138 much broken.]

The threshold . . . . . .
Unto the house on entering . . .
Shamash (is) before me,
Sin (is) behind [me],

[1] K. 224 omits.
[2] 47,852, *zu-mur-ia.*
[3] 47,852, *u.*
[4] 47,852, I-RI-PA ḪA-BA-RA-DU-UN.
[5] 47,852, *u-tam-mi-ka* . . .
[6] K. 224, *maḫ.*

[a] 47,852, "By the Great Gods I exorcise thee, that thou mayst depart!"

DINGIR - NE - URU - GAL ID - ZI - DA - [MU]
ilu Nergal ina im - ni - [ia]
DINGIR - NIN - IB ID - GUB - BU - [MU]
ilu " ina šu - me - li - ia
MULU - TUR - RA - KU TE - MAL - DA[1] - MU - NE
ana mar - ṣu[2] ina te[3] - ḫi - e - a
SAG MULU - TUR - RA - KU[4] ŠU - UŠ - GAR - RA - MU - NE
ina ḳaḳ-ḳa-du[5] mar-ṣu[2] ḳa-ti ina um-mu-di-ia
[6] UTUG- * ŠIG-GA ALAD- * ŠIG-GA DA-MU KAN-GUB
UTUG-ḪUL A-LA-ḪUL GIDIM-ḪUL MULLA-ḪUL
DINGIR-ḪUL MAŠKIM-ḪUL
TUR-RA NAM-BAD LIL-LA EN-NA KI-EL-LIL-LA
EN-NA AZAG NAM-TAR-ḪUL-ḪE-A
lu-u mur-ṣu mu-tum[7] li-lu-u li-li-tum[8] a-šak-ku
nam-ta-ru[9] lim-nu .
? IGI - MU - TA E - TA BA - RA - E
dup - pir ina pa - ni - ia iš[10] - tu bîti ṣi - i
[11] GA-E MULU-TU-TU DINGIR-EN-KI-GA ME-EN
GA-E MULU-TUR-RA-KU TU-MU MU-UN-NA-AN . . .
[12] *ana - ku ana mar - ṣu šip - tum* . . . .
UTUG-ḪUL A-LA-ḪUL GIDIM-HUL MULLA-ḪUL
[DINGIR-ḪUL MAŠKIM-ḪUL]
TUR-RA NAM-TAR LIL-LA EN-NA KI-EL-[LIL-LA EN-NA][13]
AZAG NAM-[TAR-ḪUL-ḪE-A]
? IGI-MU-TA ZI AN-NA KAN-PA [ZI KI-A KAN-PA]

---

[1] 47,852, E-NE.
[2] S. 715, *ṣi*; 47,852, *ṣa*.
[3] S. 715 and 47,852, *ṭi*.
[4] S. 715, GE.
[5] S. 715, *ḳad*, and 47,852, *ḳa-di*, for *ḳa-du*.

Nergal (is) at [my] right hand,
Ninib (is) at my left hand;
When I draw near unto the sick man,
When I lay my hand on the head of the sick man,
May a kindly Spirit, a kindly Guardian stand at my side.
Whether thou art an evil Spirit or an evil Demon,
Or an evil Ghost or an evil Devil,
Or an evil God or an evil Fiend,
Or sickness, or death, or Phantom of Night,
Or Wraith of Night, or fever, or evil pestilence,
Be thou removed from before me,
Out of the house go forth!
(For) I am the sorcerer-priest of Ea,
It is I who [recite] the incantation for the sick man
Whether thou be an evil Spirit or an evil Demon,
Or an evil Ghost or an evil Devil,
[Or an evil God or an evil Fiend],
Or sickness, or death, or Phantom of Night,
Or Wraith of Night, or disease, or evil pestilence,
Be thou removed from before me!

[6] Line translated on 47,852: *še-e-du dum-ḳi la-mas-su dum-ḳi i-da-a* . . . and on S. 715 [*še*]*-id dum-ḳi la-mas-si dum-ḳi i-da-a-a li-iz-ziz.*

[7] S. 715, *ta*; 47,852, *u-tu.*

[8] 47,852, *tu.*

[9] 47,852, *ri.*

[10] S. 715, *ul.*

[11] S. 715 translates [*a-ši*]*-pu ša* ^{ilu}*E-a*[*ana-ku*].

[12] 47,852 omits this line.

[13] 47,852, E-NE KI-EL-E-NE.

MULU - GIŠGAL - LU DU DINGIR - RA - NA BA - RA - [AN-TE-MAL-DA]

(PLATE V.)

BA - RA - AN - [GE - GE - E - NE]
ZI AN - NA KAN - PA ZI KI - A [KAN - PA]

INIM - INIM - MA UTUG - ḪUL - [A - KAN]

EN GA - E [1] DINGIR - ID ME - EN GA - E . . . .
ša *ilu* „ *ana - ku* *ša* *ilu* „ . . . .
RIG - SAR MULU - TIL - LA KALAM - MA . . . .
a - ši - pu *mu - bal - liṭ* *mâti* [2] . . .
MAŠ - MAŠ - GAL - GAL - LA URU - A GIN . . . .
„ *mut-tal-lik a-lu* . . .
GU - GIR KA ŠU - LUḪ - ḪA NUN - KI - GA . . . .
a-ši-pu *alu Eridi* *ša* *pi-i-šu* *me-su-u* . . .
MULU-TUR-RA NAM-TAR MU-UN-DIB-BI [3] AZAG . . . NA-AN-TA . . .
mar-ṣa *ša* *nam-ta-ri* [4] *iṣ-ba-tu-šu* [5] *a-šak-ku eli-šu* *šub-tum*
MULU - TUR - RA - KU TE - MAL - E [6] - NE - MU - [NE]
SA MULU - TUR - RA - KU ZU - ZU - [6] - NE . . .
bu - a - ni *mar - ṣu* [7] *ina* *la - ma - di - ia*
ID - ŠU - GIR - BI BAD - BAD - DA - [MU - NE] [8]
meš - ri - ti - šu *ina* *pu - uḳ - ḳu - di - ia*
A DINGIR-EN-KI-GE MULU-TUR-RA *SUD-*SUD-DA-MU-NE
me-e [9] *ilu E-a* [10] *mar-ṣu* [11] *ina* *sa-la-ḫi-ia*

---

[1] 47,852 inserts MULU.
[2] 47,852, *ma-a-tu*.
[3] 47,852, BA.
[4] 47,852, *tar* for *ta-ri*.

By Heaven be thou exorcised! [By Earth be thou exorcised!]
Unto the man, the son of his god, come not nigh,

(PLATE V.)

Get thee hence!
By Heaven be thou exorcised! By Earth [be thou exorcised!]

PRAYER AGAINST THE EVIL SPIRITS.

Incantation:—
Of the goddess Id[a] am I, of the god (?) . . . [am I],
A sorcerer that giveth life unto the land,
A potent wizard that patrolleth the city,
A sorcerer of Eridu whose mouth is purified [am I].
The sick man upon whom sickness hath seized,
Fever (hath taken up) its seat upon him.
When I draw near unto the sick man,
When I examine[b] the muscles of the sick man,
When I compose his limbs,
When I sprinkle the water of Ea on the sick man,

---

[5] 47,852, *tuš* for *tu-šu*.
[6] K. 8,262, DA-MU.
[7] 47,852, *ṣa*.
[8] K. 8,262 . . . PA-DA-MU-NE.
[9] K. 224, A-MEŠ for *me-e*.
[10] 47,852, NAḲBU for *E-a*.
[11] 47,852 and K. 8,262, *ṣa*.

[a] The goddess Id, according to Brünnow, *List* No. 10,223, was the mother of Ea.
[b] Lit. "learn."

MULU - TUR - RA ḪU - LUḪ - ḪA - MU - NE
mar - ṣa ina[1] *gul - lu - ti - ia*
TE MULU - TUR - RA - KU RA - RA - DA - MU - NE
li - it mar - ṣa[2] *ina*[1] *ma - ša - di - ia*
MUḪ MULU - TUR - RA - GE GU - DE - MU - NE
e - li mar - ṣi[3] *ina ša - si - e - a*
NAM-ŠUB NUN-KI-GA : *ši-pat* [alu]*Eridi ina na-di-e-a* :
SUM-MU-DA[4] - MU[4] - NE
UTUG - * ŠIG - GA ALAD - * ŠIG - GA DA - GE KAN - GUB
UTUG-ḪUL A-LA-ḪUL GIDIM-ḪUL MULLA-ḪUL
DINGIR-ḪUL MAŠKIM-[ḪUL]
DINGIR - RAB - KAN - ME DINGIR - RAB - KAN - [ME][5] - A
DINGIR-RAB-KAN-[ME-KIL]
MULU-LIL-LA KI-EL-LIL KI-EL-GID[6] - DA - KAR - RA
NAM-TAR-ḪUL-IK AZAG-GAR-GIG[7] GAR-GIG GAR-ŠA-A
GAR-ḪUL-GIM-MA
[SUR-AŠ]-ŠUB A-ḪA-AN-TUM U - ŠU[8] - ŠUB . . . .
MULU - ḪUL IGI - ḪUL
UḪ (?)[9] -ḪUL EME-ḪUL KA-ḪUL-A GAR-ŠA-A
GAR-ḪUL-GIM-MA

---

[1] 47,852, *i-na*.
[2] K. 224, *ṣi*.
[3] 47,852, *ṣa*.
[4] 35,611 omits.
[5] ME is omitted on 35,611.
[6] K. 8,262, UD.
[7] S. 996 inserts TUR-RA-NU-DUG-GA.
[8] S. 996 inserts UŠ.
[9] S. 996 . . . UḪ (?) -ZU UḪ (?) A-RI-A GAR-ŠA-A GAR-ḪUL-GIM-MA.

When I subdue[a] the sick man,
When I bring low the strength of the sick man,
When I recite an incantation over the sick man,
When I perform the Incantation of Eridu,
May a kindly Spirit, a kindly Guardian, be present
at my side.
Whether thou art an evil Spirit or an evil Demon,
Or an evil Ghost or an evil Devil,
Or an evil God or an evil Fiend,
Or Hag-demon or Ghoul or Robber Sprite,
Or Phantom of Night or Wraith of Night,
Or Handmaiden of the Phantom,
Or evil pestilence or noisome fever,
Or pain or sorcery or any evil,
[b]Or headache or shivering or (?) or terror,
Or an evil man or evil face,
Or evil spell, or evil tongue, or evil mouth, or
sorcery, or any evil,

---

[a] *Gullutia*. From *W.A.I.*, iv, 26 (4), 46, *tam-tum ši-i gal-ta-at* ("the sea heaves"), *galâtu* has evidently the meaning of "quaking" (whence its more common meaning of "quaking with fear"), but here the translation "when I have shaken the sick man" is unlikely. It is more probable that just as the magician reduces the strength of the sick man (cf. the following line), and thereby that of the devil in him, so will he frighten into subjection the evil power which has possessed the body of the patient.

[b] Restore the first characters, SUR-AŠ, and compare pl. 31, l. 102, which should read SUR-AŠ-ŠUB A-ḪA-AN-TUM U-ŠU-UŠ-ŠUB, etc. In *Devils and Evil Spirits*, vol. ii, Tablet "O," ll. 11–12, SUR-AŠ-ŠUB is translated *ṭi-'-u šu-ru-ub-bu-*[*u*]. The meaning of A-ḪA-AN-TUM is doubtful; A-ḪA-AN = *nušû* (Brünnow, *List* No. 11,704). U-ŠU-ŠUB is probably to be translated *ḫarbašu*; see pl. 46, ll. 168–169, where *ḫar-ba-šu* is certainly to be restored as the translation of U-ŠU-[ŠUB].

? -LA IGI-MU-TA ZI AN-NA KAN-PA ZI KI-A KAN-PA

INIM - INIM - MA UTUG - ḪUL - A - KAN[1]

EN [2]GA-E MULU DINGIR-EN-KI-GA ME-EN
(PLATE VI.)
[3]GA-E MULU DINGIR-DAM-GAL-NUN-NA ME-EN
[4]GA-E MULU-KIN-GA-A DINGIR-SILIG-MULU-ŠAR ME-EN
TU-MU *tu u-a tu-u ša* *ilu* *E-a*[5] TU DINGIR-EN-KI-GE
TU-TU-MU *šip-ti*[6] *šip-tum*[7] *ša* *ilu* *Marduk* TU-TU DINGIR-SILIG-MULU-ŠAR-GE
GIŠ-ḪAR DINGIR-EN-KI-GE ŠU-MU MU-UN-DA-AN-GAL
u - ṣu - rat *ilu* *E - a*[8] *ina ḳa - ti - ia ba - ša - a*
GIŠ - MA - NU GIŠ - KU - MAḪ AN - NA - GE ŠU - MU MU - UN - DA - AN - GAL
GIŠ - PA - ŠANGA PA-AN-GAL-GAL-LA ŠU-MU MU-UN-DA - AN - GAL
[9]*a-ra ša par-ṣu rabi-tu ina ḳa-ti-ia na-ša-ku*
SU - MU NAM - BA - TE - MAL - E - NE
ana zumri - ia a - a iṭ - ḫu - ni
IGI - MU - KU NAM - BA - ḪUL - E - NE
EGIR - MU - KU NAM - BA - GIN - GIN - NE
a - na ar - ki - ia a - a il - li - ku - nu
[10]I - LU KAN - GUB NAM - MU - UN - DA - UŠ - EN
KI - GUB - BU - NE BA - RA - AN - DA[11] - GUB - BU-NE-EN
a - šar az - ziz[12] *- zu la ta - az - za - zi*[13]

---

[1] 47,852, GE.
[2] 47,852 translates: *ša* *ilu* *Ea ana-ku.*
[3] 47,852 translates: *ša* *ilu* *Dam-ki-an-na ana-ku.*

Be thou removed from before me!
By Heaven be thou exorcised! By Earth be thou exorcised!

PRAYER AGAINST THE EVIL SPIRITS.

Incantation:—
The man of Ea am I,

(PLATE VI.)

The man of Damkina am I,
The messenger of Marduk am I,
My spell is the spell of Ea,
My incantation is the incantation of Marduk,
The Ban of Ea is in my hand,
The tamarisk, the powerful weapon of Anu,
In my hand I hold;
The date spathe, mighty in decision,
In my hand I hold.
Unto my body may they not draw nigh,
Before me may they wreak no evil,
Nor follow behind me.
On the threshold where I stand, let them not set themselves;
Where I stand, there stand thou not!

---

[4] 47,852 translates: *mar šip-ri ša* [ilu]*Marduk ana-ku.*

[5] 47,852, *te-e ša* [ilu] *Ea.*

[6] 47,852, *tu.*

[7] 47,852, *tu*; 38,594, *ti.*

[8] 47,852, [*u*]-*ṣur-tu* [ilu] *Ea.*

[9] 47,852, [*gi*]-*šim-ma-ri ša par-ṣi rab-bu-tu ina ḳa-ti-ia na-ša-ku.*

[10] 47,852 translates . . . *a-a ir-du-ni.*

[11] 47,852 omits.

[12] 47,852, *zi.*

[13] 47,852, *tas-za-az-zi* for *ta-az-za-zi.*

KI - TUŠ - A - MU BA - RA - AN - DA - TUŠ - U - NE - EN

a - šar uš - ša - bu la tu - uš - šab

KI - AL - GIN - A BA - RA - AL - GIN - A

a - šar al - la - ku la tal - lak

KI - TU - ṪU - DA - MU - KU BA - RA - AN - TU - TU - NE

a - šar ir - ru - bu la tir[1] - ru - ub

[2] ZI AN - NA KAN - PA ZI KI - A KAN - PA

INIM - İNIM - MA UTUG - ḪUL - A - KAN [3]

[EN] GAR-GAR-RA GAR-GAR-RA GAR-BI-KI GAR-GAR-RA-E-NE

mu-ni-iḫ mimma šum-šu mu-pa-aš-šiḫ[4] mimma šum-šu

ša ina šip-ti-šu mimma šum-šu i-pa-aš-ša-ḫu[5]

EN-GAL DINGIR-EN-KI-GE GAR-GAR-RA GAR-GAR-RA GAR-BI-KI GAR-GAR-RA-E-NE

belu rabu(u) ša ^{ilu}E - a (ditto)[6]

MULU-TUR-RA-KU TE-MAL-E-NE-MU-NE GAR[7] - KI GAR-GAR-RA-E-NE

ana mar-ṣa ina te-ḫi-e-a mimma šum-šu i-pa-aš-ša-ḫu[8]

MULU-TU-TU NUN-KI-GA-GE MU-UN[9] -UD-DA ME-EN

a-ši-pu ša ina ^{alu}Eridu ib-ba-nu-u ana-ku

NUN-KI A-ḪA-KI-KU MU-UN-NA-RI KAN-ME-EN

ša ina ^{alu}Eridi u Šu-ba-ri ri-ḫu-u a-na-ku

GA-E MULU-TUR-RA-KU MU - UN - NA - AN - TE - MAL

ana - ku ana mar - ṣa ina te[10] - ḫi - e - a

(Plate VII.)

DINGIR-EN-KI LUGAL ZU-AB-GE GA-E NU-UN-GA-ḪE-A

^{ilu}E - a šar ap - si - i ia - a - ši[11] li-iṣ-ṣur-an-ni

Where I sit, there sit thou not!
Where I walk, there walk thou not!
Where I enter, there enter thou not!
By Heaven be thou exorcised! By Earth be thou exorcised!

PRAYER AGAINST THE EVIL SPIRITS.

[Incantation :—]
He that stilleth all to rest, that pacifieth all,
That pacifieth all by his incantation,
He is the Great Lord Ea,
Stilling all to rest, and pacifying all,
Pacifying everything, whatever it be,
When I draw nigh unto the sick man,
He will pacify everything, whatever it be.
I am the magician born of Eridu,
Begotten in Eridu and Shubari.
When I draw nigh unto the sick man,

(PLATE VII.)

May Ea, King of the Deep, safeguard me:

---

[1] 47,852, *te*.
[2] 47,852 translates [*niš šame*]*e* *lu-u-ta-mat niš irṣitim*(*tim*) *lu-u-ta-mat*.
[3] 47,852, GE.
[4] 47,852, *mu-šap-ši-iḫ*.
[5] 47,852, *ḫa*.
[6] 47,852, do. do. do. do.
[7] 47,852 inserts BI.
[8] 47,852, *saḫ*.
[9] 47,852 inserts TU.
[10] 47,852, *ṭi*.
[11] 47,852, *ti*.

GI - ŠIS GI . . . . NUN - KI - GA - GE
gi (?) . . . . [1] ^{alu}*Eridi*
IGI - MU - [KU] ḪE - EN - LAḪ - LAḪ - GI - EŠ
ana pa - [ni - i]a lu - u - ka - a - a - an

[Hiatus of about four lines.]

DINGIR - NIN - A - ḪA - KUD - DU . . . .
^{ilu} " *a - ḫat* ^{ilu}*A - [nim]* . . . . .
DINGIR - ID NIN A - GUB - BA LAḪ-LAḪ-GA . . . . .
^{ilu}*Id be - lit agubbe - e el - [li]* . . . .
DINGIR-SILIG-MULU-ŠAR DU NUN-KI-GA-GE GIG-BI . . .
^{ilu}*Marduk mar* ^{alu}*Eridi mur-ṣa šu-a-tum* . . .

INIM - INIM - MA [UTUG - ḪUL - A - KAN]

EN DINGIR-EN-KI LUGAL ZU-AB-GE DI-PA-[DA] . . . .
^{ilu}*E - a šar ap - si - i a - ta - [a]* . . . . .
GA - E MULU - TU - TU URU - ZU
ana - ku a - ši - pu arad - ka
ID-ZI-DA-MU-KU GIN-NA-AB ID-GUB-BU-MU-KU DAḪ-AB
ina im-ni-ia a-lik ina šu-me-li-ia ia-ru-uṣ
TU - MU TU - AZAG - GA - ZU GAR - RA - AB
ta - a - ka el - lu ana te - e - a šu - kun
KA - MU KA - AZAG - GA - ZU GAR - RA - AB
pi - i - ka elli a - na [2] *pi - ia šu - kun*
KA - AZAG - GA - MU *ŠIG - GA - AB
a - ma - tum [3] *ellitim(tim)* [4] *dum* [5] *- mi - iḳ*
KA - TA DUG [6] - GA - MU ḪE - EN - SILIM - MA - AB
ḳi - bit pi - ia šul - lim
ME - MU EL - E - NE DUG - GA - AB
par - ṣi - ia ul - lu - lu [7] *ḳi - bi*

May the . . . . of Eridu
Stand continually before me.

[Hiatus of about two lines.]

(May) Nin-akha-kuddu, sister of Anu, . . . ,
Id, Lady of pure waters, . . .
Marduk, son of Eridu, [remove] this sickness.

PRAYER AGAINST THE EVIL SPIRITS.

Incantation :—
O Ea, King of the Deep, to see . . . .
I, the magician, am thy slave.
March thou on my right hand,
Be present[a] on my left ;
Add thy pure spell unto mine,
Add thy pure voice unto mine,
Vouchsafe (to me) pure words,
Make fortunate the utterances of my mouth.
Ordain that my decisions be happy,

---

[1] 38,594 has here *tir*, 47,852 . . . *bu ša*.
[2] Rm. 541, *ana* for *a-na*.
[3] K. 224 and Rm. 541, *ti*.
[4] K. 224, *el-li-ta* ; Rm. 541, *el-li-tu*.
[5] Rm. 541, *du-um*.
[6] Rm. 541 inserts AZAG.
[7] K. 224, *la*.

[a] *Iaruṣ* ; *arâṣu* = Syriac *era'*, "met" (Brockelmann, *Lexicon Syriacum*, p. 28, *a*).

KI - GIR GIN - NA - MU - GA AN - SI - IL
e - ma al - la - ku lu - uš - lim
MULU ŠU - TAG - GA - MU ḪE - EN - SILIM - MA - AB
amelu[1] *a - lap - pa - tu*[2] *liš - lim*

(PLATE VIII.)

IGI - MU - TA KA - GAR - *ŠIG - GA ḪE - EN - DUG - GA
ana pa-ni[3] *-ia e-gir-tum*[4] *damiḳtim(tim)*[5] *liḳ-ḳa-bi*
BAR - MU - TA ŠU - *ŠIG - GA ḪE - EN - DU - DU
ana ar-ki[6] *-ia u-ba-nu damiḳtim(tim) lit-ta-ri-iṣ*
UTUG - *ŠIG - GA - MU KAN - ME - EN
lu - u[7] *še - e - du*[8] *dùm - ḳi - ia at - ta*[9]
ALAD - *ŠIG - GA - MU [KAN - ME] - EN
lu - u[7] *la - mas - si dum - ḳi - ia at - tu*
DINGIR SILIM-MA-MU DINGIR-[SILIG-MULU-ŠAR]
ilâni^{pl} *mu - šal - li - mu* ^{ilu}*Marduk*
KI-GIR GIN-NA-MU SILIM-MA ḪE-[EN-SILIM-MA]-AB
e - ma tal - lak - ti - ia ša - la - mu liš - [lim]
DINGIR-MULU-BA-GE NAM-MAḪ-ZU ḪE-EN-IB-BA
ilu a - me - lu[10] *nar - bi - ka liḳ - bi*
MULU-GIŠGAL-LU-BI KA-TAR-ZU ḪE-EN-SI-IL-LA
[amelu][10] *šu - u da - li - li - ka lid - lul*
U GA-E MULU-TU-TU URU-ZU KA-TAR-ZU GA-SI-IL-LA
u a-na-ku a-ši-pu arad-ka da-li-li-ka lud-lul TU EN

---

[11] [INIM -]INIM - MA UTUG - ḪUL - [A - KAN]

[EN A-AN-NA] A-RI-A-MEŠ DU KI IN-TU-UD-DA-MEŠ

Let me be blessed where'er I tread,
Let the man whom I (now) touch be blessed.

(PLATE VIII.)

Before me may lucky thoughts be spoken,
After me may a lucky finger be pointed.
Oh that thou wert my guardian Genius,
And my guardian Spirit!
O god[a] that blesseth, Marduḳ,
Let me be blessed, where'er my path may be!
Thy power shall god and man proclaim;
This man shall do thy service,
And I too, the magician, thy slave.

Perform the Incantation.

PRAYER AGAINST THE EVIL SPIRITS.

[Incantation :—They are that which] was spawned in the Creation of Anu,
Children of the Earth they were born.

---

[1] K. 224, *a-me-lu*; D.T. 241, *a-mi-lu*.
[2] K. 224 and Rm. 541, *tum*.
[3] D.T. 271, *pani* for *pa-ni*.
[4] K. 224, Rm. 541, and D.T. 271, *ri*.
[5] K. 224, *da-me-iḳ-ti*.
[6] D.T. 271, *arki* for *ar-ki*.
[7] Rm. 541 omits.
[8] K. 224 and Rm. 541, *id* for *e-du*.
[9] K. 224, *tu*.
[10] K. 224, *amelu*.
[11] 38,594 omits this line.

[a] The plural here must be a scribe's mistake.

The Fourth Tablet.

COL. I (PLATE IX).

EN A-AN-NA A-RI-A-MEŠ DU[1] [KI IN-TU-UD-DA-MEŠ]
ša ri-ḫu-ut ^ilu^ *Ȧ-nim ri-ḫu-*[*u marâni* ^pl^ *irṣitim aldu*]
UMMEDA . . . .
ša ta - ri - ti . . . .
UM - ME - GA - LA ŠIS - A . . . .
ša mu - še - niḳ - ti li - [*mut - ti*] . . . . .
ARALI . . . .
ina a - ra - al - li - e . . . .
URUGAL - LA - AŠ . . . .
ina ḳab - rim . . . .
KA - GAL DINGIR - BABBAR - ŠU - [A] . . . .
ina a - bu - ul [*erib* ^ilu^ *Šamši*] . . . . .
TAK - DU - DU . . . .
ab - na [*ṣiḫirta*] . . . .
TAK - GAL . . . .
ab - [*na rabta*] . . . .
. . . .

[Hiatus of several lines.]

. . . . DINGIR-GIR BA-AN-DA(?)-TIG-IM-MI-[IN-GAR ?]
. . . . . ^ilu^ *Nergal u - kan - na -* [*šu*]
. . . DUG-KURUN-NA GAZ-ZA-GIM ḪAR-SAG-GA . . . .
šar (?) - *ḫa* (?) - *šu* (?) - *nu kima kar - pa ka - ra - ni ḫi - pi - ti* . . .
MA - DA - MA - DA - BI MU - UN - LAḪ - LAḪ - GI - [EŠ]
ma - a - ta ana ma - a - ti it - ta - na - al - la - [*ku*]

The Fourth Tablet.

COL. I (PLATE IX).

Incantation :—

They are that which was spawned in the Creation of Anu,
[Children of the Earth they were born].
They are that which a woman in travail [. . . . hath brought forth],[a]
They are that which an evil foster-mother [hath suckled],
In the Underworld [are they],
In the tomb [are they],
In the Great Gate of Sunset [are they],
A small stone . . . .
A large stone . . . .

[Hiatus of several lines.]

. . . . . . Nergal they have subdued,
Their . . . like a shattered wine goblet . . . ,
From land to land they roam,

---

[1] K. 2,410 has I (instead of DU, which is apparently the better reading from the catchline of the preceding tablet).

[a] I.e., probably abortions.

KI - EL DAGAL - A - NI - TA[1] BA - RA - GIBIŠ - NE
ar - da - tu ina maš - ta - ki - ša[2] *u - še - el - lu - u*
GURUŠ E-UR[3] - A - NI - TA BA - RA - E - NE
id - la ina bit e - mu - ti - ša[2] *u - še - ṣu - u*
DU E - AD - DA[4] - A - NI - TA BA - RA - E - NE
ma - a - ra ina bit a - bi[5] *- šu u - še -* [6]*ṣu - u*
ṬU-Ḫ̮U AB-LA-BI-TA BA - RA - AN - DIB - DIB - BI - NE
su - um - ma - ti ina a - pa - ti - ši[7]*-na i - bar - rum*
* NAMṢAB ID - BUL - BI - TA BA - RA - GIBIŠ - NE
iṣ - ṣu - ru ina ab - ri - šu u - še - el - lu - u
NAM-Ḫ̮U U-KI-* SIG-GA-BI-TA BA-AN-RA-AN-RI-RI-E-NE
si - nun - tu ina ḳin - ni - ša u - šap - ra - šu
GUD IN - GE - GE - E - NE LU IN - GE - GE - E - NE
al - pi i - šab - bi - ṭu im - me - ra i - šab - bi - ṭu
U-GAL-GAL-LA-A-MEŠ UTUG-Ḫ̮UL NIGIN-NA-MEŠ
umu (mu) rabûti^{pl} *u-tuk-ku lim-nu-tum ṣa-i-du*[8] *šu-nu*
SAG - GIŠ KALAM - MA MU - UN - RA - RA - E - NE
ša ma - a - tu i - nar - rum šu - nu

Col. II.

GAR - ERIM - MA SAG - DU . . . .
ina li - pit - tu i - šit - ti . . . .
KUR - RA DUG - SAR - GIM . . . .
DINGIR-NIN-DU-U-NA DUP-SAR-MAḪ̮ . . . .
ba - lum ^{ilu}*Be - lit ṣi - ri dup - šar -* [
GIR KUR - RA - GE NU - MU - UN . . . .
še - e - pu ana irṣitim(tim) ul . . . .
E - SU KUR - RA - GE NU - MU - UN - DA . . . .
su - li ir - ṣi - ti ul . . . . . .

[Hiatus of several lines.]

Driving the maiden from her chamber,
Sending the man forth from his home,
Expelling the son from the house of his father,
Hunting the pigeons from their cotes,
Driving the bird from its nest,
Making the swallow fly forth from its hole,
Smiting both oxen and sheep.
They are the evil spirits that chase the great storms,
Bringing a blight on the land.

COL. II.

In the enclosure . . . .
The land like a bowl . . . .
Without Beltis, mighty scribe . . . .
Foot to earth [they ?] cannot . . . .
The paths of earth [they ?] cannot . . . .

[Hiatus of several lines.]

---

[1] 36,589, TI.
[2] 36,589, *šu*.
[3] 36,589, TUM.
[4] 36,589 omits.
[5] 36,589, *abi* for *a-bi*.
[6] 36,589 inserts *iṣ*.
[7] 36,589, *šu*[*-nu* ?].
[8] K. 2,578 inserts *ti* after *du*.

. . . .

,, ,, ...

SILA SIG-GA . . . GE MU-UN-LAḪ-[LAḪ-GI-EŠ]
ina su-ḳi ša-[ḳu-um]-mi ina mu-ši it-ta-na-[al-la-ku]
TUR IN . . . . E-NE AMAŠ IN . . . .
tar-ba-ṣa i . . . . *su-pu-ra i* . . . . . .
KALAM - MA GIŠ - GAL[GIŠ - ŠAGIL]-GIM MU-UN-NA-RA-AB . . . .
ma-a-tu [*kima* (?) *dalti u*] *me-di-li it-* . . . . .
ERI - A ME - GIM MU - UN - GA - GA - E - [NE]
ina ali ki - ma ḳu - li it - ta - na - aš - ki - [*nu*]
GIŠ - GAL - A ṢIR - GIM MU - UN - SUR - SUR - E - [NE]
ina dal - ti ki - ma si - ri it - ta - na - aš - la - [*lu*]
GIŠ-ZA-RA IMI-GIM MU-UN-ZA-LA-AḪ-ḪI-E-[NE]
ina ṣir[1] *ki - ma ša - a - ri i* - [*ziḳ - ḳu*]
DAM UR MULU KA - BA - RA - AN - [NAM (?) - NE]
aš - ša - ta ina ut - li ameli i - tar - [*ru - u*]
DU DU-UB MULU KA-BA-RA-AN-ZI-[ZI-E-NE]
ma-a-ra ina b.r-ki ameli u-šat-[*bu-u*]

[The whole of Col. III is wanting.]

Col. IV.

ZI DINGIR-PA-TE-SI-GAL-ZU-AB NU-[DU-DA] A-AB . . . .
niš *ilu* ,, *la - bu - ut - te - e* . . . . .
MULU - GIŠGAL - LU DU DINGIR - [RA - NA]
(Plate X.)
ša ameli mar [*ili - šu*]
KI GUB-BA-NA BA - RA - AN - DA - [GUB - BU - NE - EN]
a - šar iz[2] *- zi - zu la ta* - [*az - zi - iz*]

Through the gloomy street by night they roam,
[Smiting] sheepfold and cattle-pen.
The land [as with door and ?] bolt they [shut up],
In the city like a snare[a] they are set,
Through the door like a snake they glide,[b]
Through the hinge[c] like the wind they blow,
Estranging the wife from the embrace of a husband,
Snatching the child from the loins[d] of a man.

[The whole of Col. III is wanting.]

COL. IV.

By the god Patesi-Gal-Zuab,[e] Chief of the Sea, [mayest thou be exorcised].

(PLATE X.)

(And) concerning the man, son of his god,

---

[1] K. 2,578 adds *ri*.

[2] K. 4,857, *az*.

[a] *Ḳulu* (Tallqvist, *Maqlu*, p. 148). As there are two different groups in Sumerian which are both rendered by *ḳulu* in these texts (ME as here, and GAR-ME-GAR, v i, 42), it is possible that there is another meaning for it besides "burning," which does not seem to fit here. Cf. the Chaldaic *ḳôlâ*, "a snare" (Levy, *Chaldäisches Wörterbuch*, vol. ii, p. 350). Cf. also Haupt, *Akkad. u. Sumer. Keils.*, p. 121, Ḳ. 5,332, *ḳulu šukun-ma manma ilu la iba'* ("Set a trap that no god can escape").

[b] *Ittanašlalu*: √*šalâlu*, "to steal," and so in a passive conjugation, "to go stealthily." Cf. Heb. *yithgannêbh*, 2 Sam. xix, 4, "go by stealth," and Syr. *g'nab naphsheh*. See also Tablet V, i, 33.

[c] *ṣir* (v. *ṣirri*, Tablet V, i, 35). Cf. Syr. *ṣ'iar'tha*, "a hinge."

[d] *birki*, literally "knees."

[e] "Great Ruler of the Deep."

KI TUŠ-A-NA BA-RA-AN-DA-TUŠ-[U-NE-EN]
a-šar uš-ša-bu la tu-[uš-šab]
[KI] AL-GIN-A BA-RA-AL-GIN-[A]
[a-šar] il[1] *-la-ku la tal-lak*
KI [TU-TU-DA-MU]-KU BA-RA-AN-DA-TU-TU-NE
[a-šar ir]-ru-bu la tir-ru-ub
. . . . BA-RA-AN-DA-UŠ-EN
[a-na?] . . . šu la te-rid-di-šu
KI-[A ID]-DA-GE BA-RA-AN-DA-AN-BUR-RI[2]
ina ki-bir na-a-ri la tap-pa-aš-šir-šu
KIR A-[AB]-BA-GE BA-RA-AN-DA-PAL-E
ina ki-rib tam-tim la te-ib-bir-šu
ZI DINGIR-GAL-GAL-LA-E-NE-GE KAN-RI-PA
ḪA-BA-RA-DU-UN
niš ilâni^{pl} *rabûti*^{pl} *u-tam-mi-ka*
lu-ta-at-tal-lak

INIM-INIM-MA UTUG-ḪUL-A-KAN

EN EN-E ANA-GAL-TA KI-DAGAL-KU
GIŠ-KU-PI-GA-A-NI NAM . . . .
be-lum iš-tu šame(e) rabûti^{pl} *irṣitim(tim)*
rapaštim(tim) u-zu-un-[šu iš-kun]
EN-GAL DINGIR-EN-KI-GE ANA-GAL-TA KI-DAGAL-KU . . .
[be-lum] rabu(u) ^{ilu}*E-a [irṣitim(tim)*
rapaštim(tim)] . . . . .

[Hiatus of several lines.]

Where he standeth,[a] there stand thou not!
Where he is seated,[a] there sit thou not!
[Where] he goeth,[a] there go thou not!
[Where] he entereth,[a] there enter thou not!
[Unto his . . .] pursue him not!
On the bank of a river loose[b] him not!
In the middle of the sea over him pass not!
By the Great Gods I exorcise thee,
That thou mayest depart!

PRAYER AGAINST THE EVIL SPIRITS.

Incantation :—
The lord from the broad heavens unto the wide earth [inclined his] ear,
The great lord Ea from the broad heavens unto the wide earth . . . . .

[Hiatus of several lines.]

---

[1] K. 4,857, *al.*
[2] K. 4,857, *ra.*

[a] K. 4,857 uses the first person.
[b] I.e., his boat.

. . . .

. . . *irṣitim(tim)* . . . .

NU - GIG . . . .

ana ḳa-diš-[ti] . . . .

ŠU - BAD A . . . .

ḳa - ti mu - u - tum li (?) - pi - tum . . . . . .

[1] DINGIR-NIN-UK DINGIR-NIN-ME DINGIR . . .

DINGIR-NIN-KI-GAL : *ilu* „ *al-ti* [*ilu* „ :] DAM DINGIR-[NIN-A-ZU]

A NU-MU [2] -ŠU-NAG KA-NU-MU-UN-[ ]-IB-[PIŠ?]

mê pl ul ir - mu - ku ul u - šal - li - [šu ?]

DAK - KI - GAL [3] - E - NE DAK - AZAG - [GA] . . .

ina šu-ba-ti ra-ba-[ti] [4] *šub-tum el-li-[tum]* . . .

GIDIM KUR - TA [5] GIBIŠ [6] - IB - IB ME - [EN]

lu-u e-kim-mu ša iš-tu-u irṣitim(tim) il-la-a-[ku at-ta]

MULU-LIL-LA KI-NA-A NU-TUK-A KAN-ME-EN

lu-u li-lu-u ša ma-a-a-al-tum la i-šu-u at-ta

KI - EL NU - UN - ZU - A - AN KAN - ME - EN

lu - u ar - da (?) - tum la la - mit - tum at - ta

GURUŠ ID - NU - E [7] KAN - ME - EN

[lu - u id] - lu la muš - te - en - nu - u at - ta

MULU - EDIN - NA ŠUB - BA KAN - ME - EN

[lu - u ša ina] ṣi - e - ri na - du - u at - ta

MULU-EDIN-NA BA . . NE IŠ NU-DUL-LA KAN-ME-EN

[lu-u ša ina ṣi-e-ri] na-du-u e-pi-ri la kat-mu at-ta

MULU-EDIN-NA . . . . KAN-ME-EN

lu-u ša [ina ṣi-e-ri] . . . .

MULU . . . .

[Some lines wanting.]

. . . earth . . . .
Unto the harlot . . . .
The hand of death (?) . . . .
Ninuk, Ninme, (and) . . . .
Ninkigal, the wife of [Ninazu].
They pour forth no water, they utter no spells,[a]
In a lofty, shining abode . . . .
Whether thou art a ghost that hath come from the earth,
Or a phantom of night that hath no couch,
Or a woman (that hath died) a virgin,[b]
Or a man (that hath died) unmarried,[c]
Or one that lieth dead in the desert,
Or one that lieth dead in the desert, uncovered with earth,
Or one that in the desert . . . .
Or one that . . . .

[Some lines wanting.]

[1] 45,744 translates this line *[ilu]* ,, *[ilu]* ,, *u* . . . .
[2] 45,744 inserts UN.
[3] 45,744 inserts LA.
[4] 45,744 for this has *šu-ba-a-tum rab-ba-a-tum.*
[5] 45,744, RA.
[6] 45,744, MULU . . (?).
[7] 45,744 has . . . LAL-E.

[a] *Ušalli*[*šu* ?]; *šalâšu* = "to do something three times," probably for reciting incantations. Cf. the *Legend of the Worm* (vol. ii), *r.* 26, *šipti III-šu ana eli tamannu*(*nu*). The first half of the line refers to libations as offerings.

[b] *Lamittum*; *lamâdu* = "to learn," probably here with an ulterior meaning, like the Hebrew *yada'*, "to know."

[c] *Muštennû* = "one that changes the condition of." From the parallel passage in the previous line it evidently has the meaning of "marrying," and possibly affords a clue to the interpretation of the Hebrew *šânâ* in Esther ii, 9.

Col. V.

[MULU GIŠ]-GIŠIMMAR-TA BA-AN-ZI-IR-ZI-IR-RI-DA KAN-ME-EN
[lu-u] ša iš-tu gi-šim-ma-ri iḫ-ḫi-il-ṣa-a at-tu
[MULU GIŠ] - MA - BI A * SIG - GA KAN - ME - EN
[lu-u] ša ina e-lip-pi ina me-e it-bu-u „
GIDIM MULU KI-ʾNU-TUM-MA KAN-ME-EN
lu-u e-kim-mu la ḳib-rum „
GIDIM MULU SAG-LI-TAR NU-TUK-A KAN-ME-EN
lu-u e-kim-mu ša pa-ḳi-da la i-šu-u „
GIDIM MULU KI-* SIG-GA NU-TUK-A KAN-ME-EN
lu-u e-kim-mu ša ka-sap ki-is-pi la i-šu-u „
GIDIM MULU A-DE-A NU-TUK-A KAN-ME-EN
[lu-u] e-kim-mu ša na-aḳ me-e la i-šu-u „
[GIDIM] MULU MU-PA-DA NU-TUK-A KAN-ME-EN
[lu-u] e-kim-mu ša za-kar šu-me la i-šu-u „
[DINGIR] - RAB - KAN - ME KAN - ME - EN
[lu] - u la - bar - tum „
[DINGIR - RAB - KAN - ME] - A KAN - ME - EN
[lu - u la - ba] - ṣu „
[DINGIR - RAB - KAN - ME - KIL] KAN - ME - EN
[lu - u aḫ - ḫa - zu] „
[NU - GIG ŠA - TUR - RA] KAN - ME - EN
[lu-u ḳa-diš-tu ša lib-ba-ša . . . „]
[UMMEDA KAN - ME - EN]
[lu - u ta - ri - tu „]
[UM - ME - GA - LA KAN - ME - EN]
lu - u mu - še - [niḳ - tu „]
IR - RA UM - [ME - GA - LA KAN - ME - EN]
lu - u ba - ki - tu mu - [še - niḳ - tu „]

Col. V.

Or one that hath been torn from a date-palm,
Or one that cometh through the waters in a boat,
Or a ghost unburied,
Or a ghost that none careth for,
Or a ghost with none to make offerings,
Or a ghost with none to pour libations,
Or a ghost that hath no posterity,[a]
Or a hag-demon,
Or a ghoul,
Or a robber-sprite,
[Or a harlot (that hath died) whose body is sick],
[Or a woman (that hath died) in travail],
Or a woman (that hath died) with a babe at the breast,
Or a weeping[b] woman (that hath died) with a babe at the breast,

---

[a] *Zakar šume*, i.e., one that carries on the family name.

[b] From this it must be inferred that the ghost is that of a nursing woman whose babe is dead.

MULU-ḪUL-IK : *lu-u lim-*[*nu* „ : KAN-ME-EN]
UTUG - ḪUL - IK [KAN - ME - EN]
lu - u u - [*tuk - ku lim - nu* „]
UB - DA - GUB - [GUB - BU KAN - ME - EN]
lu - u mut - [*ta - al - lik tub - ḳi* „]
DA - GUB - [GUB - BU KAN - ME - EN]
lu - u mut - ta - [*al - lik ša - ḫa - ti* „]
U - ŠU - UŠ GA - BA - DA - AN - [KU KAN - ME - EN]
lu - u ša uma(ma) it - ti - šu [*lu - kul* „]
U - ŠU - UŠ GA - BA - DA - AN - [NAK KAN - ME - EN]

(Plate XI.)

lu - u ša uma(ma) it - ti - šu [*lu - uš - ti* „]
U - ŠU - UŠ GA - BA - DA - AN - ŠEŠ [KAN - ME - EN]
lu-u ša uma(ma) it-ti-šu lu-[*up*]*-pa-šiš* [„]
U - ŠU - UŠ GA - BA - DA - AN - KU KAN - ME - EN
lu-u ša uma(ma) it-ti-šu lul-ta-biš „
GA - AN - TU GA - BA - DA - AN - KU KAN - ME - EN
lu-u ša lu-ru-um-ma it-ti-šu lu-kul „
GA - AN - TU GA - BA - DA - AN - NAK KAN - ME - EN
GA - AN - TU GA - BA - DA - AN - ŠEŠ KAN - ME - EN
GA - AN - TU GA - BA - DA - AN - KU [KAN - ME - EN]
[ŠA-GAR]-TUK-A-MU-NE GAR GA-BA-DA-AN-KU [KAN-ME-EN]
[*lu-u*] *ša ina bu-ri-ia a-ka-la*[1] *it ti*[2]*-šu lu-kul* „
[IMMA - TA - TUK] - A - MU - NE A GA-BA-DA-AN-NAK KAN-ME-EN
[3] [IḪ-TAG]-GA-A-MU-NE NI GA - BA - DA - AN - ŠEŠ KAN-ME-EN

Or an evil man (that hath died),
Or an [evil] spirit,
Or one that haunteth [the neighbourhood],
Or one that haunteth [the vicinity].
Or whether thou be one with whom on a day [I have eaten],

(PLATE XI.)

Or with whom on a day [I have drunk],
Or with whom on a day I have anointed myself,
Or with whom on a day I have clothed myself,
Or whether thou be one with whom I have entered and eaten,
Or with whom I have entered and drunk,
Or with whom I have entered and anointed myself,
Or with whom I have entered and clothed myself,
Or whether thou be one with whom I have eaten food when I was hungry,
Or with whom I have drunk water when I was thirsty,
Or with whom I have anointed myself with oil when I was sore,

---

[1] K. 5,020, *lu*. [2] K. 5,020, *itti* for *it-ti*.
[3] K. 5,020 translates . . .*-ia šam-na it-ti šu lu-up-pa-šiš* ,,

[A-ŠED-DE-TUK]-A-MU[1]-NE UR-RA-NA-KU GA-BA-DA-AN-KU KAN-ME-EN

[lu-u ina ku-uṣ]-ṣi-ia ina ut-li-šu ṣu-ba-tu itti-šu lul-ta-biš at-tu

[SU] MULU-GIŠGAL-LU DU DINGIR-RA-NA

[ ] *zu-mur ameli mar ili-šu*

[EN-NA BA-RA-AN]-TA-RI-EN-NA-AŠ EN-NA BA-RA-AN-TA

ZI-GA-EN-NA-AŠ

[a-di la ta]-as-su-u a-di la ta-as-su-ḫu

[U BA-RA-AN-DA]-AB-KU-E A BA-RA-AN-DA-AB-NAK-E

[a-ka-la e] ta-kul me-e e tal-ti

[GIŠ-BANŠUR A]-A MUḪ-ZU DINGIR-EN-LIL-LA-GE ŠU-ZU BA-RA-NE-IN-TUM

[paššuri] a-bi ^{ilu}*Bel [a-li]-di-ka ḳa-at-ka e tu-bil*

[A A-AB-BA A-DUG]-GA A-ŠIS [A ID]-MAS-TIG-GAR

[me-e tam]-ti u me-e ṭa-bu-[ti me-e lim-nu-ti me-e ^{nâru}*]I-di-iḳ-lat*

[A ID-UD-KIB]-NUN-KI-NA A PU-[TA A ID-DA BA-RA-AN]-ŠU-ŠU-NE

[me-e Pu]-rat-ti „ bu-ri [„ na-a-ri e takkatim]

[ANA-KU] BA-RI-EN PA-[NA-AN-TUK-TUK-E]

[ina šame(e)] nap-riš-ma kap-[pi e te-ir-ši]

COL. VI.

KI-KU BA-GUB-BA TUŠ NAM-BI-GA-GA

ina irṣitim(tim) nik-la-ma šub-ta e [ta-aš-kun]

MULU-GIŠGAL-LU DU DINGIR-RA-NA BA-RA-AN-TE-MAL-[DA]

BA-RA-AN-GE-GE-E-[NE]

SAG-ZU SAG-GA-NA NAM-BA-DA-AB-MUK . . .

ḳaḳ-ḳad-ka ana ḳaḳ-ḳa-di-šu la ta-šak-kan

Or with whom when I was cold I have clothed
his nakedness with a garment,
(Whatever thou be) until thou art removed,
55. Until thou departest from the body of the man,
the son of his god,
60. Thou shalt have no food to eat,
Thou shalt have no water to drink,
Thou shalt not stretch forth thy hand
Unto the [table] of my father Bel, thy creator,
Neither with sea [water], nor with sweet water,
Nor with bad water, nor with Tigris water,
65. Nor with Euphrates [water], nor with pond water,
[Nor with river water] shalt thou be covered.
If thou wouldst fly up to heaven
Thou shalt have no wings,

COL. VI.

If thou wouldst lurk in ambush on earth
Thou shalt secure no resting-place.
Unto the man, the son of his god, come not nigh,
Get thee hence!
5. Place not thy head upon his head,

[1] K. 5,020, . . . TAG-GA for the beginning of this line.

[ŠU] - ZU ŠU - NA NAM - BA - DA - AN - GA - GA
[ḳa - ti] - ka ana ḳa - ti - šu la ta - šak - kan
GIR - ZU GIR - NA NAM - BA - DA - AN - GA - GA
še - ip - ka ana še - pi - šu la ta - šaḳ - kan
ŠU - ZU ŠU - NA AB - TAG
ina ḳa - ti - ka la ta - lap - pat - su
TIG - ZU [ ] - BU - I
ki - šad - ka [la ta] - sa - ḫar - šu
IGI - ZU [ ] ŠU - DA - AB - IL - LA
in - ka [la taš - ša - a]
EGIR - ZU [ ] ŠI - NA - AN - ŠI - IN - BAR - RI
ana arki - ka la tap - pal - la - as
MUḪ - NA GU - BA - RA - AN - DA - AB - [DE - E]
e - li - šu la ta - ša - as - si
E - A - KU NAM - BA - TU - TU - NE
a - na bi - ti [la te - ru - ub]
* UR - A - KU NAM - MU - [UN] - DA - PAL - E
a - na u - ri [la tab - bal - kit]
E - KI - TUŠ - A - NA NAM - BA[1] - TU - TU - NE
a - na bit [šub - ti] la te - ru - ub - šu
ŠA - ERI - A - TA NAM - MU - UN - DA[2] - NIGIN - E - NE
ina lib - bi ali[3] la tal - ta - nam - mi - šu[4]
BAR-TA-BI-KU NAM - MU - UN - DA[5] - NIGIN - E - NE
ina a - ḫa - a - ti[6] la ta - ṣa - na - aḫ - ḫar[7] - šu
I DINGIR-EN-KI-GE MULU-GIŠGAL-LU DU DINGIR RA-NA
ina a - mat ilu E - a[8] ameli mar[9] ili - šu
ḪE-EN-AZAG-GA ḪE-EN-EL-LA ḪE EN-LAḪ-LAḪ-GA[10]
DUG - BUR - ŠAGAN - GIM U - ME - NI - ḪU[5] - LUḪ - LUḪ
ki - ma bu - ri šik - ka - ti lim - te - is - si[11]

Place not thy [hand] upon his hand,
Place not thy foot upon his foot,
With thy hand touch him not,
Turn [not] thy back upon him,
Lift not thine eye [against him],
Look not behind thee,
Gibber not against him,
Into the house enter thou not,
Through the fence break thou not,
Into the chamber enter thou not,
In the midst of the city encircle him not,
Near him make no circuit;
By the Word of Ea
May the man, the son of his god,
Become pure, become clean, become bright!
Like a vessel of lard[a] may he be cleansed,

---

[1] 45,744, MU-UN.

[2] 45,744, BA for MU-UN-DA.

[3] 45,744, *a-lu*.

[4] 45,744, *miš* for *mi-šu*.

[5] 45,744 omits.

[6] 45,744, *tum*.

[7] 45,744, *tas-tan-na-ḫar* for *ta-ṣa-na-aḫ-ḫar*.

[8] 45,744, *Ea* for *E-a*.

[9] 45,744, *a-me-lu ma-ri* for *ameli mar*.

[10] 45,744 translates *li-lil li-bi-ib li-nam-mi-ri*.

[11] 45,744, for this line *kima bu-ur šik-kat lim-te-si*.

[a] *Šikkatu* has a variant *šappatu* in the twelfth tablet of the Gilgamish Epic (Haupt, *Beiträge*, i, 48; K. 3,475, i, l. 45, and K. 2,774, ii, l. 22) which is probably to be connected with the Syriac *shûphia*, adeps, lardum (Payne Smith, *Thesaurus*, 4,261).

DUG-BUR-NI-NUN-NA-GIM U-ME-NI-SU[1]-UB-SU[1]-UB

ki - ma bu - ri[2] *ḫi - me - ti*[3] *liš - ta - kil*[4]

DINGIR-BABBAR SAG-KAL DINGIR-RI-E[5]-NE-GE ŠU-NA U-ME-NI-SUM

. *ana* ^{ilu}*Šamši a - ša - rid ilâni*^{pl} *pi - ḳid - su-ma*

DINGIR-BABBAR SAG-KAL DINGIR-RI-E[5]-NE-GE SILIM-MA-NA ŠU-* ŠAG[6]-GA DINGIR-RA-NA-KU[7] ḪE - EN - ŠI - IN - GE - GE

ana ^{ilu}*Šamši a-ša-rid ilâni*^{pl} *šal-mu-us-su ana ḳa-at dam-ḳa-a-tu*

ša ilâni^{pl} *lip - pa - ḳid* TE EN

INIM - INIM - MA UTUG - ḪUL - A - KAN

---

[8]EN A - ZA - AD GAR - ŠE BA - NIGIN - NA - BA - E

. . . A - DUG - GA - NA UTUG - ḪUL A - RI - A

Duppi IV^{KAM-MA} UTUG - ḪUL - MEŠ[9]

Mât $^{m\ ilu}$*Aššur - [bani - apli]*

šar kiššati šar $^{matu\ ilu}$*Aššuri*

Like a vessel of butter may he be clean!
Unto Shamash, Chief of the gods, commend him,
Through Shamash, Chief of the gods,
May his welfare be secured at the kindly hands of the gods.

Exorcism, incantation.

PRAYER AGAINST THE EVIL SPIRITS.

Incantation:—

Cold and rain that minish all things . . .
They are the evil Spirits in the Creation of Anu spawned.

FOURTH TABLET OF THE SERIES "THE EVIL SPIRITS."

---

1 45,744, ŠU.

2 K. 2,410, *kima* for *ki-ma*.

3 K. 5,123, *mi*.

4 45,744, for this line *kim-ma bu-ru ḫi-me-tum liš-tak-kil-nu*.

5 45,744 transposes RI and E.

6 45,744, * SIG.

7 45,744, RI-NE-GE for RA-NA-KU.

8 45,744 here has IM-DUP *ša arki-šu*, "Tablet which follows it," and then the line EN A-ZA-AD GAR-ŠE-GAR-ŠE ? -GAR NIGIN-NA-BA-E-NE.

9 K. 2,410 states that it was copied from a Babylonian original.

The Fifth Tablet.

Col. I (Plate XII).

EN A-ZA-AD GAR-ŠE BA-NIGIN-NA-BA-E
. . . [A-DUG-GA-NA] UTUG-ḪUL A-RI-A
šu-ru-ub-bu-u ḫar-ba-šu mu-na-aš-šir nap-ḫar
. . . šu u-tuk-ku lim-nu ša ri-ḫu-ut ^{ilu}*A-nim ri-ḫu-u*
NAM-TAR DU KI-*AG-GA DINGIR-EN-LIL-LA
U-TU-UD-DA DINGIR-NIN-KI-GAL-LA-GE
nam-ta-ru ma-ru na-ram ^{ilu}*Bel*
i-lit-ti ^{ilu}*Nin-ki-gal*
AN-NA GUR-RU[1]-UŠ NE-IN-SIR-RU-UŠ
KI-TA KAR-RA NE-IN-SIG-GA
e-liš ig-ṣu-ṣu-ma šap-liš kar-ra id-du-u
E-NE-NE-NE DIM-MA ARALI MEŠ
šu-nu bi-nu-ut A-ra-al-li-e šu-nu
AN-TA GU-DE-DE-A-MEŠ KI-TA GU-BAL-BAL-A-MEŠ
e-liš i-šag-gu-mu šap-liš i-ṣab-bu-ru šu-nu
*UḪ ṢI DINGIR-RI-E-NE MEŠ
i-mat mar-ti ša ilâni^{pl} *šu-nu*
U-GAL ANA-TA ŠU-BAR-RA MEŠ
ûmu(mu) rab-bu-tum ša ul-tu šame(e)
uš-šu-ru-ni šu-nu
DINGIR-NIN-BUL-BUL-ḪU URU-A ? GA-GA-A-MEŠ
eš-še-pu ša ina ali i-šag-gu-mu šu-nu
A-AN-NA A-RI-A-MEŠ DU KI-IN-GUB TU-UD-DA-A-MEŠ
ša ri-ḫu-ut ^{ilu}*A-nim ri-ḫu-u marâni*^{pl} *i-lit-ti*
irṣitim(tim) šu-nu

The Fifth Tablet.

OBVERSE.

COL. I (PLATE XII).

Incantation :—

Cold and rain that minish all things, . . .
They are the evil Spirits[a] in the creation of Anu spawned.
Plague Gods,[a] the beloved sons[a] of Bel,
The offspring of Ninkigal.
Rending in pieces on high,
Bringing destruction below,
They are the Children of the Underworld.
Loudly roaring on high,
Gibbering[b] below,
They are the bitter venom of the gods.
The great storms directed from heaven—those are they,
The owl,[c] that hoots over a city—that is they,
They are the children born of Earth,

---

[1] K. 4,943 omits.

[a] Singular in the text.

[b] Cf. *W.A.I.*, ii, 20, 48–49, *ṣabarum ša iṣṣuri* ("chirping of a bird"), i.e. the Syriac *ṣ'bar*, garrivit. Cf. also *ina šerim lam iṣṣuru ṣabari*, "in the morning before a bird chirps" (D.T. 57, rev. 2).

[c] *Eššepu*, the Hebrew *yanšuph* according to Delitzsch, *Prolegomena*, p. 80.

* UR-BAD-DA * UR-DAGAL-LA A-MI-GIM NI-UL-UL-NE
u-ri e-lu-ti u-ri rap-šu-ti ki-ma a-gi-e i-šur-rum
E - TA E - A - KU IN - BAL - BAL - E - NE
iš[1] *- tu bi - ti ana bi - ti it - ta - nab - lak - ka - tu*
E - NE - NE - NE GIŠ - GAL NU - UN - GA - A - MEŠ
GIŠ - ŠAGIL NU - UN - GA - A - MEŠ
šu - nu dal - tu ul i - kal - lu - šu - nu - ti
me - di - lu ul u - tar - [šu] - nu - ti
GIŠ-GAL-A ṢIR-GIM MU-UN-SUR-SUR-[RI]-E-NE
ina dal - ti ki - ma ṣi - ri it - ta - [na - aš] - la - lu
GIŠ-ZA-RA IMI-GIM MU-UN-ZA-LA-[AḪ-ḪI]-E-NE
[ina] ṣir - ri ki - ma ša - a - ri i - ziḳ - ḳu
DAM UR MULU - GE[2] BA - RA - AN - NAM - NE
aš - ša - ta ina ut - li ameli i - tar - ru - u
DU DU - UB[3] MULU - GE[4] BA-RA-AN-ZI-ZI-E-NE
ma - ru[5] *ina*[6] *bir - ki ameli u - šat - bu - u*
GURUŠ E - UR - A - NI - TA[7] BA - RA - GIBIŠ[8] - NE
id - la[9] *ina bit*[10] *e - mu - ti - šu u - še - iṣ - ṣu - u*
E - NE - NE - NE U - DI GAR - ME - GAR[11] EGIR - BI
MULU - RA UŠ - SA[12]
šu-nu ḳu[13]*-lu ku*[13]*-ru ša ar-ki*[14] *ameli rak-su šu-nu*
DINGIR MULU-GIŠGAL-LU SIBA U-ḲI-ḲI-GA[15]
MULU-GIŠGAL-LU
[16]*ilu ameli ri-'-um*[17] *muš-te-'-u ri-ta ana*[18] *ameli*
DINGIR-DINGIR-RA-NA-KU[19] SUK-KU MU-UN-DIB-BI[20]-EŠ
ša ili-šu ana[21] *ku-ru-um-ma-ti*[22] *iṣ-ba-tu-šu*

That in the creation of Anu were spawned.
The highest walls, the thickest walls,
Like a flood they pass.
From house to house they break through,
No door can shut them out,
No bolt can turn them back,
Through the door like a snake they glide,
Through the hinge like the wind they blow;
Estranging the wife from the embrace of a husband,
Snatching the child from the loins of a man,
Sending the man forth from his home.
They are the burning pain
That bindeth itself upon the back of a man.
The god of the man is a shepherd
Who seeketh pasture for the man,
Whose god unto food leadeth him.

---

[1] K. 4,943, *ul*.
[2] 46,296, DAM MULU-KA . . .
[3] 46,296, BIR for DU-UB.
[4] 46,296, KA.
[5] K. 10,175, *a-ra*; 46,296, *ri*.
[6] 46,296, *i-na*.
[7] 46,296, *ḫi-bi*, "broken," for E-UR-A-NI-TA.
[8] K. 3,121 and 46,296, UD-DU.
[9] 46,296, *lu*.
[10] 46,296, *bi-it*.
[11] 46,296, GAL.
[12] 46,296, U-DI for UŠ-SA.
[13] 46,296 inserts *u*.
[14] K. 3,121, *arki*, 46,296, *ar-ka*, for *ar-ki*.
[15] 46,296 omits.
[16] 46,296, *ilu a-me-lu ri-e-*[’?]*-u mu-uš-te-mu-u ri-’-tu ana a-me-lu*.
[17] K. 3,121, *u*.
[18] K. 3,121, *a-na*.
[19] K. 3,121 omits *ra*: it is doubtful whether K. 2,507 had more than one DINGIR: 46,296 has DINGIR-RI-E-NE-KU.
[20] 46,296, DIB.
[21] K. 3,121 and K. 10,175, *ina*.
[22] 46,296, *tum*.

DINGIR - LUGAL - KAN - ME[1] KAN - ME - EN
DINGIR - LUGAL - KAN - ME - A KAN - ME - EN
DINGIR - LUGAL - KAN - ME - KIL KAN - ME - EN
NU - GIG ŠA - TUR - RA KAN - ME - EN
UMMEDA[2] KAN - ME - EN
IR UM[MEDA[2]] KAN - ME - EN
MULU - ḪUL - IK KAN - ME - EN
UTUG - ḪUL KAN - ME - EN
UB - DA - GUB - GUB - BU KAN - ME - EN
DA - GUB - GUB - BU KAN - ME - EN
U - ŠU - UŠ [GA - BA - DA - AN - KU KAN] - ME - EN
U - ŠU - UŠ [GA - BA - DA - AN - NAK KAN] - ME - EN
U - SU - UŠ [GA - BA - DA - AN - ŠEŠ KAN] - ME - EN
U - SU - UŠ [GA - BA - DA - AN - KU KAN] - ME - EN
GA - AN - TU [GA - BA - DA - AN - KU KAN] - ME - EN
GA - AN - TU GA - [BA - DA - AN - NAK KAN] - ME - EN
GA - AN - TU GA - BA - [DA - AN - ŠEŠ]KAN - ME - EN
GA - AN - TU GA - BA - [DA - AN - KU]KAN - ME - EN
ŠA-GAR-TUK-A-MU-NE GAR GA - BA - DA - AN - KU KAN - ME - EN
IMMA-TA-TUK-A-MU-NE A GA-BA-DA-AN-NAK KAN-ME-EN

[1] K. 3,121 translates: *lu* . . .
[2] 46,296, GA-LA for ME-DA.

Whether thou be a hag-demon,
Or a ghoul,
50. Or a robber-sprite,
Or a harlot (that hath died) whose body is sick,
Or a woman (that hath died) in travail,
Or a weeping woman (that hath died) with a babe at the breast,
Or an evil man (that hath died),
55. Or an evil spirit,
Or one that haunteth the neighbourhood,
Or one that haunteth the vicinity,
Or whether thou be one with whom on a day [I have eaten],
Or with whom on a day [I have drunk],
60. Or with whom on a day [I have anointed myself],
Or with whom on a day [I have clothed myself],
Or whether thou be one with whom I have entered and eaten,
Or with whom I have entered and drunk,
Or with whom I have entered and anointed myself,
65. Or with whom I have entered and clothed myself,
Or whether thou be one with whom I have eaten food when I was hungry,
Or with whom I have drunk water when I was thirsty,

Col. II.

IḪ-TUK[1] - A-MU-NE NI GA-BA-DA-AN-ŠEŠ KAN-ME-EN

A-ŠED-DE-TUK[2] - A-MU-NE UR-RA-NA-KU GA-BA-DA-AN-KU KAN-ME-EN

AZAG SAG-BA DINGIR-A-NUN-NA-GE-E-NE SAG-KI[3] - BI KAN-PA

a-šak-ku ma-mit ^{ilu}*A-nun-na-ki u-tam-me-ka*

MULU-ḪUL[4] AZAG SAG-BA DINGIR-A-NUN-NA-GE-E-NE SAG-KI[3] - BI KAN-PA

lim-nu a-[šak]-ku ma-mit ^{ilu}*A-nun-na-ki*[5] *u-tam-me-ka*

[AZAG] MU - UN - NA - TE - GA MULU - TUR - RA - KU MU - UN - NA - TE - GA[6]

(Plate XIII.)

a-šak-ku ša te-iṭ-ḫu-u ana mar-ṣi e ta-aṭ-ḫi

AZAG ZI AN-NA KAN-PA ZI KI-A KAN-PA

a-šak-ku niš šame(e) lu-u-ta-ma-a-ta niš irṣitim(tim) „

ZI DINGIR - EN - KI - E - NE KAN - PA

ZI DINGIR - NIN - KI - E - NE KAN - PA

ZI DINGIR - EN - UL - E - NE KAN - PA

ZI DINGIR - NIN - UL - E - NE KAN - PA

ZI DINGIR - EN - KUR - KUR - E - NE KAN - PA

ZI DINGIR - NIN - KUR - KUR - E - NE KAN - PA

ẒI DINGIR - EN - DA - ŠURIM - MA KAN - PA

ZI DINGIR - NIN - DA - ŠURIM - MA KAN - PA

ZI DINGIR - EN - DUL - AZAG - GA KAN - PA

ZI DINGIR - NIN - DUL - AZAG - GA KAN - PA

ZI DINGIR - EN - UD - TIL - LA KAN - PA

COL. II.

Or with whom I have anointed myself with oil when I was sore,
Or with whom when I was cold I have clothed his nakedness with a garment,
O fever, I exorcise thee by the ban of the Spirits of Heaven.
O evil one, O fever, I exorcise thee by the ban of the Spirits of Heaven.
O fever that hath come nigh,

(PLATE XIII.)

Come not nigh unto the sick man,
O fever! By Heaven be thou exorcised! By Earth be thou exorcised!
By Ea mayest thou be exorcised,
By Damkina mayest thou be exorcised,
By En-ul mayest thou be exorcised,
By Nin-ul mayest thou be exorcised,
By En-kur-kur mayest thou be exorcised,
By Nin-kur-kur mayest thou be exorcised,
By En-da-shurimma mayest thou be exorcised,
By Nin-da-shurimma mayest thou be exorcised,
By En-dul-azagga[a] mayest thou be exorcised,
By Nin-dul-azagga mayest thou be exorcised,
By En-ud-tilla mayest thou be exorcised,

---

[1] K. 3,121, TAG-GA.
[2] K. 3,121, SA-TAG-GA for DE-TUK.
[3] K. 3,121, DUL.
[4] K. 3,121, ḪUL-IK.
[5] K. 3,121 ,, for *A-nun-na-ki.*
[6] K. 3,121, NA.

[a] I.e., probably Nabu (cf. Brünnow, No. 9,609). *Nindul azagga* should therefore be Tashmitum.

ZI DINGIR - NIN - UD - TIL[1] - LA KAN - PA

ZI DINGIR - EN - ME - ŠAR - RA KAN - PA

ZI DINGIR - NIN - ME - ŠAR - RA KAN - PA

ZI DINGIR-EN-AMA-A-A DINGIR-EN-LIL-LA-GE KAN-PA

niš be-el[2] *a-bi um-mi*[3] *ša* *ilu* *Bel lu-u-ta-ma-a-ta*[4]

ZI DINGIR-NIN-AMA-A-A DINGIR-NIN-LIL-LA-GE KAN-PA

nis be-el-ti[5] *a-bi um-mi*[6] *ša* *ilu* „ [7] *lu-u-ta-ma-a-ta*[4]

ZI DINGIR-SIS-KI GIŠ[8] - MA SAG-BA-DA-A-NI ID-DA

NU-BAL-E-MA[3] KAN-PA

niš *ilu* *Sin ša e-lip*[9] *ta-me*[10]*-šu na-a-ru*[11] *la ib-bi-ru*[11]

lu-u-ta-ma-a-ta[4]

ZI DINGIR-BABBAR LUGAL DIKUD[12] DINGIR-RI-E-NE-GE

KAN-PA

niš *ilu* *Šamši be-ili*[13] *da-a-a-ni*[14] *ša ilâni* *pl*

lu-u-ta-ma-a-ta[15]

ZI DINGIR-NINNI DUG-GA-A-NI[16] DINGIR-A-NUN-NA

I-A-AN SAG-NU-UN-GA-GA DA-KAN[17]

niš *ilu* *Iš-tar ša a-na*[18] *ḳi-bi*[19] *- ti-ša*[20] *ilu* *A-nun-na-ki*

[21] *iš-ta-nu la i-ir-ru lu-u-[ta-ma-a-ta]*

ZI DINGIR-ID AMA DINGIR-EN-KI-GA-GE KAN-PA

niš *ilu* „ *um-me*[22] *ilu* *E-a lu-u-[ta-ma-a-ta]*[15]

ZI DINGIR-NINA DU-SAL DINGIR-EN-KI-GA-GE KAN-PA

niš *ilu* „ *mar-ti* *ilu* *E-a [lu-u-ta-ma-a-ta]*[23]

ZI DINGIR-NIN-TAR-A AB-KU UTUL-LU-U-A KAN-PA

niš *ilu* „ *ri-'-i*[24] *u-tul-la-ti* „

By Nin-ud-tilla mayest thou be exorcised,
By En-me-sharra mayest thou be exorcised,
By Nin-me-sharra mayest thou be exorcised,
By the lord, the father and mother of Bel, mayest thou be exorcised,
By the lady, the father and mother of Beltis, mayest thou be exorcised,
By Sin, whose Bark of Destiny crosses no river, mayest thou be exorcised,
By Shamash, lord judge of the gods, mayest thou be exorcised,
By Ishtar, at whose word each of the Anunnaki standeth fast, mayest thou be exorcised,
By Id, the mother of Ea, mayest thou be exorcised,
By Nina, daughṭer of Ea, mayest thou be exorcised,
By Ṇin-tara, the shepherd of flocks, mayest thou be exorcised,

---

[1] 46,296, BAD(TIL).
[2] 46,296, *ili*.
[3] 46,296, *mu*.
[4] 46,296, *lu-u-ta-mat*.
[5] 46,296, *tum*.
[6] 46,296, *ma*.
[7] 46,296, NIN-LIL.
[8] 46,296 omits.
[9] 46,296 inserts *-pi*.
[10] 46,296, *mi*.
[11] 46,296, *ri*.
[12] 46,296, *ḫi-bi*, "broken," for DINGIR-BABBAR LUGAL DIKUD.
[13] 46,296, *bêlu* for *be-ili*.
[14] 46,296, *nu*.
[15] 46,296, *lu-u-ta-mat*; K. 2,954, probably „
[16] K. 2,954, NA for A-NI.
[17] 46,296, E-NE-KAN-PA : . . *ru* for DA-KAN.
[18] K. 2,954, *ana* for *a-na*.
[19] 46,296, *bit*.
[20] 46,296, *šu*.
[21] 46,296, *iš-ṭin la'-ir* ditto.
[22] K. 2,954, *mi*.
[23] K. 2,954 „
[24] K. 2,954 . . *i*; 46,296, *ri-e-um*.

ZI DINGIR-GIŠ-BIL SAG . . . AD[1] (?) KUR-RA-GE-KAN
niš ilu „ šak-ka-nak-ka[2] *irṣitim(tim)* „
ZI DINGIR-NIN-GIŠ-ZI-DA GU-ZA-LA KUR-RA-GE KAN
niš ilu „ gu-za-[lu-u ša irṣitim(tim) „]
ZI GIŠ - GAL KUR - RA IMINA - BI KAN
niš da - [lat irṣitim(tim) si - ba „]
ZI GIŠ - ŠAGIL KUR - RA IMINA - BI KAN
ZI DINGIR-NE-GAB NI-GAB-GAL KUR-RA-GE KAN
niš ilu „ „ *irṣitim(tim) lu-u-ta-ma-tu*
ZI DINGIR - ḪUŠ - BI - ŠANGA DAM DINGIR - NAM - TAR - RA - GE KAN
niš ilu „ *al - ti Nam - ta - ri* „
ZI DINGIR-GAN-DIM-AZAG DU-SAL ZU-AB-GE KAN
niš ilu „ *mar-ti ap-si-i lu-u-ta-ma-tu*
[3] MULU - GIŠGAL (?) - LU DU - DINGIR - RA - NA
EN - NA BA - RA - AN - TA - RI - IN - NA - AŠ EN - NA BA-RA-AN-ZI[4] -GA-EN-NA-AŠ
U BA-RA-AN-DA-AB-KU-E A BA-RA-AN-DA-AB-NAK-E
GIŠ-BANŠUR A-A MUḪ-ZU DINGIR-EN-LIL-LA-GE ŠU-ZU BA-RA-NE-IN-GUB[5]
A A-AB-BA A-DUG[6] A-ŠIS[6] A ID-MAS-TIG-GAR A ID-UD-KIB-NUN-KI
A PU - TA A ID - DA BA - RA - AN - ŠU - ŠU - DA

[1] 46,296 . . . KAN(?)UŠ. [2] K. 3,121, *ki.*
[3] K. 12,000, *n.* inserts [ZI AN-NA KAN-PA Z]I KI-A [KAN-PA].
[4] K. 12,000, *k*, *n* insert TA. [5]. K. 3,218 and K. 12,000, *k*, TUM.
[6] K. 12,000, *k* inserts A.

By Gishbil, high priest of the earth, mayest thou be exorcised,
By Ningishzida, throne-bearer of the earth, mayest thou be exorcised,
By the Seven Gates of the Earth mayest thou be exorcised,
By the Seven Bolts of the Earth mayest thou be exorcised,
By Negab, the great Warden of the Earth, mayest thou be exorcised,
By Khushbishanga, the wife of Namtar, mayest thou be exorcised,
By Gan-dim-azag, the daughter of the Ocean Deep, mayest thou be exorcised:
(Whatever thou be) until thou art removed, until thou departest
From the man, the son of his god,
Thou shalt have no food to eat,
Thou shalt have no water to drink,
Thou shalt not stretch forth thy hand
Unto the table of my father Bel, thy creator.
Neither with sea-water, nor with sweet water,
Nor with bad water, nor with Tigris water,
Nor with Euphrates water, nor with pond water,
Nor with river water shalt thou be covered.

ANA - KU BA - RI - EN PA - NA - AN - TUK - TUK - E[1]
KI - KU BA - GUB - BA KU - NAM - BI - GA - GA
MULU-GIŠGAL (?) -LU DU-DINGIR-RA-NA BA-RA-AN-TE-MAL-DA BA-RA-AN-GE-GE-E-NE

INIM - INIM - MA UTUG - ḪUL - A - KAN

EN U - ŠU - UŠ IMI - ḪUL - GIM - MA A - MEŠ
ûmu(mu) ub-bu-tum ša-a-ri lim-nu-tum[2] *šu-nu*

Col. III.

U - ḪUL IM - ḪUL ŠI - GAB - A - MEŠ
ûmu(mu) ša limuttim(tim) im-ḫul-lu a-me-ru-ti[3] *šu-nu*
U - ḪUL IM - ḪUL ŠI - GUB - A - MEŠ
ûmu(mu) ša limuttim(tim) im-ḫul-lu a-lik maḫ-ri šu-nu

DU AŠ - A - MEŠ IBILA AŠ - A - MEŠ
ma-ru-u[4] *git*[5]*-ma-lu-tum ap-lu git*[5]*-ma-lu-tum šu-nu*
MULU - KIN - GA - A LIL - LA - DA - RA A - MEŠ
marâni^{pl} *šip - ri ša nam - ta - ru*[6] *šu - nu*
GU - ZA - LA DINGIR - NIN - KI - GAL A - MEŠ
gu - za - lu - u ša ^{ilu} „ [7] *šu - nu*
A - MA - TU KALAM - MA NIGIN[8] - NA - MEŠ
a-bu-bu ša ina mâti iṣ-ṣa-nun-du šu-nu
VII - A - AN DINGIR ANA - DAGAL - LA - MEŠ
si - bit ilâni^{pl} *šame(e) rap - šu - ti*
VII-A-AN DINGIR KALAM-MA-DAGAL-LA-MEŠ
si - bit ilâni^{pl} *ma - a - ti ra - pa - aš - ti*
VII-A-AN DINGIR-UR-UR-RI-A[4] - MEŠ : *si-bit ilâni*^{pl} *maš-ši-'-u-ti*
VII-A-AN DINGIR *VII*-A-AN-MEŠ[4]: *si-bit ilâni*^{pl} *kiš-ša-ti*

If thou wouldst fly up to heaven
Thou shalt have no wings,
If thou wouldst lurk in ambush on earth
Thou shalt secure no resting-place.
Unto the man, the son of his god,
Come not nigh,
Get thee hence!

Prayer against the Evil Spirits.

Incantation :—
Destructive storms (and) evil winds are they,

Col. III.

An evil blast that heraldeth[a] the baneful storm,
An evil blast, forerunner of the baneful storm.
They are mighty children, mighty sons,
Heralds of the Pestilence,
Throne-bearers of Ninkigal,
They are the flood which rusheth through the land.
Seven gods of the broad heaven,
Seven gods of the broad earth,
Seven robber gods are they.
Seven gods of might,

---

[1] K. 3,218 omits.
[2] K. 3,218, *ti*.
[3] K. 3,218, *tum*.
[4] K. 3,121 omits.
[5] K. 3,121, *git*(*kit*).
[6] K. 3,121, *ri*.
[7] K. 3,121, *Nin-ḳi-gal*.
[8] K. 3,121, KIL-KIL.

[a] Literally "beholdeth."

VII - A - AN DINGIR - ḪUL - A - MEŠ
si - bit ilâni [pl] *lim - nu - tum*
VII - A - AN DINGIR - LUGAL - KAN - ME ḪUL - A - MEŠ

(PLATE XIV.)

si - bit la - bar - ti[1] *lim - nu - tum*
VII-A-AN DINGIR-RAB-KAN-ME-A ŠED-DE ḪUL-A-MEŠ
si - bit la - bar - tum[2] *li - ' - bu lim - nu - tum*
ANA *VII* - A - AN KI *VII* - A - AN
ina šame(e) si-bit ina irṣitim(tim) si-bit-ma
UTUG - ḪUL A - LA - ḪUL GIDIM - ḪUL MULLA - ḪUL
DINGIR - ḪUL MAŠKIM - ḪUL
ZI AN - NA KAN - PA ZI KI - A KAN - PA
ZI DINGIR-EN-LIL-LA LUGAL KUR-KUR-RA-GE KAN-PA
niš ilu „[3] *be-el ma-ta-[a-ti]*[4] *lu-u-ta-ma-tu*[5]
ZI DINGIR-NIN-LIL-LA NIN KUR-KUR-RA-GE KAN-PA
niš ilu „ *be - lit mâtâti lu - u - ta - ma - tu*[5]
ZI DINGIR-NIN-IB IBILA E-ŠAR-RA-GE KAN-PA
niš ilu „ *apil E - šar - ra* „
ZI DINGIR - NINNI NIN KUR - KUR - RA - GE GIG
ŠI - IN - BABBAR - RA - GE KAN - PA
niš ilu „ *be-lit mâtâti* [pl] *mu-nam-mi-rat mu-ši*
lu-u-ta-ma-tu[5]
EN-NA SU MULU-GIŠGAL (?)-LU DU DINGIR-RA-NA
[6] U BA-RA-AN-DA-AB-KU-E A BA-RA-AN-DA-AB-NAK-E

[7] ———————————

[8] EN NAM - TAR AZAG KALAM - MA ZI - ZI
nam-ta-ru[9] *a-šak-ku ša mâti i-na-as-sa-ḫu*

Seven evil gods,
Seven evil demons,[a]
(PLATE XIV.)
Seven evil demons of oppression,
Seven in heaven and seven on earth.
Evil Spirit, evil Demon, evil Ghost,
Evil Devil, evil God, evil Fiend.
By Heaven be thou exorcised![b] By Earth be thou exorcised!
By Bel, Lord of the World, mayest thou be exorcised,
By Beltis, Lady of the World, mayest thou be exorcised!
By Ninib, son of Esharra, mayest thou be exorcised!
By Ishtar, Mistress of the World,
Who enlighteneth the night, mayest thou be exorcised!
Until thou art removed, until thou departest
From the body of the man, the son of his god,
Thou shalt have no food to eat,
Thou shalt have no water to drink.

Incantation :—
Pestilence and fever that ravage the land,

---

1 K. 3,121, *tum*.
2 K. 3,121, *la-ba-ṣi* for *la-bar-tum*.
3 K. 3,121, *Bel*.
4 K. 2,528 and K. 3,121, *mâtâti*[pl].
5 K. 2,528 ,,
6 K. 2,528 here inserts the following line:—U . . . -EN-NA-AŠ EN NA BA-RA-AN-ZI-GA-EN-NA-AŠ.
7 38,798, INIM-INIM-MA . . . , omitting l. 38.
8 K. 2,528, INIM-INIM-MA UTUG-ḪUL-A-KAN.
9 38,798, *ri*.

a *labartu*.
b Or "be ye exorcised!" and so on all through. See variant l. 65.

TUR - RA ŠI - LUL KALAM - MA ZI - IR - ZI - IR
mur - ṣu[1] *di - lib - ti ša mâti i - aš - ša - šu*

SU - NU - DUG - GA BAR - RA - NU - *ŠIG - GA
ša a-na[2] *ši-i*[3] *-ri la ṭa-a-bu ana zu-um-ri la dam-ḳu*

UTUG-ḪUL A-LA-ḪUL GIDIM-ḪUL MULLA-ḪUL
DINGIR-ḪUL MAŠKIM-ḪUL[4]

MULU - ḪUL IGI - ḪUL KA - ḪUL EME - ḪUL

MULU - GIŠGAL (?) - LU DU DINGIR-RA-NA SU-NI-TA
KAN-NI-IB-TA-E BAR-RA-NI-TA KAN-RI-IB-E-NE
ša ameli mâr ili-šu ina zumri[5] *-šu li-is-su*[6] *-u*
ina zumri[5] *-šu li-iṣ*[7] *-ṣu-u*

SU-MU : *ana zu-um-ri-ia a-a iṭ-ḫu-ni* : NAM-BA-TE-MAL-DA

IGI - MU : *ana pani - ia a - a u - lam - me - nu - ni* :
NAM - BA - ḪUL - E - NE

EGIR - MU : *ana arki - ia a - a il - li - ku - u - ni* :
NAM - BA - GIN - GIN - NE

E-MU : *ana biti-ia a-a i-ru-bu-u-ni* : NAM-BA-TU-TU-NE

*UR - MU NAM - BA - BAL - BAL - E[7] - NE
ana u - ri - ia a - a ib - bal - ki - tu - ni

E - KI - TUŠ - A - MU NAM - BA - TU - TU - NE
ana bît šub - ti - ia a - a irubu^{pl} *- ni*

ZI AN - NA KAN - PA ZI KI - A KAN - PA
ni-iš šame(e) lu-ta-ma-tu ni-iš irṣitim(tim)
lu-ta-ma-tu

ZI DINGIR-EN-LIL-LA LUGAL KUR-KUR-RA-GE KAN-PA

ZI DINGIR-NIN-LIL-LA NIN KUR-KUR-RA-GE KAN-PA

ZI DINGIR-NIN-IB UR-SAG-LIG-GA DINGIR-
EN-LIL-LA-GE KAN-PA

ZI DINGIR-NUZKU LUḪ-MAḪ DINGIR-EN-LIL-LA-GE
KAN-PA

Sickness and woe that oppress the land,
Harmful to the flesh, unclean to the body.
Evil Spirit, evil Demon, evil Ghost,
Evil Devil, evil God, evil Fiend,
Evil man, evil face, evil mouth, evil tongue,
From the man, the son of his god,
May they depart from his body
And from his body may they issue forth!
Unto my body may they not draw nigh,
Before me may they wreak no evil,
Nor follow behind me,
Into my house may they not enter,
My fence may they not break through,
Into my chamber may they not enter.
By Heaven be thou exorcised! By Earth be thou exorcised!
By Bel, Lord of the World, mayest thou be exorcised,
By Beltis, Lady of the World, mayest thou be exorcised,
By Ninib, the mighty warrior of Bel, mayest thou be exorcised,
By Nuzku, the powerful minister of Bel, mayest thou be exorcised,

---

[1] K. 3,528 . . *uṣ*; 38,798, *mu-ru-uṣ*.
[2] K. 2,528 and 38,798, *ana* for *a-na*.
[3] K. 2,528 omits.
[4] Latter half of line added from K. 2528 and K. 9,405.
[5] K. 2,528 and K. 9,405, *zu-um-ri*.
[6] K. 2,528, *šu*.
[7] K. 2,528 and K. 9,405 omit.

ZI DINGIR-EN-ZU-NA DU-SAG DINGIR-EN-LIL-LA-GE
KAN-PA

ZI DINGIR-NINNI NIN KI-SU-LU-KU-GAR-RA[1]-GE
KAN-PA[2]

niš ^{ilu}*Iš-tar be-lit um-ma-ni lu*[3]*-ta-ma-tu*[4]

Col. IV.

ZI DINGIR-NI LUGAL GU-DUG-GA-GE [5]KAN-PA[2]
niš ^{ilu}*Adadi be-ili*[6] *ša ri-gim-šu ṭa-a-bu* „

ZI DINGIR-BABBAR LUGAL SA-DA[7]-GE [5]KAN-PA[2]
niš ^{ilu}*Šamši be-ili*[8] *di-ni lu-u-ta-ma-tu*[9]

ZI DINGIR-A-NUN-NA[10] DINGIR-GAL-GAL[11]-E-NE[12]
KAN-PA[2]
niš ^{ilu}*A-nun-na-ki*[13] *ilâni*^{pl} *rabûti*^{pl} „

INIM-INIM-MA UTUG-ḪUL-A-KAN

EN ANA-KI-BA MULU-KI-BA ALAD KI-BA-E
mu-na[14]*-šir šame(e) u irṣitim(tim) še-e-du*
mu-na-aš-šir ma-a-ti

ALAD KI-BA ŠU-AN-NA-GE
še-e-du mu-na-aš-šir ma-a-ti ša e-mu-ḳa-šu ša-ḳa-a

ŠU-AN-NA-GE GIR-GIN-NA AN-NA-GE
ša e-mu-ḳa-šu ša-ḳa-a tal-lak-ta-šu ša-ḳa-at

MULLA GUD-UL-UL GUD-MAḪ-E
gal-lu-u al-pu na-ki-pu e-kim-mu ra-bu-u

GUD E-DU-A : *e-kim-mu ša kal bîti*^{pl} *it-ta-nab-lak-ka-tum* :
BAL-BAL-E-MEŠ

MULLA UR NU-TUK *VII*-NA A-MEŠ
gal-lu-u ša bul-ta la i-šu-u si-bit-ti šu-nu

By Sin, the firstborn of Bel, mayest thou be exorcised,
By Ishtar, mistress of mankind, mayest thou be exorcised,

Col. IV.

By Adad, the lord of goodly sound, mayest thou be exorcised,
By Shamash, the lord of judgment, mayest thou be exorcised,
By the Anunnaki, the great gods, mayest thou be exorcised,

Prayer against the Evil Spirits.

Incantation :—

Spirits that minish heaven and earth,
That minish the land,
Spirits that minish the land,
Of giant strength,
Of giant strength and giant tread,
Demons (like) raging bulls, great ghosts,
Ghosts that break through all houses,
Demons that have no shame,
Seven are they!

[1] K. 2,528 omits.
[2] 45,539 omits PA.
[3] K. 2,528 and 45,539 insert *u*.
[4] 45,539, *mat* for *ma-tu*.
[5] 45,539 adds ,,
[6] K. 5,096, *lim*.
[7] 45,539, TAR.
[8] K. 3,121, *el*.
[9] K. 3,121 ,, for *lu-u-ta-ma-tu*.
[10] K. 5,096 inserts GE-NE.
[11] 45,539 inserts LA.
[12] 45,539 inserts GE.
[13] K. 5,096 ,, for *A-nun-na-ki*.
[14] K. 3,121 and K. 5,096 insert *aš*.

SAL-DUG-GA : *kun-na-a ul i-du-u* : NU-UN-ZU-MEŠ

KALAM - MA ZID - GIM MU[1] - MU[1] - MEŠ

ma - a - tu[2] *ki - ma ḳi - me*[3] *i - ḳam - mu - u*

KAR - RA NU - UN - ZU - MEŠ

e - ṭi - ra[4] *ul i - du - u*

UKU - KU [5]ZI - GA - A[6] - MEŠ

a - na niše^{pl} *na - ad - ru*

SU NE[7] - IN-KU-KU-MEŠ MUD SUR-SUR[8] - MEŠ

UŠ NAK-NAK-[MEŠ]

a-kil ši-i-ri mu-ša-az-nin da-me[3] *ša-tu-u uš-la-ti*

. . BA (?)-A KI * SIG-ALAM-BI DINGIR-RI-E-NE-MEŠ

i (?)*-nu-šu a-šar bu-un-na-an-ni-e*[9] *ša ilâni*^{pl} *šu-nu*

É-BI DINGIR-DUL-AZAG-GA DINGIR-ŠURIM DINGIR-ŠE-

TIR MU-UN-SI-EŠ-A-AN

ina bi-ti ^{ilu}*Dul-azag-ga ša laḫ-ra* ^{ilu} „ *du-uš-šu-u*

MULLA GAR - NE - ŠUB TIG - DIR - MEŠ

gal-lu-u ša rag-gu ma-lu-u šu-nu

UŠ KU - KU - MEŠ ŠUD - NU - DU - MU MEŠ

a - kil da - mi la mu - par - ku - ti šu - nu

NAM - NE - ŠUB - MA U - ME - NI - KUD UB-DA-BI-KU

NAM-BA-GUR-RU-DA

ma-mit tum-me-šu-nu-ti-ma ana tub-ḳi u ša-ḫa-ti

a-a i-tu-ru-ni.

(Plate XV.)

ZI AN-NA KAN-PA-NE-EŠ ZI KI-A KAN-PA-NE-EŠ

Knowing no care,
They grind the land like corn;
Knowing no mercy,
They rage against mankind;
They spill their blood like rain
Devouring their flesh (and) sucking their veins,
[a] Where the images of the gods are, there they quake (?)
In the Temple of Nabû,[b] who fertilizeth the shoots (?) of wheat.
They are demons full of violence,
Ceaselessly devouring blood.
Invoke the ban against them,
That they no more return to this neighbourhood.

(PLATE XV.)

By Heaven be ye exorcised! By Earth be ye exorcised!

---

1 K. 3,121, TU.
2 K. 3,121, *tum*.
3 K. 3,121, *mi*.
4 K. 3,121, *ru*.
5 K. 3,121 inserts ŠU.
6 K. 3,121 omits.
7 K. 3,121, BI.
8 K. 3,121 inserts RA.
9 K. 3,121, *i*.

a The mutilated condition of this and the following line prevents any trustworthy rendering. The *i* in *inusu* is very doubtful; *laḫra* is doubtful, although justified as a translation of DINGIR-ŠURIM by Brünnow, No. 10,252. *Laḫra* is supposed to be the Hebrew *râḫêl*, a ewe (Muss-Arnolt, *Dictionary*, p. 479), and there seems to be a parallel in the Arabic root *raghala*, suxit *matrem*; iv, lactavit; grana in spicis producere coeperunt *sata*; cf. also *raghlun* (Freytag, *Lexicon*, ii, p. 169*a*).

b "God of the holy mound."

INIM - INIM - MA UTUG - ḪUL - A - KAN

EN GAR-UD-DU GAR-UD-DU GAR-NAM-MA UŠ-ŠIR
[ḫa]-a-a-ṭu ḫa-a-a-i-ṭu mur-te-id-du-u mimma šum-šu
. . . . - DIM - MA - BI A AN - NA - GE
[i] - na irṣitim(tim) ri - ḫu - ut šame(e)
. . . . . ANA - GIM ŠU NU - TE - MAL
. . . . *ki - ma šame(e)*
. . . . *[la iṭ] - ḫu - u*
. . . . BI

[Hiatus of about eight lines.]

DINGIR - NIN . . . .
ilu „ *be* - . . . . *- ṣa - '*
ḪUL-DUB . . . . [ZI AN-NA KAN-PA ZI KI]-A
KAN-PA.

INIM - INIM - MA UTUG - ḪUL - A - KAN

EN UR - SAG [*VII*] - NA A - DU *II* - NA - MEŠ
ḳar - ra - [du sibitti] a - di ši - na šu - nu

Col. V.

A-RI-A AŠ A-MEŠ A-RI-A BA-AN-NA-GE TU-UD-DA-MEŠ
ša ri-ḫu-su-nu iš-ta-at (?) *ina ri-ḫu-ut ilu A-nim*
ib-ba-nu-u šu-nu
E - NE - NE - NE LIL - LA KAS[1] - KAS[1] MEŠ
šu-nu za-ḳi-ḳu mut-taš-ra-bi-ṭu-ti[2] *šu-nu*
DAM NU - TUK - MEŠ DU NU - TU - UD - DA - MEŠ
aš-ša-tu ul aḫ-zu ma-ru[3] *ul al-du šu-nu*

Prayer against the Evil Spirits.

Incantation :—

Uprooting everything, uprooting everything,
Overthrowing everything, whatever its name ;
On earth the spawn of heaven
. . . . like heaven
. . . . they shall not draw nigh
. . . .

[Hiatus of about four lines.]

Beltis (?), lady of . . . .
. . . [By Heaven be ye exorcised ! By Earth] be ye exorcised !

Prayer against the Evil Spirits.

Incantation :—

Wárriors twice seven are they,

Col. V.

That in a single (?) spawning in the creation of Anu were spawned ;
They are the roaming windblast ;
No wife have they, no son do they beget,

[1] K. 3,121, SIR.
[2] K. 3,121, *tu*.
[3] K. 3,121, *a-ra*.

BANDA NU - UN - ZU - MEŠ

ta - šim - tu[1] *ul i - du - u*

ANŠU - KUR - RA ḪAR - SAG - TA E - A - MEŠ

si - su - u ša ina šadi(i) ir - bu - u šu - nu

DINGIR-EN-KI-GE : *ša* ^{ilu}*E-a lim-nu-tum šu-nu* :

ŠIS - A - MEŠ

GU-ZA-LA : *gu-uz*[2]*-za-lu-u ša ilâni*^{pl} *šu-nu* :

DINGIR-RI-E-NE[3]-MEŠ

E - SIR - RA LU - LU - A SILA - A GUB - BA - MEŠ

su-la-a a-na[4] *da-la-ḫi ina šuḳi*[5] *it-ta-nam-za-az-zu šu-nu*

IGI DINGIR-NE-URU-GAL UR-SAG-LIG-GA DINGIR-EN-LIL-LA-GE MU-UN-LAḪ-LAḪ-GI-EŠ

ina ma-ḫar ^{ilu} „ *ḳar-ra-du*[6] *dan-nu*[7] *ša* ^{ilu}*Bêl*[8] *it-ta-na-al-la-ku šu-nu*

[9]ZI AN - NA KAN - PA[10] ZI KI - A KAN - PA[11]

ZI DINGIR-EN-ZU-NA EN AN-AŠ-GIRI-BAR-RA-GE KAN-PA

ni-iš[12] ^{ilu}*Sin bel*[13] *nam-ra ṣi-it lu-ta-ma-tu*

ZI DINGIR-PA-SAG-GA GIR SILA-A SIG-GA-GE KAN-PA

ni-iš[14] ^{ilu}*I-šum na-gir su-ḳi ša-ḳu-um-mi lu-ta-ma-tu*[15]

SU MULU - GIŠGAL (?) - LU DU DINGIR - RA - NA BA-RA-AN-TE-MAL-DA BA-RA-AN-GE-GE-NE

ana zumur ameli mar ili-šu la te-ṭi-iḫ-ḫi la tasaniḳ

Sense they know not.
They are as horses reared among the hills;
The Evil Ones of Ea,
Throne-bearers to the gods are they;
They stand in the highway to befoul the path,
Marching before the Plague God, the mighty warrior of Bel.
By Heaven be thou exorcised! By Earth be thou exorcised!
By Sin, lord of the Brilliant Rising, mayest thou be exorcised,
By Ishum, overseer of foul streets, mayest thou be exorcised,
Unto the body of the man, son of his god,
Approach not nor draw nigh!

---

[1] K. 3,121, *tum*.
[2] K. 8,508 omits.
[3] K. 2,528 and K. 4,658 insert A.
[4] K. 2,528, *ana* for *a-na*.
[5] K. 2,528 and K. 4,658, *su-ḳi*.
[6] K. 2,528 and K. 4,658, *di*.
[7] K. 2,528 and K. 4,658, *ni*.
[8] K. 2,528 and K. 4,658 ,,
[9] K. 8,508 translates *niš šame(e) lu-u-ta-*[*mat niš irṣitim lu-u-ta-mat*].
[10] K. 2,528 and K. 4,658 insert NE-EŠ.
[11] K. 2,528 inserts NE-EŠ.
[12] K. 4,658 and K. 8,508, *niš* for *ni-iš*.
[13] K. 2,528 and K. 4,658, *be-el*.
[14] K. 4,658, *niš* for *ni-iš*.
[15] K. 2,528 ,, for *lu-ta-ma-tu*.

IGI - NA BAD - DU [1] A - GA - NA BAD - DU [1]
ana pa-ni-šu i-si ana ar-ki-šu i-si

INIM - INIM - MA UTUG - ḪUL - A - KAN

EN VII - NA - MEŠ VII - NA - MEŠ
si - bit - ti šu - nu si - bit - ti šu - nu [2]
IDIM - ZU - AB - TA VII - NA - MEŠ
ina na - ḳab [3] *ap - si - i si - bit - ti šu - nu*
ŠE - IR - KA ANA - DUG - GA - NA VII - NA - MEŠ
zu-'-u [4] *- nu-ti* [5] *ina šame(e) si-bit-ti šu-nu*
IDIM - ZU - AB - TA E - ZIL - TA E - A - MEŠ
ina na - ḳab ap - si - i ina ku - um - me
ir - bu - u šu - nu
U SAL NU - MEŠ U UŠ NU - MEŠ
ul zi [6] *-ka-ru šu-nu ul sin-niš-a-ti* [7] *šu-nu*
E - NE - NE - NE LIL - LA KAS [8] - KAS [8] - MEŠ
šu - nu za - ḳi - ḳu mut - taš - rab - bi - ṭu - ti [9] *šu - nu*
DAM NU - TUK - A - MEŠ DU NU - TU - UD - DA - MEŠ
aš-ša-tu [7] *ul aḫ-zu ma-ri* [10] *ul al-du šu-nu*
GAR - ŠU AG - AG - DA NU - UN [11] - ZU - MEŠ
e - ṭi - ra ga - ma - lu [12] *ul i - du - u*
A-RA-ZU SIGIŠŠE (?)-SIGIŠŠE (?)-RA GIŠ-NU-TUK-A [11] -MEŠ
ik - ri - bi [13] *taš - li - tu* [14] *ul i - šim - mu - u*
AṄŠU - KUR - RA ḪAR - SAG - TA E - A - MEŠ
si-su-u ša ina šadi(i) ir-bu-u šu-nu
DINGIR - EN - KI - GE ŠIS - SI [15] - MEŠ
ša ^{ilu}*E - a lim - nu - ti šu - nu*
GU - ZA - LA DINGIR - RI - E - NE MEŠ
gu - za - lu - u ša ilâni ^{pl} *šu - nu*

25. Get hence from before him, get hence from behind him!

PRAYER AGAINST THE EVIL SPIRITS.

Incantation:—

Seven are they, seven are they,
30. In the Ocean Deep seven are they,
Battening[a] in Heaven seven are they,
35. In the Ocean Deep as their home they were reared,
Nor male or female are they,
40. They are as the roaming windblast,
No wife have they, no son do they beget;
Knowing neither mercy nor pity,
45. They hearken not unto prayer or supplication.
They are as horses reared among the hills;
50. The Evil Ones of Ea,
Throne-bearers to the gods are they.

[1] K. 3,121, DA.
[2] K. 3,121 „ for *si-bil-ti šu-nu*.
[3] K. 3,121, *nak-bi* for *na-ḳab*.
[4] K. 3,121 and K. 4,658 omit.
[5] K. 3,121, *tu*; K. 4,658, *tum*.
[6] K. 4,658, *zik*.
[7] K. 3,121, *tum*.
[8] K. 3,121, SIR.
[9] K. 3,121, *tu*.
[10] K. 3,121, *ru*.
[11] K. 3,121 omits.
[12] K. 3,121, *la*.
[13] K. 3,121, *ba*.
[14] K. 3,121, *ta*.
[15] K. 3,121, A.

[a] *Zu'unuti*, Hebrew *zûn* (Jer. v, 8).

[1] E - SIR - RA LU - LU - A SILA - A GUB - BA - MEŠ
[1] *su-la-a ana da-la-ḫi ina su-ḳi it-ta-na-za-zu šu-nu*
ŠIS-SI-MEŠ: *lim-nu-ti*[2] *šu-nu lim-nu-ti*[2] *šu-nu*:
ŠIS - SI [3] - MEŠ
VII-NA-MEŠ *VII*-NA-MEŠ *VII*[4] - A-DU *II*-NA-MEŠ
si-bit-ti šu-nu si-bit-ti šu-nu si-bit a-di ši-na šu-nu
ZI AN-NA KAN-PA-NE-EŠ ZI KI-A KAN-PA-NE-EŠ

(Plate XVI.)

INIM - INIM - MA UTUG - ḪUL - A - KAN

Col. VI.

. . . . UTUG - ḪUL MU - UN - DA - RU - UŠ
. . . . *u - tuk - ku lim - nu i - ta - ru - uš*
. . . . MUD - NA - A IM - MA - AN - UŠ
. . . . *-ši la na - bu - u ir - te - di - šu*
[MULU] SU - BI NU - E - NE IM - MA - AN - UŠ
ša ina zu - mur la šu - pu - u ir-te-di-šu
ŠU - NI IN - RA SU - A - NI - KU IM-ME-IN-GAR
ḳa-as-su im-ḫaṣ-ma ana ḳa-ti-šu iš-kun
GIR-NI IN-RA GIR-A-NI-KU IM-ME-IN-GAR
še-ip-šu im-ḫaṣ-ma ana še-pi-šu iš-kun
SAG-GA-NI IN-RA SAG-GA-A-NI-KU IM-ME-IN-GAR
ḳaḳ-ḳa-su im-ḫaṣ-ma ana ḳaḳ-ḳa-di-šu iš-kun
NAM-BI-KU GE-BARA-KI AZAG-GA-TA IM-MA-DA-
[AN-TU-TU]
ana šim-[ti-šu ana gi-pa-a-ri el-li e-ru-ub-ma]

[Hiatus of about four lines.]

They stand in the highway to befoul the path,
Evil are they, evil are they!
Seven are they, seven are they,
Twice seven are they!
By Heaven be ye exorcised! By Earth be ye exorcised!

(PLATE XVI.)

PRAYER AGAINST THE EVIL SPIRITS.

COL. VI.

[Incantation]:—
An evil spirit . . . hath overcome him,
[Something] unnamed hath seized upon him,
Something impure for the body hath seized upon him,
His hand it hath smitten and his hand it hath set upon,
His foot it hath smitten and his foot it hath set upon,
His head it hath smitten and his head it hath set upon;
[a] Unto a pure field for his fate it hath entered and

[Hiatus of two lines.]

[1] Line omitted on K. 3,121.
[2] K. 3,121, *tum*.
[3] K. 3,121, A.
[4] K. 3,121 inserts NA.

[a] Restored from the explanatory text S. 48. Apparently it means that the evil spirit has entered the "pure field" to seize upon the man.

UTUG . . . .
u - tuk - ku . . . .
ana bi - ti a - a i - ru - [ub] . . . .
UTUG-ḪUL DIB-BA-A-NI BAR-KU ḪE-IM-TA-GUB
u-tuk-ku lim-nu ka-mu-šu ina a-ḫa-ti li-iz-ziz
UTUG-*ŠIG-GA ALAD-*ŠIG-GA ḪE-EN-LAḪ-LAḪ-GI-EŠ

INIM - INIM - MA UTUG - ḪUL - A - KAN

EN UTUG - ḪUL - IK GIDIM BAD KUR - RA

Duppi V KAM-MA UTUG - ḪUL - A - MEŠ

The [evil] spirit . . . .
Let it not enter the house . . .
May the evil Spirit that hath seized him stand aside,
May a kindly Spirit, a kindly Guardian be present.

Prayer against the Evil Spirits.

Incantation: "The Evil Spirit, the Ghost that destroyeth the land."

Fifth Tablet of the Series "The Evil Spirits."

The Tenth Tablet.

OBVERSE.

(PLATE XVII.)

. . . .

. . . . . *a* . . *šap*(?)*-la-a-ti ša ap-si-*[*i*] . .

. . . [MULU]-ŠAR UKU ŠAR-TA(?)-U-TU ZU-AB-TA ME-EN

. . . *kiš-šat niši*^{pl} *ša ap-si-i a-na-ku*

. . . MULU-ŠAR DUL-DUL UTUG-ḪUL DIB-BA ME-EN

. . . *-bi-ib u-tuk-ḳu lim-nu ka-mu-u a-na-ku*

. . . [MULU]-ŠAR DUL-DUL A-LA-ḪUL DIB-BA ME-EN

. . . [*-bi-ib*] *a-lu-u lim-nu ka-mu-u a-na-ku*

. . . [MULU-ŠAR] DUL-DUL GIDIM-ḪUL DIB-BA ME-EN

. . . [*-bi-ib e-kim*]*-mu lim-nu ka-mu-u ạ-*[*na-ku*]

. . . [MULU - ŠAR DUL - DUL] MUL - LA - ḪUL DIB - [BA ME - EN]

. . . [*-bi-ib gal*]*-lu-u lim-nu ka-*[*mu-u a-na-ku*]

. . . [MULU-ŠAR DUL]-DUL DINGIR-ḪUL DIB-[BA ME-EN]

. . . [*-bi-ib i*]*-lum lim-nu ka-*[*mu-u a-na-ku*]

. . . [MULU-ŠAR DUL-DUL MAŠKIM-ḪUL DIB-BA ME-EN]

. . . [*-bi-ib ra-bi-ṣu lim-nu ka-mu-u a-na-ku*]

. . . [MULU-ŠAR DUL-DUL LUGAL-RAB-KAN-ME DIB-BA ME-EN]

PART XVII (PLATE XLIX).

. . . [*-bi-ib*] *la-bar-tum* [*ka-mu-u a-na-ku*]

. . . [MULU-ŠAR] DUL-DUL LUGAL-RAB-KAN-ME-A DIB-BA [ME-EN]

. . . [*-bi-ib*] *la-ba-ṣu ka-mu-u* [*a-na-ku*]

. . . [MULU-ŠAR] DUL-DUL LUGAL-RAB-KAN-ME-KIL DIB-BA [ME-EN]

. . . [*-bi-ib*] *aḫ-ḫa-zu ka-mu-u a-na-*[*ku*]

The Tenth Tablet.

OBVERSE.

(PLATE XVII.)

. . . .

. . . . . of the Deep . . . .

. . of multitudes of people of the Deep am I,

. . . of Marduk (?), who . . . . the evil Spirit seizeth, am I,

. . . [of Marduk (?), who . . .] the evil Demon seizeth, am I,

. . . [of Marduk (?), who . . .] the evil Ghost seizeth, am I,

. . . [of Marduk (?), who . . .] the evil Devil seizeth, [am I],

. . . [of Marduk (?), who . . .] the evil God seizeth, [am I],

. . . [of Marduk (?), who . . . the evil Fiend seizeth, am I],

PART XVII (PLATE XLIX).

. . . [of Marduk (?), who . . .] the Hag-demon [seizeth, am I],

. . . [of Marduk (?), who . . .] the Ghoul seizeth, [am I],

. . . [of Marduk (?), who . . .] the Robber-sprite seizeth, am I,

. . . [MULU-ŠAR DUL]-DUL MULU-LIL-LA DIB-BA ME-EN

. . . *[-bi-ib] li-lu-u ka-mu-u a-na-[ku]*

. . . [MULU-ŠAR DUL]-DUL KI-EL-LIL-LA DIB-BA ME-EN

. . . *[-bi-ib li-li]-ti ka-mu-u a-na-ku*

. . . [MULU-ŠAR DUL-DUL KI-EL]-UD-DA-KAR-RA DIB-BA ME-EN

. *[-bi-ib ar-da-at li]-li-i ka-mu-u a-na-ku*

. . . . DIB-BA ME-EN

. . . . *[ka]-mu-u a-na-ku*

. . . . [DIB-BA] ME-EN

. . . .

REVERSE.

. . . .

(b) . . . . . *tul-lal* (c) . . . . . *tamannu(nu)* (d) . . . . . . ^{ilu}*E* (e) . . . . . *tanakkas(kas)* (f) . . . . *tanaḳḳi(ḳi)* (g) . . . . ^{siru}*šume tu-ṭaḫ-ḫa* (h) . . . . *-mu ana bît ili šuâti riksi* (i) . . . . *kima ṣit* ^{ilu}*Šamši* (j) . . . . ^{ilu}*E-a* ^{ilu}*Šamšu* (k) . . . . [^{ilu}SILIG]-MULU-ŠAR *tanakkas(kas)* (l) . . . . GAR-MEŠ *tašakkan(an)* (m) . . . . . . *ḫımeti tašakkan(an)* (n) . . . . . . *saluppi* KU-A-TIR *tasarraḳ(aḳ)* (o) . . . . *tukan(an)* (p) . . . . . *tanaḳḳi(ḳi)* (q) . . . . . [^{siru}*ḫin*]*ṣa*(?) *u* ^{siru}*šume* (r) [*tuṭaḫḫa*] . . . BI *tanaḳḳi(ḳi)* (s) . . . . ^{ilu}*Šamši* . . . *tamannu(nu)*

.

. . . *dup-pir lim-nu še-e*(?) . . . .

[*Dup*]*pi X* ^{KAM} UTUG-ḪUL-MEŠ

. . . [of Marduk (?), who . . .] the Phantom of Night seizeth, am I,

. . . [of Marduk (?), who . . .] the Night Wraith seizeth, am I,

. . . [of Marduk (?), who . . .] the handmaiden of the Phantom seizeth, am I,

. . . . seizeth, am I,

. . . . [seizeth], am I.

. . . .

[The Reverse contains fragmentary directions for ceremonies.]

. . . . remove, the evil . . . . . .

TENTH TABLET OF THE SERIES "THE EVIL SPIRITS."

The Fifteenth Tablet.

OBVERSE.

(PLATE XVIII.)

EN DINGIR-EN-KI-E-NE [DINGIR-NIN-KI-E-NE A-MEŠ]
ša ilu „ šu-nu ša ilu „ šu-[nu]
DINGIR-EN-KI DINGIR-NIN-KI EN . . . .
ša ilu „ u ilu „ be-lu „ šu-nu
NUN-KI KI-TUŠ-AZAG-GA-NI-KU ŠUB-NA-EŠ-A-AN
[ina] alu Eridi šub-ta el-li-ti uš-bu-ni
MULU-TUR-RA DU DINGIR-RA-NA ŠI-MU-UN-ŠI-IN-BAR-RA-EŠ-A-AN
MU-UN-NA-TE-EŠ
mar-ṣi mâr ili-šu ip-pal-su-šu iṭ-ḫu-šu
. . . . NUN-KI-GA GU-[MU-UN-NA-]AN-DE-EŠ-A-AN ID-BA-[AN]-DA-AN-AG-EŠ
ina alu Eridi is-su-ma u-ma-'-i-ru
. . . KI GANA GA MU-RA-AB-BI (?) . .
. . . *me* (?) *ilu ka* (?) *-a* (?) *-i-nu e-ši-tum*
. . . . . MULU . . GA-A MU-RA-AB-BI (?) . .
. . . . *nu šar-ri-iḫ-tum* (?)
. . . . . . *alu Eridu* NUN-KI-GA . .
. . . . AZAG-GA GA DU . . .
. . . . *-tu aš-ri el-li . . . šu* (?) *-ni*
. . . . ME (?) . . . . .
. . . . *ma* (?) . . .
. . . . ḪAR-SAG-GE
. . . . *ša-di-i*
. . . .

REVERSE.

. . . .
[UTUG]-ḪUL [A-LA-ḪUL BAR-KU ḪE-IM-TA-GUB]
UTUG-* ŠIG-GA AL[AD * ŠIG-GA ḪE-EN-LAḪ-LAḪ-GI-EŠ]

INIM-INIM-MA UTUG-ḪUL-[A-KAN]

EN U-DU-DU-MEŠ [DINGIR-ḪUL-A-MEŠ]

The Fifteenth Tablet.

OBVERSE.

(PLATE XVIII.)

Of Ea are they, of [Damkina] are they,
Of Ea and Damkina, the lord . . . are they,
In the hallowed dwelling Eridu they were seated,
(And) they beheld the sick man, the son of his god,
(And) drew nigh unto him,
In Eridu they shrieked and hastened on;

. . . .

REVERSE.

[May the] evil [Spirit, the evil Demon, stand away from him],
[May a] kindly Spirit, [a kindly] Guardian, [be present].

PRAYER AGAINST THE EVIL SPIRITS.

Incantation:—
"[The Evil Gods] are raging storms."[a]

---

[a] According to the colophon, No. 47,736 was made for Marduk-bani-apli, the son of Mukalmu, the Priest of Marduk, by Itti-Marduk-balaṭu, the son of Miṣirai:—

ki-ma labiri-šu ša-ṭir-ma up-pu- . . . .
a-na ḳa-bi e-li mâti . . . .
za-mar šu-bal-ku-tu dup-pi $^{m\ ilu}$*Marduk-bani-apli*
mâr ^{m}*Mu-kal-mu* ^{am} *bari* ^{ilu} *Marduk*
ḳatâ ^{II} ^{m}*Itti-* ^{ilu}*Marduk-balaṭu mâr* ^{m}*Mi-ṣir-a-a.*

The Sixteenth Tablet.

(PLATE XIX.)

EN U - DU - DU - MEŠ DINGIR - ḪUL - A - MEŠ
ûmi[pl] mut-tak-pu-tum ilâni[pl] lim-nu-tum šu-nu
ALAD UŠ - NU - KU DU - ḪE - A SIG - GA - MEŠ
še-e-du la pa-dû-tum[1] *ša ina šu-puk šame(e)*
ib-ba-nu-u šu-nu
E - NE - NE - NE GAR - GIG ŠA - A - MEŠ
šu - nu e - piš ma - ru - uš - ti šu - nu
SAG-ḪUL ḪA-ZA[2]-MEŠ U-ŠU-UŠ-E GAR-ḪUL DIB-BA
SAG - GIŠ - RA - RA - E - NE . . . . .
mu-kil ḳakḳad limuttim(tim)[3] *ša ûmi(mi)-šam-ma*
ana limutti . . .
nir - tu ana na - a - ri . . . . . [*šunu*]
VII-BI-TA UŠU-A-AN IM-GIŠGAL-[LU] . . .
ina si-bit-ti šu-nu [. . .] *šu-u-tu* . . .
II-KAM-MA UŠUMGAL KA-GAL KAB(?) MULU NA
ME . . MU-UN . . .
ša-nu-u u-šum-gal-lum ša pi-i-šu pi-tu-u . . .
ma - am[4] *- ma* [*la*] . . . .
III-KAM-MA GIR-DU ḪUŠ . . . . . KAR-RA BA(?) . . .
šal-šu[5] *nim-ru*[6] *iz-zu ša pi-i-ri e*(?)-[*ki-mu*] . . .
IV-KAM-MA ṢIR-AGA ḪU-LAḪ-ḪA . . . .
ri - bu - u šib - bu gal - ti . . . . . .
V-KAM-MA GIR-KU(?)-ZI-GA A-GA-BI-KU TU . . NU-UN . .
ḫa-aš-ša ab-bu[7] *na-ad-ru*[8] *ša ana arki*[9] *- šu*
ni-'-a la . . . .
VI-[KAM-MA] . . . ZI-GA DINGIR-LUGAL-LA-KU . . . . .
siš-[*šu*] . . . *-u ti-bu-u ša ana ili u šarri* . . . .

The Sixteenth Tablet.

(PLATE XIX.)

The Evil Gods are raging storms,
Ruthless spirits created in the vault of heaven;
Workers of woe are they,
That each day raise their evil heads for evil,
To wreak destruction . . . . .
Of these seven [the first] is the South Wind . .
The second is a dragon with mouth agape
That none can [withstand?],
The third is a grim leopard that carries off (?) young . . . .
The fourth is a terrible serpent . . . .
The fifth is a furious beast (?),[a] after which no restraint (?) . . . .
The sixth is a rampant . . . which against god and king . . .

---

[1] 34,106, *tu*.
[2] 34,106 inserts A.
[3] 34,106, *li-mut-tum*.
[4] 34,106, *man* for *ma-am*.
[5] K. 4,904, *ši*.
[6] 34,106 and K. 4,904, *ri*.
[7] 34,106, *bi*.
[8] 34,106, *ri*.
[9] K. 4,870, *ar-[ki]*.

[a] *Abbu*, the meaning of which is at present quite uncertain. From the Sumerian GIR in the line above (since GIR-DU is translated *nimru* in l. 18), this would seem to be the name of a wild beast. Cf. also the Arabic حُباب, "serpent," which Wellhausen (*Skizzen*, iii, 171, 217) suggests in comparison with the Hebrew name *Ḥôbâb*.

VII-KAM-MA IM-MIR-RA IM-ḪUL-A GE (?) . . . .
si-bu-u me-ḫu-u ša-a-ru lim-nu ša gi (?)-*iš* . . .
VII-BI E-NE MULU-KIN-GA-A ANA LUGAL-LA A-MEŠ
si-bit-ti šu-nu mâr šip-ri ša ^ilu^ *A-nim šar-ri šu-nu*
ERI - ERI - A - AN AN - USAN - DA GA - GA - MEŠ
a-li ana a-li da-um-ma-ta i-šak-ka-nu šu-nu
IM-DAL-ḪA-MUN AN-NA-GE ŠUR-BI NIGIN-NA-MEŠ
a-šam-šu-tum ša ina šame(*e*) *iz-zi-iš iṣ-ṣa-nun-du šu-nu*
IM-DIR[1]-SIR-RA AN-NA-GE IM-A-AN-ḪI-ŠI IN-GA-GA-MEŠ
ir-pi-tum ša-pi-tum ša ina šame(*e*) *da-um-ma-ta i-šak-ka-nu šu-nu*
IM-DAL-ZI-GA U-LAḪ-GA ḪI-ŠI MI-NI-IN-GAR-RI-EŠ
zi-iḳ[2] *ša-a-ri te-bu-tum ša ina ûme*(*me*) *nam-ri e - ṭu - ta i - šak - ka - nu šu - nu*
IM - ḪUL IM - ḪUL - BI - TA DU - DU - MEŠ
it-ti im-ḫul-li ša-a-ri lim-ni i-šur-ru šu-nu
U - NE - RA - RA I (?) - I (?) KA - ḪAR -AK - DA - MEŠ
ri-ḫi-iṣ-ti ^ilu^ *Adadi te-šu-u ḳar-du-te šu-nu*
ID - ZID - DA̤ DINGIR - NI LAḪ - LAḪ - MEŠ
ina i - mit - ti ^ilu^ *Adadi il - la* - [*ku šu - nu*]
AN - UR - RA NIM - GIR - GIM . . . .
ina i-šid šame(*e*) *ki-ma bir-ḳi it-ta*-[*nab-ri-ḳu šu-nu*]
SAG - GIŠ - RA - RA - E - NE SAG - TA . . . . .
ni-ir-tu ana na-a-ri ina maḫ-ri il-la-ku [*šu-nu*]
ANA-DAGAL-LA KI-TUŠ DINGIR-LUGAL-LA-GE ḪUL-DIB-BI LAḪ-GA-[MEŠ]
GAB - RI NU - TUK - A - MEŠ
ina šame(*e*) *rap-šu-ti šu-bat* ^ilu^ *A-nim šar-ri lim-niš iz-za-zu-ma ma-ḫi-ra ul i-šu-u*

The seventh is an evil windstorm which . . .
These seven are the Messengers of Anu, the king,
Bearing gloom from city to city,
Tempests[a] that furiously scour the heavens,
Dense clouds[a] that bring gloom over the sky,
Rushing windgusts,[a] casting darkness over the brightest day,
Forcing their way with the baneful windstorms.
Mighty destroyers are they, the deluge of the Storm-God,
Stalking at the right hand of the Storm-God.
In the height of heaven like lightning they [flash],
To wreak destruction they lead the way,
In heaven's breadth, the home of Anu, the king,

---

[1] 36,690 inserts E.

[2] 36,690 inserts *ḳu*.

[a] Singular.

U-BI-A DINGIR-EN-LIL-LA DIMMU-BI GIŠ-NE-IN-TUK-A
I ŠA-BI-KU BA-AN-BU-I
i-nu-šu ^{ilu}*Bel* *ṭe-e-ma* *šu-a-tum* *iš-me-ma*
a-ma-ta *ana* *lib-bi-šu* *iš-du-ud*
DINGIR-EN-KI-DA MAS-SU-MAḪ DINGIR-RI-E-NE-GE
AD-BA-NI-IB-GE-GE
it-ti ^{ilu}*E-a* *mas-si-e* *ṣi-ri* *ša* *ilâni*^{pl} *im-ta-lik-ma*
DINGIR-ŠIS-KI DINGIR-BABBAR DINGIR-NINNI-GE
DU-ḪE-A SI-DI-E-NE
IM-MA-NI-IN-GAR
^{ilu}*Sin* ^{ilu}*Šamšu* *u* ^{ilu}*Iš-tar* *šu-puk* *šame(e)* *ana*
šu-te-šu-ri *uk-tin-nu*
ANA-DA NAM-EN-NA KIŠ AN-NA-GE
MU-UN-NE-ŠI-IN-ḪAL-ḪAL-LA
it-ti ^{ilu}*A-nim* *be-lu-ut* *kiš-šat* *šame(e)* *i-zu-us-su-nu-ti*
III-A-AN-NE-NE DINGIR-DU-NE-NE-IR
(PLATE XX.)
ana *še-lal-ti-šu-nu* *ilâni*^{pl} *mârâni*^{pl}*-šu*
GIG-ANA-NE-GA-E BA-GUB-BA SUḪ-NU-GUB-MA
E-NE-NE-NE MU-UN-NE-ŠI-IN-AG-GI-EŠ
mu-ša *u* *ur-ra* *u-zu-uz-zu* *la* *na-par-ka* *šu-nu-ti*
u-ma-'-ir-šu-nu-ti
U-BI-A *VII*-BI DINGIR-ḪUL-A-MEŠ DU-ḪE-A DU-DU-MEŠ
i-nu-šu *si-bit-ti-šu-nu* *ilâni*^{pl} *lim-nu-ti*
ina *šu-puk* *šame(e)* *i-šur-ru*
UM-SAG-TA UD-SIR DINGIR-EN-ZU-NA ŠUR-BI
BA-AN-DIB-BI-EŠ
ina *ma-ḫar* ^{ilu}*Nannari(ri)* ^{ilu}*Sin* *iz-zi-iš*
il-ta-nam-mu-u
ŠUL DINGIR-BABBAR DINGIR-NI °UR-SAG ID-NI-KU-A
BA-NI-IB-GE-GE-EŠ
id-la[1] ^{ilu}*Šamšu* ^{ilu}*Adadu* *kar-du* *ana* *i-di-šu-nu*
ut-tir-ru

They take their stand for evil, and none oppose.
When Bel heard these tidings and pondered in his heart,
With Ea, the mighty Guide[a] of the gods, he took counsel,
And Sin, Shamash, and Ishtar,[b]
Whom he had set to rule the firmament
With Anu,[c] apportioning among them
The dominion of the heavenly host.

(PLATE XX.)

These three gods, his offspring,
He ordained to stand by night and day unceasingly.
When the seven evil gods
Forced their way into the vault of heaven,
They clustered angrily round before the Crescent of the Moon God,
(And) won over to their aid Shamash the mighty and Adad the warrior,

[1] S. 1,448, *lu*.

[a] *Massu*, of which the exact meaning is at present unknown.

[b] The Moon, the Sun, and Venus.

[c] The heavens.

DINGIR-NINNI-GE ANA-DA[1], KI-TUŠ-AZAG[2] MU-UN-RI NAM-LUGAL-LA
AN - NA - KU IR - ḪU - MU - UN - ŠA
^{ilu}*Iš-tar it-ti* ^{ilu}*A-nim šar-ri šub-tu ellitim(tim)*
ir-me-ma ana šarru-ut šame(e) i-kap-pu-ud
DINGIR-LUGAL-E-A DINGIR-GAL-GAL . . . . . .
. . . .
E - NE - DA - NU - ME - A . . . .
ša ina ba - li - šu me . . . .
U - BI - A *VII* . . . .
i - nu - šu si - bit . . . .
SAG TAB KALAM (?) KALAM . . . .
. . . . ḪUL A-AN (?) . . . .
ina ri-eš šur-ri-i ana e . . . .
li - mut - tu . . . .
SIR (?)-TA KA-AZAG-GA-TA MU . . . .
ana (?) *ša-at-ti pi-i-šu el-[li]* . . . .
[DINGIR]-EN-ZU-NA ZIR NAM-[MULU-GIŠGAL-LU] . . .
^{ilu}*Sin* . . -'- . . . *zi-ir a-me-lu-[ti]* . . .
. . . *[dal ?] - ḫa - ti ma - a - ti* . . . . .
. . . . . . LU SIG - SIG - GA - BI BA - TIL
. . . . . . *-tum id-da-li-iḫ-ma ša-ḳu-um-miš i-šib*
. . . . NI-IN-SU-MU-UG-GA KI-TUŠ NAM-EN-NA NU-TUŠ
[muša (?) *u] ur-ra a-dir ina šu-bat be-lu-ti-šu ul a-šib*
[DINGIR]-ḪUL-A-MEŠ MULU-KIN-GA-A DINGIR-LUGAL-LA-MEŠ
ilâni^{pl} *lim-nu-tum mâr-šip-ri ša* ^{ilu}*A-nim šar-ri šu-nu*
SAG - ḪUL ḪA - ZA - MEŠ GIG BA - UR - UR - RA - MEŠ
mu-kil ḳakḳad limuttim(tim) ina mu-ši it-ta-na-ar-ra-ru šu-nu

(And) Ishtar who with Anu the king
Hath founded a shining dwelling,
And hath planned the dominion of the heavens,
God and king the great gods . . . . .
Without whom . . . .
When [those] seven . . . .
At the first [began to work ?] evil . . . .
. . his pure mouth . . . .
Sin . . . the seed of mankind . . . .
. . . . troubling (?) the land,
. . . was troubled and sate in gloom,
[By night and] day he was dark,
Nor dwelt in the seat of his rule.
The evil gods, the messengers of Anu the king,
Raising their evil heads went to and fro[a] through the night,

[1] S. 1,448, AN-NA-GE for GE ANA-DA.

[2] S. 1,448 inserts GA.

[a] Literally, "shook themselves."

GAR - ḪUL - A KIN - KIN - NA MEŠ

li- mut- tu iš- te- ni- '- u šu- nu

ANA-ŠA-GA-TA IMI-GIM KALAMA-TA ZI-GA-MEŠ

iš-tu ki-rib šame(e) ki-ma ša-a-ri ana ma-a-ti it-te-bu-ni šu-nu

DINGIR - EN - LIL - LA ŠUL DINGIR - EN - ZU - NA SU - MU - UG - GA - NI

^{ilu} „ *ša id - li* ^{ilu}*Sin na - an - dur - ša*

AN - NA IGI - GAB - MU - UN - E - A

ina šame(e) i - mur - ma

EN LUḪ - A - NI DINGIR - NUZKU - RA GU - MU - UN - AN - DE - E

be-lum ana suk-kal-li-šu ^{ilu}*Nuzku i-šis-si*

[1] LUḪ-MU DINGIR-NUZKU I-MU ZU-AB-KU TUM-MA-AB

suk-kal-li ^{ilu}*Nuzku a-ma-ti ana ap-si-i bi-i-li*

DIMMU DU - MU DINGIR - EN - ZU - NA AN - NA SU-MU-UG-GA-BI GIG-GA

ṭe-im ma-ri-ia ^{ilu}*Sin ša ina šame(e) mar-ṣi-iš* [']-*ad*-[*ru*]

DINGIR-EN-KI ṬU-RA . . ŠU-A-AŠ-AN-NA-AN-GI

a-na ^{ilu}*E-a ina ap-si-i šu-un-ni-šum-ma*

DINGIR - NUZKU I LUGAL - LA - GE SAG - SAR - A - BA - ŠI - IN - NA - AG

^{ilu}*Nuzku a - mat be - ili - šu it - ta - ' - id - ma*

DINGIR - EN - KI - GE ṬU - RA - GE GIR - PAP - ḪAL - LA MU - UN - GIN

a - na ^{ilu}*E - a. ina ap - si - i pu - ri - du il - lak*

DINGIR-NUN MAS-SU-MAḪ EN DINGIR-NU-DIM-MUD-RA

a-na ru-bi-e mas-su-u ṣi-i-ri belu ^{ilu} „

105. Searching out wickedness,
Rushing loose over the land
Like the wind from the depths of the heavens.
110. Bel saw the darkening of the hero Sin in heaven,
And the lord spake unto his minister Nuzku:
115. "O my minister Nuzku!
"Bear my message unto the Ocean Deep,
"Tell unto Ea in the Ocean Deep
"The tidings of my son Sin,
"Who in heaven hath been grievously bedimmed."
120. And Nuzku, praising the message of his master,
Went therefore unto Ea in the Ocean Deep;
125. Unto Ea the prince, the mighty guide and lord,

[1] K. 4,904 begins DINGIR . . . . .

DINGIR-NUZKU I LUGAL-LA-GE ḪAL-BI-ŠU-A BA-AN-NA-AN-GI

[ilu]Nuzku a-mat be-ili-šu a-ḫi-en-na-a uš-[ta]-an-na-[a]

DINGIR-EN-KI-KA-GE ṬU-RA-GE I-BI GIŠ-NE-IN-TUK

[ilu]E-a ina ap-si-i a-ma-tu[1] *šu-a-tu iš-me*[2]*-ma*

SU-BI KA-NE-IN-TAR 'U-A KA-BI NE-IN-SI

ša-pat-su iš-šuk[3]*-ma 'u-a pi-i-šu um-tal*[4]*-li*

DINGIR-EN-KI DU-NI DINGIR-SILIG-MULU-ŠAR GU-NAM-MI-IN-DE I MI-NI-IN[5]-DIB-BA

[ilu]E-a mâri-šu[6] *[ilu]Marduk is-si-ma a-ma-ta u-šaḫ-ḫaz*[7]

GIN-NA DU-MU DINGIR-SILIG-MULU-ŠAR

a-lik ma-ri [ilu]Marduk

DU-KU[8] UD-SIR DINGIR-EN-ZU-NA[9] AN-NA SU-MU-UG-GA-BI GIG-GA

mar[10] *ru-bi-e na-an-na-ri*[11] *[ilu]Sin ša ina šame(e) mar-ṣi-iš '-ad-ru*

(PLATE XXI.)

SU-MU-UG-GA-BI AN-NA[9] MAS-TIG-GAR-MU-UN-E-A

na-an[12]*-dur-šu ina šame(e) šu-pu-u*

VII-BI-E-NE DINGIR-ḪUL-A-MEŠ MULU-BAD-GA[13]-MEŠ IM-NU-TE-MAL-DA-MEŠ

si-bit-ti šu-nu ilâni[pl][14] *lim-nu-tum*[15] *muš-mi-tu-ti*[16] *la a-di-ru-ti šu-nu*

VII-BI-E-NE DINGIR-ḪUL-A-MEŠ A-MA-TU-GIM ZI KALAM-MA

BA-AN-UR-UR-A-MEŠ

si-bit-ti šu-nu ilâni[pl][14] *lim-nu-tum*[15] *ša kima*[17] *a-bu-bi*[18]

ti[19]*-bu-ma mâti i-ba-'-u šu-nu*

ḲALAM-MA IM-MIR-RA-GIM ZI-ZI-MEŠ

ana[20] *ma-a-ti ki-ma me*[21]*-ḫi-e ti*[19]*-bu-ni šu-nu*

Nuzku there repeated the message of his master.
Ea in the Ocean Deep heard this message,
And bit his lip and filled his mouth with wailing.
Ea called unto his son Marduk,
And with a message entrusted him:
"Go, my son Marduk,
"Son of a Prince, the Crescent of the Moon God
"In heaven hath been grievously bedimmed;

(PLATE XXI.)

"The darkening thereof is visible throughout the heavens.
"Those seven evil gods, death-dealing without fear,
"Those seven evil gods, rushing on like a flood,
"Have scoured the land,
"Have attacked the land like a storm,

---

[1] K. 4,904, *mat* for *ma-tu*.
[2] K. 4,904, [*m*]*i-e*.
[3] K. 4,904, *šu-uk*.
[4] K. 4,904, *ta-al*.
[5] K. 4,904, MU-UN for MI-NI-IN.
[6] 33,712, [*ma*]-*ra-a-šu*.
[7] K. 4,904, *ḫa-az*.
[8] K. 4,904 omits KU; 33,712, NUN-NA for KU.
[9] K. 4,904 omits.
[10] 33,712, *ma-ri*.
[11] K. 4,904, *ṭe-mi mâri-ia* for the beginning of this line.
[12] K. 4,904 ’ .
[13] K. 4,904 inserts A.
[14] K. 4,904 omits ^{pl}.
[15] K. 4,904, *ti*.
[16] K. 4,904, *tu*.
[17] K. 4,904, *ki-ma*.
[18] K. 4,904, *bu*.
[19] K. 4,904, *te*.
[20] K. 4,904, *a-na*.
[21] K. 4,904, *mi*.

DUP-SAG-TA UD-SIR DINGIR-EN-ZU-NA SUR-BI BA-AN-DIB-BI-EŠ
ina ma-ḫar na-an-na-ri ^{ilu}*Sin iz zi-is il-ta-nam-mu-u*

ŠUL DINGIR-BABBAR DINGIR-NI UR-SAG A[1]-NI-KU-A BA-NI-IB-GE-GE-EŠ
id-la [^{ilu}]*Šamšu* [^{ilu}]*Adadu ḳar-du a-na i-di-šu-nu ut-tir-ru*

. . . . IM-MI-IN-DIB-BI-E-NE
. . . . *ra-a-ti i-taḫ-zu*

[Hiatus of about fourteen lines.]

(168) MI . . . (169) . . : (170) SI (?) . . . (171) . . .
(172) . . . . . (173) . . . (174) E (?) . . GAR . . . .

ina bît bal-ti u meš-ri . . . .
me-lam-me i-šu-u tap-pi . . . . .

KA E-GAL-LA-GE GU *II* TAB . . . . . .
ina ba-ab e-kal-li ḳa-a . . . .

KU-U-LI-IN TAR-A SIG-RIK-KAR . . . . .

SIG-SAL-?-UŠ-NU-ZU U-ME-NI-NU-NU
u-li-in-na bur-ru-um-ta ša-rat u-ni-ki
la pi-ti-ti ša-rat bu-ḫat-ti la pi-te-te ṭi-me-ma

LUGAL-E DU-DINGIR-RA-NA ID-ŠU-GIR-BI U-ME-NI-KEŠDA-KEŠDA

LUGAL-E DU-DINGIR-RA-NA UD-SIR-DINGIR-EN-ZU-NA-GIM ZI KALAM-MA ŠU-UL

šar-ru mâr ili-šu ša ki-ma na-an-na-ri ^{ilu}*Sin na-piš-ti mâti u-kal-lu*

UD-SIR-BIL-GIM SAG-BI SU-ŠI GUR-RU-A
ki-ma na-an-na-ri id-di-ši-i ina ri-ši-šu ša-lum-[*ma-ti iš-šu*]

[Hiatus of about eleven lines.]

"Clustering angrily round the Crescent of the Moon God,
"Have won over to their aid Shamash the mighty and Adad the warrior.
"Holding . . . .

[Hiatus of about ten lines.]

In the Home of Plenteous Increase . . . .
They have power . . . .
In the palace-gate a cord . . . .
Weave thou a two-coloured cord[a] from the hair of a virgin kid and from the wool of a virgin lamb,
Upon the limbs of the king,[b] son of his god, bind it,
Then shall the king,[b] the son of his god
Who holdeth the life of the land like the Crescent of the Moon God,
Placing it as a glory on his head,
Like the new Crescent of the Moon,

[Hiatus of about five lines.]

---

[1] K. 5,156, ID.

[a] *Ulinnu*. Cf. Syriac *helânâ*, in *kel'tha d'helânâ*, stola seu orarium (Brockelmann, *Lexicon Syriacum*, p. 83, *b*).

[b] The use of the word *šarru* here instead of the common *amelu* is very similar to that in certain of the Prayers of the Raising of the Hand (King, *Bab. Magic and Sorcery*, xxiii), e.g., No. 2, l. 26, dupl. D, "I, thy servant, Ashurbanipal, the son of his god. . . ."

GAR - ḪUL . . . .
lim - nu · in - na . . . .
GIŠ-MA-NU GIṢ̌-KU-LIG-GA-TA KA-[KA] SAG-GA-NA
U-ME-NI-GAR
e-ra kak-ka dan-na rig-ma(?)-ta ina ri-ši-šu
šu-kun-ma
NAM - ŠUB NUN - KI - GA U - ME - NI - SUM
ši - pat ^{alu}*Eridi* *i - di - ma*
GAR - NA GI - BIL - LA U - ME - NI - E
A - GUB - BA A - AZAG - GA NA - RI - GA - A - AN
„ *- a* *mê*^{pl} *el - u - ti* *ul - lil - šu - ma*
LUGẠL - E DU - DINGIR - RA - NA U - ME - NI - EL
U - ME - NI - LAḪ - LAḪ - GA
UTUG-ḪUL A-LA-ḪUL GIDIM-ḪUL MULLA-ḪUL
DINGIR - ḪUL MAŠKIM - ḪUL
E - [A] NAM - BA - TU - TU - NE
ana [bîti] a - a i - ru - bu - ni
DA E - GAL - LA - GE NAM - BA - TE - MAL - NE
i - da - at ekalli a - a iṭ - ḫu - u - ni
LUGAL - LA - RA NAM - BA - TE - MAL - NE
ana šar - ri a - a iṭ - ḫu - u - ni
ERI - A NAM - BA - NIGIN - E - NE
å - na a - li a - a is - saḫ - ru - u - ni
. . . . NAM - BA - TU - TU - NE
. . . . *a - a i - ru - bu - u - ni*

[Hiatus of about three lines.]

. . . . RI - EŠ

Evil . . . .
Place at his head the tamarisk,
The mighty weapon of . . . . ,
Perform the Incantation of Eridu,
Bring unto him a censer, a torch,
With the purest water wash him,
And cleanse and purify the king,[a] the son of his god.
Evil Spirit, evil Demon, evil Ghost, evil Devil,
Evil God, evil Fiend,
Into the [house] may they not enter,
Unto the walls of the palace may they not draw nigh,
Unto the king may they not draw nigh,
Around the city may they not circle,
. . . . may they not enter.

[Hiatus of about two lines.]

[a] See note *b*, p. 101.

INIM - INIM - MA [UTUG - ḪUL - A] - KAN

EN . . UL . . . . MEŠ
MI (?) - RA - A . . . . MEŠ
. . . . *u* . . . . *šu - nu*
SAG - BU - BU - I . . . . MEŠ

(Plate XXII.)

šar - ri - ru la (?) . . . . [*šu*] - *nu*
E - NE - NE - NE . . . . MEŠ
šu - nu ûmu(*mu*) *la pa - ḳu* (?) - *u* (?) . . . *šu-nu*
E - NE - NE - NE . . . . MEŠ
e-la ša šu-nu . . šame(*e*) *ilu ma-am-man ul in-nam-bi*
ANA DINGIR-EN-LIL-LA GU-NAM-MI-IN-DE-EŠ
ilu A - nu - um u ilu Bel im - bu - šu - nu - ti
DINGIR-EN-ZU-NA [ANA]-ŠA-TA SU-MU-UG-GA-GI-EŠ
ilu Sin ina [*lib*] *šame*(*e*) *u - ša - di - ru*
. . . . SIG - SIG - GI - EŠ
. . . . *iš - ḫu - ṭu*
. . . . EŠ

[Hiatus of several lines.]

. . . *ṭu* . . . .
. . . GAL . . . .
. . MULU DU - DINGIR - RA - NA . . . .
URUDU-GAR-LIG-GA UR-SAG AN-NA-[GE ZA-PA-RAM]-
ME-NE-[A-NI]
ḪU-LUḪ-ḪA GAR-ḪUL BA-AB-SIR-RI ŠU-U-ME-TI
GIŠ-MA-NU GIŠ-KU-LIG-GA-TA ḲA-KA U-ME-NI-IN-GAR
NAM - ŠUB NUN - KI - GA U - ME - NI - SUM

PRAYER AGAINST [THE EVIL SPIRITS].

Incantation :—

[Raging storms ?] . . . . . . are they,
Brilliant . . . . are they,

(PLATE XXII.)

They are the storm . . . .
Over that which is theirs in heaven
No god hath been proclaimed,
Anu and Bel proclaimed them.
They have darkened the Moon God in the heavens,
They have torn away . . . .

[Hiatus of several lines.]

. . The man, son of his god . . . .
Take thou the potent meteorite[a] of heaven,
Which by the roar of its awful might removeth all evil,
Place the tamarisk,
The mighty weapon of . . . ,
Perform the Incantation of Eridu,

[a] URUDU-GAR-LIG-GA ; GAR-LIG-GA=*e-ru-u* (*Cun. Texts*, part xii, pl. 36, cols. iii–iv, 45) ; URUDU-GAR-LIG-GA = *e-ra-a dan-nu* (*W.A.I.*, iv, 13, i, 18–19 : *at-ta e-ra-a dan-nu ki-ma maš-ki* . . . "Thou (bendest ?) strong copper like skin"). URUDU-GAR-LIG-GA from its determinative is evidently some metal or metal object. From the description of it given here ("the potent *erû* of heaven, which by the roar of its awful might") and the addition on Tablet "A," i, 30, "Place him where the thunder roars," it is probable that it signifies a meteorite or meteoric iron.

U - UL - UL - MEŠ DINGIR - ḪUL - [A - MEŠ]
ZI ANA-DINGIR-EN-LIL-LA-BI[1] KAN-[PA] . . . . .
GABA - ZU ZI - BA - RA - AB . . . .
i - rat - ka . . . .
A - GA - ZU - KU . . . .
ana ar - ki - ka . . . .
E - A NAM - BA - [TU - TU - NE]
GIŠ - ZA - RA[2] NAM - BA - IM - [IM - E - NE]
ERI - A[3] NAM - BA - [NIGIN - E - NE]
E - TA[4] BA - RA - E[5]
U - UL - UL - MEŠ DINGIR - ḪUL - [A - MEŠ]
UTUG - ḪUL A - LA - ḪUL GIDIM - ḪUL
MULLA - ḪUL DINGIR - [ḪUL MAŠKIM - ḪUL]
ZI AN - NA[6] KAN - PA ZI KI - A [KAN - PA]

INIM - INIM - MA UTUG - ḪUL - A - KAN

EN U-GAL ANA-TA ŠU-BAR-RA-MEŠ [DINGIR-ḪUL A-MEŠ]
[7] *ûmu(mu) rabûti*[pl] *ša* [*ultu šamê*] *uš-šu-ru-*[*ni ilâni limnuti šunu*]

[Hiatus of several lines.]

---

[1] 34,106 translates: *niš* [ilu] *A-nim* . . . .
[2] 34,106 translates: *ina ṣir-ri* . . . .
[3] 34,106 translates: *ana a-li a-a is-* . . . .
[4] 34,106 translates: *iš-tu lib bîti li-ṣu-* . . . .
[5] K. 2,406 translates: *ul* . . . .
[6] K. 2,406 omits.
[7] 34,106 ends here with (a) *kima labiri-šu šaṭir-ma* . . . (b) . . . [m ilu] *Nabu* . . . .

O raging storms, ye evil gods!
By Anu and Bel may ye be exorcised!
Thy breast . . . .
Behind thee . . . .
Into the house may they not [enter],
Through the hinge [may they not crawl [a]],
Around the city may they not circle!
Go ye forth from the house,
O raging storms, ye evil gods!
Evil Spirit, evil Demon, evil Ghost,
Evil Devil, [evil] God, [evil Fiend],
By Heaven be ye exorcised! By Earth be ye exorcised!

Prayer against the Evil Spirits.

Incantation:—
Great storms directed from heaven,
They are the evil gods!

[Hiatus of several lines.]

---

[a] The Sumerian IM (Brünnow, No. 4,822) has the value *šalû*, "to sink" (into water), and we must supply some such meaning here. *Iziḳku* is used of spirits *blowing* through the hinge elsewhere (Tablet V, i, 35).

. . . . *id ki* . . . .

[DINGIR-SILIG-MULU-ŠAR : GAR-GA]-E : GIN-NA DU-MU

. . . . RAM - ME - NE . . .

. . . .

. . . .

. . . .

U-GAL ANA-TA ŠU BAR-RA-MEŠ DINGIR-Ḫ̮UL-A-MEŠ

AN - NA Ḫ̮A - BA - GIBIŠ - NE KI - TUŠ - BI - KU

Ḫ̮A - BA - AN - GE - GE - E - NE

ana šame(e) li-lu-u-ma ana šab-ti-šu-nu li-tu-ru

UTUG-Ḫ̮UL A-LA-Ḫ̮UL KI-TUŠ Ḫ̮A-BA-GIBIŠ-NE

u-tuk-ku lim-nu a-lu-u lim-nu ana irṣitim(tim) li-ri-du

GIDIM-Ḫ̮UL MULLA-Ḫ̮UL ERI-TA Ḫ̮A-BA-RA-E

e-kim-mu lim-nu gal-lu-u lim-nu iš-tu ali li-ṣu-u

ZI DINGIR - GAL - GAL - E - NE - GE U - MU - UN - NI - PA

E - A NAM - BA - TU - TU - NE

*UR - RA NAM - MU - UN - DA - PAL - E

DA - DA E - GAL - LA - GE NAM - BA - TE - MAL - E - NE

BAD NA - AN - . . . .

ALAD E - GAL . . . .

E - SIR - RA . . . .

ERI - A . . . .

[Hiatus of several lines.]

Marduk hath seen him : (etc.)
"What I : (etc.)
"Go, my son : (etc.)[a]

[Hiatus of several lines.]

. . . .[b]
. . . .
. . . .
Great storms directed from heaven,
They are the evil gods!
Unto heaven may they ascend,
Unto their abodes may they return!
May the evil Spirit, the evil Demon,
Into the earth descend!
May the evil Ghost, the evil Devil,
Go forth from the city!
By the great Gods may ye be exorcised!
Into the house may they not enter,
The fence may they not break through,
Unto the neighbourhood of the palace may they not draw nigh,
The wall . . . .
The guardian spirit of the palace . . . .
The street . . . .
The city . . . .

[Hiatus of several lines.]

[a] See Tablet "A," l. 17.
[b] Cf. l. 247.

. . . . ḪUL . . . .
. . . UḪ (?) -ZU UḪ (?) -RI-A GAR-ŠA-A GAR-ḪUL-A . .
ZI AN - NA KAN - PA ZI KI - A KAN - PA

INIM - INIM - MA DINGIR - ḪUL TAR - RU - DA - KAN

---

[1] EN GI - AZAG GI - GAL - GAL - LA GI-SUK-AZAG-GA
GIŠ - BANŠUR - EL - LA [2] DINGIR - RI - E - NE - GE
GI - URUDU - ŠUN - TAB - BA SU - ZI RI - A
ḳa - an pa - aš - tı ša ša - lum - ma - tu ra - mu - u
GA-E MULU-KIN-GA-A DINGIR-SILIG-MULU-ŠAR ME-EN
mâr - šip - ri ša [ilu]*Marduk a - na* [3] *- ku*
NAM - ŠUB NA - RI - GA NE - IN - SUM
sip - tum ellitum(tum) ina na - di - e - a
A - * SIR GIŠ - ŠA - KA - NA - TA KI - TA IM - MI - IN - RI
id - da - a it - ti „ *šap - liš ar - me - ma*
(PLATE XXIII.)
DINGIR - E - A E - A KAN - TI
[ilu]*E ina bîti li - šib*
UTUG- * ŠIG-GA ALAD- * ŠIG-GA E-A ḪE-EN-TU-TU-NE
UTUG - ḪUL A - LA - ḪUL GIDIM - ḪUL

---

[1] K. 2,406 translates [*ḳa-nu-u el-lu ḳa-nu*]*-u ra-bu-u ḳa-an ap-pa-ri el-lu.*

[2] K. 2,406 translates [*ḳa-an pa*]*-aš-šu-ri el-lu ša ilâni*[pl].

[3] K. 2,406, *ana* for *a-na.*

[a] *Pašti.* It is possible that this is the same as the Hebrew *pišteh,* "flax," but the Sumerian seems to suggest a copper vessel.

[b] GIŠ ŠA-KA-NA, for which no Assyrian equivalent has been given. It occurs also in Tablet "C" (pl. 32), l. 163 [GIŠ-GAM]-MA (= *kippati*) GIŠ-ŠA-KA-NA-GE. Now *kippatu* is the Syriac *kappetha*

. . . witchcraft, sorcery, enchantment, and all evil,
By Heaven be ye exorcised! By Earth be ye exorcised!

PRAYER AGAINST THE EVIL GOD WHICH CUTTETH OFF.

Incantation :—
A clean reed, a long reed,
A reed from an undefiled brake,
A clean vessel of the gods,
A stalk of flax [a] encircled with a glory.
I am the messenger of Marduk,
As I perform the pure incantation,
I put bitumen on the door [b] beneath,

(PLATE XXIII.)

That Ea may rest within the house.
May a kindly Spirit, a kindly Guardian,
Enter the house.
May no evil Spirit or evil Demon,

(Brockelmann, *Lexicon*, p. 163, *a*), "arch," so that "Arch of the GIŠ-ŠA-KA-NA" clearly points to the meaning "door" for the latter word (i.e., the actual door as the Sumerian "wood : middle : door" shows, and not merely the whole doorway, gateposts and all). This is still further borne out by the present passage "I put bitumen on the door beneath," in order that Ea (the god of the water supposed to be spilt on the floor) may remain within the house, and not drain away over the threshold into the street.

MULLA - ḪUL DINGIR - ḪUL MAŠKIM - ḪUL
LUGAL - RA NAM - BA - TE - MAL - E - NE
ZI AN - NA KAN - PA ZI KI - A KAN - PA

INIM - INIM - MA GI - DUR - GIL - MA - KAN

EN SIG - UZ . . . .
. . . .
ša - rat en - [zi] . . . .
. . . .
DINGIR - NIN - NI (?) . . . .
ilu . . . .
AMAŠ . . . .
ina [supuri] . . . .

[Hiatus of several lines.]

E - GAL - LA - KU NAM - BA - TU - TU - NE
LUGAL - LA - RA NAM - BA - TE - MAL - E - NE
ZI AN - NA KAN - PA ZI KI - A KAN - PA

INIM-INIM-MA SIG-UZ-SIG-GA RIK-KAR-KAN

EN MULU-ḪUL MULU-ḪUL MULU-BI MULU-ḪUL
lim - nu li - mun a - me - lu šu - u li - mun
MULU - BI NAM - MULU - GIŠGAL - LU MULU - ḪUL
MULU - BI MULU - ḪUL
a - me - lu šu - u ina ni - ši li - mun „ „

Or evil Ghost or evil Devil,
Or evil God or evil Fiend,
Draw nigh unto the King.
By Heaven be ye exorcised! By Earth be ye exorcised!

Prayer of the Reed . . . . . . (?).

Incantation:—
Goat's hair . . . .
. . . .
The goddess . . . .
In the cattle-pen . . . .

[Hiatus of several lines.]

Into the house may they not enter,
Unto the King may they not draw nigh.
By Heaven be ye exorcised! By Earth be ye exorcised!

Prayer of the Hair of the Yellow Goat (and) the Kid.

Incantation:—
He that is evil is evil,
That man is evil:
That man among men is evil,
That man is evil.

[ŠA]-TUR NAM-MULU-GIŠGAL-LU ṢIR TIK-KIL-DUG-GA
ina ša - sur ni - ši ṣira u - kan - ni - nu
MULU-BI NAM-MULU-GIŠGAL-LU GU I (?) SA-A LAL-E
amelu[1] *šu - u ina ni - ši ḳa - a e - ša - a*
ana še - e - ti tar - ṣu
NI - BI - A KA - RU - A GU - DE - A - NI - TA
UḪ (?) MULU - RA SU - SU
pu - luḫ - ta - šu ṣa - ' - i - rat ri - gim - šu
im - tu amelu i - sal - [laḫ]
KI GIG - GA - BI ḪUL - A - NI DU . . . .
ŠA - BI GUR UŠ - NU - UN - GIR (?) . .
a - šar ma - ru - uš - ti - šu lim - [ni] . . .
lib - ba - šu i - ḳaṣ - ṣa - aṣ . . .
[2] ALAD IGI - ḪUL DINGIR - ḪUL . . . .
[3] TUR - RA NE - IB - DIB . . . .
AMAŠ - A NE - IB - DIB . . . .
IḌ - BI MULU - NU - NA . . . .
. . . . . *ma* (?) *uš* (?) . . . .
ŠA - BI - A DINGIR - BABBAR BA . . . . .
BI . . . .
ana lib-bi-šu ^{ilu}*Šamšu ul* . . . . *i-ḳab-bi*
DINGIR-BABBAR NE-E-TA ŠU-[BI] . . SIR-RA-A-AN
^{ilu}*Šamšu ina an - ni - ti ḳat - su li - is - suḫ*
LUGAL - MU DINGIR - EN - KI - GE *ŠAG - GA
TAG - TAG - GUB - BI ZA - A - KAN

INIM-INIM-MA DINGIR-ḪUL TAR-RU-DA-KAN

EN [4] U AŠ DINGIR [erasure] ḪUL
Duppu XVI ^{KAM} UTUG - ḪUL - MEŠ
Ekal $^{m\ ilu}$*Aššur-bani-apli šar kiššati šar* $^{m\bar{a}tu\ ilu}$*Aššuri* ^{KI}
(Etc.)

In the midst[a] of mankind
They have let (him) lurk[b] (like) a snake;
That man is set among men as a cord that is stretched out for a net
He hath sprinkled the man as with venom,
The terror of him stifling his cries.
Where his evil pain [hath smitten]
It hath torn his heart . . .
Spirit, evil eye, evil god . . .
Hunting the sheepfold . . . . .
Hunting the cattle-pen . . . . .
His side the man . . . . .
Unto his heart Shamash . . . hath spoken
By this (incantation) may Shamash remove his hand,
O my lord Ea! Thine is the power to brighten and bless!

Prayer against the Evil God which cutteth off.

Incantation:—"A storm [*erasure*] evil.

Sixteenth Tablet of the Series "The Evil Spirits."

[1] K. 5,238, *a-me-lu*.
[2] K. 5,238 translates *še-e-du ša* . . . .
[3] K. 5,238 translates *ṭar-ba-ṣa i-ba* (?) . . . .
[4] K. 2,977, . . *bîtu nu-ru* . . K. 4,627, DINGIR-ḪUL (?) . . .

[a] *Šasur*, apparently literally "the womb."
[b] *Ukanninu*: cf. *W.A.I.*, iv, 43, iii, 6, *ilâni kima kalbi kunnunu* (parallel to *rabṣu*), "The gods crouched like dogs."

Tablet "A."

Obverse.

Col. I (Plate XXIV).

. . . . BU E . .

. . . . *ar*

. . . . *pak* (?) - *ku*

. . . . NU - KU

. . . . . . *ina* *ṣi-e-*[*ri*] . . . . [*la*] *i-pa-du-u*

. . . [DINGIR-RAB]-KAN-ME-A EGIR MULU-RA SU-SU

. . . . . *la-ba-ṣu* *arki* *ameli* *i-sal-la-ḫu*

[ŠA-GIG LIKIR-GIG] TUR-RA SAG-GIG GIŠGAL-LU MULU-RA DUL-LA

[*mu-ru-uṣ* *lib*]-*bi* *ki-iṣ* *lib-bi* *mur-ṣu* *ṭi-'-i* *a-lu-u* *ša* *ameli* *kat-me*

[MULU . .]-GIN U-GIM MU-UN-DA-RU-UŠ ṢI-NA BA-NI-IN-SU-EŠ

a-me-lu *mut-tal-lik* *kima* *ûmu*(*mu*) *iḫ-mu-šu-ma* *mar-tu* *iṣ-ṣa-nu-uš*

MULU-GIŠGAL-LU-BI ZI-NI-TA NI-BAL-BAL-E ZI-GIM MU-UN-ZI

a-me-lu *šu-u* *it-ti* *na-piš-ti-šu* *it-ta-nab-kat* [sic] *ki - ma* *a - gi - i* *i - sa - ap - pu - '*

U NU-UN-DA-AB-KU-E A NU-UN-DA-AB-NAK-E

'U-U-A A-A U-ME-NI-IB-ZAL-ZAL : *ina u-a-a ûmi*(*mi*)-*šam* *uš - tab - ri*

Tablet "A."

Obverse.

Col. I (Plate XXIV).

. . . .
. . . in the desert . . . they spare not,
. . . the ghoul after the man hath sprinkled
Spreading heart disease, heartache,
Sickness (and) disease over the city [a] of the man,
Scorching [b] the wanderer like the day,
And filling him with bitterness;
Like a flood they are gathered together,[c]
(Until) this man revolteth against himself.
No food can he eat, no water can he drink,
But with woe each day is he sated.
Marduk hath seen [d] (him and
(Into the house of his father Ea hath entered and spoken,
("Father, ..."

---

[a] Or "Heart disease, heartache, sickness, disease, the demon which envelopeth the man."

[b] *Iḫmušu*; cf. Syriac *ḫ'ma*, aruit.

[c] *Ĭsappu'*; cf. Syriac *s'pha*, coacervavit.

[d] The following lines are abbreviated in the text (as they frequently are) by division-marks. The incident is given in full in part xvii, pl. 26, Tablet "P," the only difference being in the line which Marduk speaks to his father, which is the first line of the tablet. Similarly, in the sixth tablet of the series *Shurpu* (*W.A.I.*, iv, 7, i, 16–32), where the lines are also written out, Marduk quotes the first line of the tablet. Unfortunately, here it cannot be supplied.

DINGIR-SILIG-MULU-ŠAR IGI : GAʼR-GA-E : GIN-NA DU-MU

A DUG - A - SA - AM U - ME - NI - DE

mê[pl] *a - sa - am - me - e* *šu - pu - uk - ma*

GIŠ - ŠINIG U - IN - NU - UŠ ŠA - BI U - ME - NI - ŠUB

A - BI NAM - ŠUB NUN - KI - GA U - ME - NI - SUM

[1] MULU-GIŠGAL-LU-BI A U-ME-NI-SU : [2] GAR-NA GIBILLA U-ME-NI-E

NAM-TAR SU MULU KA-NI-GAL-LA A-GIM ḪE-IM-MA-AN-SUR-SUR-RI

nam-ta-ri[3] *ša ina zu-mur ameli ba-šu-u kima me-e li-iṣ-ru-ur*

URUDU-GAR-LIG-GA UR-SAG AN-NA-GE ZA-PA-RAM-ME-NE-A-NI ḪU-LUḪ-ḪA

GAR - ḪUL BA - AB - SIR - RA ŠU - U - ME - TI

"-*u ḳar-ra-du*[4] [ilu]*A-nim ša ina ri-gim me-lam-mi-šu gal-tu*

mimma lim-nu i-na-as-sa-ḫu li-ḳi-e-ma

---

[1] K. 4,965 inserts translation *amelu šu-[a-tu]* . . .

[2] K. 4,965 inserts translation GAR-NA *nak* . . .

[3] K. 4,965, *ru*. [4] K. 4,965, *rad* for *ra-du*.

[a] *Bînu*; see Brockelmann, *Lexicon*, p. 37, *b*, under the Syriac *bîna*.

[b] The line GAR-NA GI-BIL-LA U-ME-NI-E is translated in *Cun. Texts*, part xvii, pl. 5, iii, 5, by " " *-a šu-bi-ʼ-šu-ma*.

[c] *Liṣrur*; the word *ṣarâru* appears to have the meaning of *trickling* when used in conjunction with liquids: cf. *W.A.I.*, iv, 20, 3, obv. 16, *kakkaka ušumgallu ša ištu pišu imtu la inattuku*, "Thy weapon is a serpent whose mouth is unslavered with venom," paralleled in the next line by *damu la iṣarruru*, "not slobbering blood"; *natâku* is the Hebrew *nâthak*, "to pour out." When used of a star, *ṣarâru* seems to mean "to appear" or "flash into

(Twice he hath said unto him,
("What this man shall do he knoweth not whereby he may be relieved."
(Ea hath answered his son Marduk,
("O my son, what dost thou not know, what more can I give thee?
("O Marduk, what dost thou not know, what can I add unto thy knowledge?)
"What I (know, thou knowest also),
"Go, my son, (Marduk);
"Pour forth water from an *asammu*-vessel,
"Lay a sprig[a] of *mashtakal* on his heart,
"With the water perform the Incantation of Eridu,
"Sprinkle this man with the water,
"Bring unto him a censer,[b] a torch,
"That the Plague-demon, which resteth in the body of the man,
"Like the water may trickle away![c]
"Take thou the potent meteorite of heaven,
"Which by the roar of its awful might removeth all evil.

---

appearance"; cf. *Cun. Texts*, part xvii, pl. 19, l. 12, *kima kakkab šamame iṣarrur*, "(Headache) like a heavenly star comes on"; part xvi, pl. 25, l. 53, ... *limniš kima kakkabu iṣarru*[*r*], ". . . banefully like a star comes on." Cf. also the astrological texts, e.g., my *Reports of the Magicians and Astrologers*, No. 28, rev. 2, [*Ana*] *kakkabu iṣrurma*, etc. The idea of motion is shown in Tablet "V," part xvii, pl. 34, l. 28, where *iṣarruru* is parallel to *'irru*, and again pl. 35, l. 59, where it is parallel to *iziḳḳu*.

KI ZA-PA-RAM SUM-MU U-ME-NI-DE-A DAḪ-ZU-ḪI (?)-A

a-šar ri-gim[1] *na-du-u u-šub-šum-ma lu-ri-ṣu-ka*

TU-DUG-GA[2] I DINGIR-EN-KI-GA-GE

[3] URUDU-GAR-LIG-GA UR-SAG AN-NA-GE ZA-PA-RAM-ME-NE-A-NI ḪU-MU-RA-AB-DAḪ-E

UTUG-ḪUL A-LA-ḪUL ḪA-BA-RA-E

u-tuk-ku lim-nu a-lu-u lim-nu lit-ta-ṣi

GIDIM-ḪUL MULLA-ḪUL ḪA-BA-RA-E : DINGIR-ḪUL MAŠKIM-ḪUL : „

(PLATE XXV.)

DINGIR-LUGAL-KAN-ME DINGIR-LUGAL-KAN-ME-A EGIR MULU-RA SU-SU ḪA-BA-RA-E

ŠA-GIG LIKIR-GIG TUR-RA SAG-GIG-GA GIŠGAL-LU MULU-RA DUL-LA

ZI DINGIR-GAL-GAL-E-NE-GE U-ME-NI-PA . . ḪA-BA-RA-E

ḪA-BA-RA-AN-LAḪ-LAḪ-GI-EŠ

SILIM-MA-NA ŠU-*ŠIG-GA DINGIR-RA-NA-KU ḪE-EN-ŠI-IN-GE-GE

INIM-INIM-MA UTUG-ḪUL-A-KAN

EN UTUG-ḪUL A-LA-ḪUL MULU GIG-BAR-A-KU SILA-A KIL-BA

u-tuk-ku lim-nu a-lu-u lim-nu ša ana mu-u-ši-i ina su-u-ḳa par-ku

GIDIM-ḪUL MULLA-ḪUL MULU GIG-BAR-A-KU E-SIR KIL-BA

e-kim-mu lim-nu gal-lu-u lim-nu ša ana mu-u-ši-i ina su-la-a par-[*ku*]

. . BAD-ŠA-AN-ŠA-ŠA GAR-NAM-MA NU-UN-KAD-KAD . .

[*e*]-*mu-ḳis taš-ša-aš-šu ša mimma šum-šu la iz-zi-bu*

"Place him where the thunder roar is uttered, that it may help thee,
"By the magic of the word of Ea
"May the potent meteorite of heaven
"With its awful roar help thee,
"That the evil Spirit and the evil Demon may go forth,
"That the evil Ghost and the evil Devil may go forth,
"That the evil God and the evil Fiend may go forth,

(PLATE XXV.)

"That the Hag-demon and the Ghoul may go forth
"That have sprinkled (water) after the man,
"That have spread heart disease, heartache,
"Sickness (and) disease over the city of the man."[a]
By the Great Gods I exorcise you,
That ye may go forth, and get hence!
May his welfare be secured at the kindly hands of the gods.

PRAYER AGAINST THE EVIL SPIRITS.

Incantation:—

O evil Spirit, O evil Demon, that have power by night over the street,
O evil Ghost, O evil Devil, that have power by night over the path,
O thou that bringest affliction in thy might, and leavest nothing untouched,

---

[1] K. 4,965, *rig-mu* for *ri-gim*.
[2] K. 4,965 inserts translation: *ina* ,, . . .
[3] K. 4,965 inserts translation ,, *-u ḳar-rad* . . .
[a] See note *a* on p. 117.

. . . IGI - ḪUŠ - A MELAM ZAG - SIR . . .

. . . *ša pa-ni iz-zu me-lam-mu ki-iṣ-ṣu-*[*ru*]

. . . . . A *ŠUG-GA NU-UN-ZU A . . . . . .

. . . . . *na* (?)-*'-i-ri ša ma-ga-ri la i-du-*[*u*] . . .

. . . . . . ḪUL-ḄI-TA MUL-GIM SUR-SUR-RI-E-[NE]

. . . . . *lim-niš kima kak-ka-bu i-ṣar-ru-*[*ru*]

. . . . RA MULU GIG-BAR-A-KU E-A-NI KU-BA . .

. . . . [*ša*] *ana mu-u-ši-i ana bîti* . . .

[Cols. II and III fragmentary.]

REVERSE.

COL. III, 45.

INIM - INIM - MA [UTUG - ḪUL - A - KAN]

EN UTUG-ḪUL [EDIN-NA-ZU] . . . .

u-[*tuk-ku lim-nu a-na ṣi-ri*] . . . . . .

COL. IV.

[A - LA - ḪUL] EDIN - NA - ZU . . . .

a - lu - [*u*] *lim - nu a - na ṣ*[*i - ri*] . . . . .

[GIDIM - ḪUL] EDIN - NA - ZU . . . .

e-kim-[*mu*] *lim-nu a-na ṣi-*[*ri*] . . . . . .

[MULLA - ḪUL] EDIN - NA - ZU . . . .

. *gal-lu-*[*u*] *lim-nu a-na ṣi-*[*ri*] . . . .

. . . . . . ZU ŠU - KAN - NE - IN - [TIL - LA]

. . . . *at*[1] - *ka li*[2] - *ḳi*

[PAD] - ZUN - ZU ŠU - KAN - NE - IN - TIL - [LA]

ku - ru - um - mat[3] - *ka li*[2] - *ḳi*

. . . whose face is wrathful, girt about with brilliance,

. . . . . . that knoweth no kindness,

. . . . . . banefully like a star cometh on,

. . . . by night unto the house . . . .

[Cols. II and III fragmentary.]

REVERSE.

COL. III, 45.

PRAYER [AGAINST THE EVIL SPIRITS].

Incantation :—

O evil Spirit, [get thee (?) to the desert !]

COL. IV.

O evil Demon, [get thee (?)] to the desert !

O evil Ghost, [get thee (?)] to the desert !

O evil Devil, [get thee (?)] to the desert !

Take thy couch (?),

Take thy food,

---

[1] 46,288 has . . . *na'-la* . . .
[2] K. 4,856 inserts *i*.
[3] 46,288, *kur-um-mat*.

SU - A - LIL - LA - ZU ŠU - KAN - NE - IN - TIL - [LA]
na - ru[1] - ḳa - ki[2] li[3] - ḳi
KI-GUB - BA - ZU DINGIR - BABBAR - E - A[4] NU - ME - A
man - za - az - ka ul ša ṣi - it ilu Šamši(ši)
ḲI - TUŠ - A - ZU DINGIR - BABBAR - ŠU - A[5] NU - ME - A
šu - bat - ka ul ša e - rib ilu Šamši(ši)
U - KU - ZU U - KU GIDIM - MA - GE
ma - ka - lu - ka ma - ka - lu - u[6] e - kim - mu
A - NAK - ZU A - NAK GIDIM - MA - GE
maš - ḳit[7] - ka maš - ti - ti e - kim - mu

(PLATE XXVI.)

MULU - GIŠGAL - LU DU DINGIR - RA - NA
a - me - lu ma - ri[8] ili[9] - šu
UḄ - UB - TA[10] NAM - BA - GUB - BU - NE
ina tub - ḳa - a - ti[11] la ta - at - ta - nam - za - zu
DA - DA - TA[10] BA - RA - AN - KU - U - NE
ina ša-ḫa-a-ti[11] la ta - at - ta - na - aš - ša - ab - šu
ŠA - ZU - A - TA NAM - BA - GA - E - NE
ina lib[12] [ali[13]] la ta - nam - miš[14]
KI - TA (?) - BI - KU NAM - BA - NIGIN - E - [NE]
ina[15] a - ḫa - a - tu la ta - sa - na - ḫar - šu
KI . . NA KUR-RA-KU[16] GIG-GIG-GA-ZU-KỤ GIN-NA
ana ḳib-ru uš(?) . . irṣitim(tim) ana ik-li-ti-ka at-lak
ZI DINGIR-GAL-GAL-E-NE-GE I-RI-PA ḪA-BA-RA - DU - UN

Take thy girdle.[a]
Sunrise is no standing-place for thee,
15. Sunset is no seat for thee,
Thy food is the food of ghosts,
20. Thy drink is the drink of ghosts;

(PLATE XXVI.)

Stand not in the vicinity,
25. Sit not in the neighbourhood
Of the man, the son of his god.
In the city circle him not,
30. Nor go about at his side.
Get thee to the tomb (?) . . . of earth to thy darkness!
By the Great Gods I exorcise thee, that thou mayest depart.

---

[1] K. 4,856 and K. 4,965, *ruḳ*.
[2] K. 4,856, K. 4,965, and 46,288, *ka*.
[3] K. 4,856 inserts *i*.
[4] K. 4,856, NE.
[5] K. 4,856 adds KU.
[6] K. 4,856 . . . . *e*.
[7] K. 4,965, *ma-al-ti-it*; 46,288, *maš-ti-it*.
[8] K. 4,965, *mâr* for *ma-ri*.
[9] 46,288 inserts *pl*.
[10] 46,288 . . . AN-DA.
[11] 46,288, *tu*.
[12] 46,288, *lib-bi*.
[13] 46,288, *a-lu*.
[14] 46,288, *mi-*[*iš*].
[15] K. 4,965, *i-na* (?).
[16] 46,288, GE.

[a] *Naru(ḳ)ḳa*; evidently an article of leather for binding or girdling (cf. Brünnow, *List*, No. 244). Possibly it is connected with the Syriac *'erḳetha*, a girdle (Brockelmann, p. 262, *a*).

EN ḪUL-IK KAN-ME-EN ḪUL-IK KAN-ME-EN
kima labiri - šu šaṭir - ma bâri
duppi $^{m\ ilu}$*Bel - epuš aplu ša*
^{m}*Mu - na - pir - ili - šu apil* ^{m}*Eṭir* (?) - *iḳbi* (?)
^{m}*Beli - šu - nu aplu ša*
[$^{m\ ilu\ (?)}$] *Marduk* (?) - *lu - ud - da*
. . . . *sig ûmu IV*^{KAM} *šattu IC VIII*^{KAM}
[*ša* ^{m}*Si - lu*] - *uk - su u*
[*šattu XLIV* ^{m}*An - ti - uk - su*] *šarrâni*^{pl}

Incantation :—"Whether thou art an evil man, whether thou art an evil man."

Like its former copy, written and explained.

Tablet of Bel-epuš, the son of

Munapir-ilišu, the son of Eṭir (?)-iḳbi (?)

[by the hand of (?)] Belišunu, the son of

Marduk (?) -ludda.

Month . . . . fourth day, one hundred and eighth year[a]

[of Sele]ucus and

[the forty-fourth of Antiochus], the kings.

---

[a] I.e., 204 B.C.

Tablet "B."

Obverse.

(Plate XXVII.)

EN ḪUL-IK KAN-ME-EN ḪUL-IK KAN-ME-EN
lu-u lim-nu at-tu lu-u lim-nu at-ta

A LA-ḪUL-IK : *lu-u a-lu-u lim-nu at-ta* : KAN-ME-EN

A-LA-ḪUL INGAR-DIRIG-GA-GIM MULU-RA IN-GUL-'U-A KAN-ME-EN
„ *ša ki-ma i-ga-ri i-ḳup-pu-ma eli ameli ib-ba-tu at-tu*

A-LA-ḪUL KA A (?) . . . . IB-SAR-SAR . . . . KAN-ME-EN
„ *ša pa-a i-pa-šu-u-[ma (?) ḳa (?)]-ti (?) u še-pi (?) [u]-kas-su-u at-tu*

A-LA-ḪUL KA NU-TUK-[A] KAN-ME-EN
„ *ša pa-a la i-šu-u at-ta*

A-LA-ḪUL ME-GIM NU-TUK-A KAN-ME-EN
„ *ša bi-na-a-ti la i-šu-u at-ta*

A-LA-ḪUL GIŠ-NU-TUK-A KAN-ME-EN
„ *la še-mu-u at-ta*

[A]-LA-ḪUL ŠI-GU NU-TUK-A KAN-ME-EN
„ *ša zi-mi la i-šu-u at-ta*

[A]-LA-ḪUL KI DINGIR-BABBAR KAM IGI-NA-AN-GAB-RU-'U-A KAN-ME-EN
„ *ša it-ti* ^{ilu} *Šamši [ina (?) dikari (?)] i-nam-ma-ru at-ta*

[A-LA]-ḪUL KI-NA GIG-A MULU U-DI IN-UR-RA[1]-'U-A KAN-ME-EN
„ *ša ina ma-a-a-al mu-ši amelu ina šit-ti i-ri-iḫ-hu-u at-ta*

A-LA-ḪUL U-DI[2] KAR-KAR-RI MULU-A[3] GUB MU-NE-IN-GUB-BU . . KAN-ME-EN
„ *e-kim šit-ti ša ameli ana ta-ba-li iz-[zi-zu at-ta]*

Tablet "B."

OBVERSE.

(PLATE XXVII.)

Incantation :—

Whether thou art an evil man, whether thou art an evil man,
Or an evil demon,
Or an evil demon that hath fallen like a wall
And hath crushed the man,
Or an evil demon that gibbereth
And bindeth hands and feet (?),
Or an evil demon that hath no mouth,
Or an evil demon that hath no limbs,
Or an evil demon that cannot hear,
Or an evil demon that hath no form,
Or an evil demon that in a goblet (?) flasheth in the sun,
Or an evil demon that the man hath created
On a bed by night in sleep,
Or an evil demon stealing sleep away
Ready to carry off the man,

---

[1] K. 4,661 . . UR for UR-RA.
[2] K. 4,661, KA-AN-USAN for U-DI.
[3] K. 4,661 omits.

A-LA-ḪUL DINGIR GIG-A GIN-GIN ŠU BIL-LA NI-NU-TEMEN-[NA KAN-ME-EN]

„ *ilu mut-tal-lik mu-ši ša ḳa-ti lu-'-a-ti la pa-*[*al-ḫa at-ta*]

A-LA-ḪUL MULU-RA NA-A ANŠU-GIM NI-KABAR . . . . [KAN-ME-EN]

„ *ša e-li ameli rab-ṣu-ma kima imeri* [*ir-ta-bi* (?) *at-ta*]

A-LA-ḪUL SIGIŠŠE-SIGIŠŠE NU-UN-ZU-A KU-ḲUR-GA . . . . [KAN-ME-EN]

„ *ša ni-ḳa-a la i-du-u-ma as-pa* (?)-[*as-ti* (?) . . . *at-ta*]

A-LA-ḪUL MULU-RA . . . . . GIM . . . . [KAN-ME-EN]

„ *ša ameli ki*-[*ma* . . . . *at-ta*]

A-LA-ḪUL MULU-RA . . . . . GIM . . . . [KAN-ME-EN]

„ *ša ameli* [*ki-ma*] . . . *ir ši* (?) . . . . . [*at-ta*]

A-LA-ḪUL MULU-RA DA GIM ŠU-NE-IN . . . . [KAN-ME-EN]

„ *ša ameli ki-ma*[1] *šu*[2] (?) . . . *ti u-šar* . . . [*at-ta*]

A-LA-ḪUL SU-DIN-ḪU KI-IN-TAR-GIM GIG-A IN . . . [KAN-ME-EN]

„ *ša ki-ma ṣu-ud-din-nu ina ni-gi-iṣ-ṣi ina mu-ši* . . . [*at-ta*]

(Plate XXVIII.)

[A-LA-ḪUL] . . . . KI GIG-GIG-GA-NI . . . IN-RI . . [KAN-ME-EN]

„ *ša kima iṣ-ṣur-ru mu-ši a-šar ik-li-ti it-ta-ap-*[*raš at-ta*]

Or an evil demon, a god that roameth by night,

Whose unclean hands know no reverence,

Or an evil demon, couching like an ass,

That lurketh in wait for the man,

Or an evil demon that knoweth not sacrifice of beasts or herbs (?)[a]

Or an evil demon that like . . . . the man,

Or an evil demon that like . . . . the man,

Or an evil demon that like . . . . the man,

Or an evil demon that like a bat (?) [dwelleth] in caverns by night,

(PLATE XXVIII.)

Or an evil demon that like a bird of night flieth in dark places,

---

[1] 35,056, *kima* for *ki-ma*.

[2] Or *su*, or *ša*.

[a] *Aspasti* (?). For this word see *Cun. Texts*, xiv, pl. 50, l. 62, and Meissner, *Zeits. für Assyr.*, vi, p. 296.

[A-LA]-ḪUL MULU-RA SA-DUL-GIM ÁB[1]-DUL-'U-A KAN-ME-EN
„ *ša ameli ki-ma*[2] *ka-tim-ti*[3] *i-kat-ta-mu at-ta*
A-LA-ḪUL MULU-RA SA-AL-ḪAB-GIM AB-ŠU-ŠU-'U[4]-A KAN-ME-EN
„ *ša ameli ki-ma*[2] *al-lu-ḫap-pi*[5] *i-saḫ-ḫa-pu at-ta*
A-LA-ḪUL GIG-U-NA-GIM ŠI-GAB NU-TUK-A KAN-ME-EN
„ *ša ki-ma*[2] *mu-ši ni-iṭ-la*[6] *la i-šu-u at-ta*
A-LA-ḪUL LUL-A-ERI-SIG-GA-GIM GIG-A NI-DU-DU[7] KAN-ME-EN.
„ [8]*ša ki-ma*[2] *še-lib*[9] *ali ša-ḳu-miš*[10] *ina mu-ši i-dul*[11] *at-ta*
GA-E MULU-TU-TU MULU[12]-SANGA-MAḪ ME-AZAG-GA NUN-KI-GA ME-EN
a-ši-pu ša-an[12]*-gam-ma-ḫu mu-ul*[13]*-lil par-ṣi ša* *[alu]Eridi a-na*[14]*-ku*
MULU-KIN-GA-A IGI-GIN-RA DINGIR-EN-KI-GE ME-EN
mâr[15] *šip-ri a-lik maḫ-ri ša* *[ilu]E-a*[16] *a-na*[14]*-ku*
DINGIR-SILIG-MULU-ŠAR MAŠ-MAŠ AZAG-ZU DU-SAG DINGIR-EN-KI-GE MULU-KIN-GA-A ME-EN
ša *[ilu]Marduk maš-maš*[17] *en-ḳi mâru*[18] *riš-ti-i*[19] *ša* *[ilu]E-a*[16] *mâr*[15] *šip-ri-šu a-na*[20]*-ku*
GU-TU-GAL NUN-KI-GA-GE NAM-ŠUB-GALAM-MA ME-EN
a-šip[21] *[alu]Eridi ša ši-pat-su nak-lat*[22] *a-na*[14]*-ku*

[1] 35,056, IB.
[2] 35,056, *kima* for *ki-ma.*
[3] 35,056, *tum.*
[4] 35,056 inserts *u.*
[5] 35,056, *pu.*
[6] 35,056, *lu.*
[7] K. 3,152, DU-DU . . . ; 35,056, BUR-BUR-'-U-U-A for DU-DU.
[8] 35,056 originally *a-lu-u lim-nu,* in place of „ from ll. 5–45.
[9] 35,056, *šil-li-bu* for *še-lib.*
[10] 35,056, *um-mi-iš* for *miš.*
[11] K. 3,152, *du-*[*ul*]; 35,056, *dul-lu.*
[12] 35,056 omits.

Or an evil demon that envelopeth the man
As it were with a coverlet,
Or an evil demon that enshroudeth the man
As it were with a sack,
Or an evil demon that like night hath no brightness,
Or an evil demon that by night
Like a pariah dog[a] prowleth[b] in the mud,[c]
The Sorcerer-priest that maketh clear the ordinances of Eridu am I,
The Herald that goeth before Ea am I,
Of Marduk, sage magician (and) eldest son of Ea,
The Herald am I,
The Exorciser of Eridu, most cunning in magic am I;

---

[13] 35,056, *mul* for *mu-ul*.
[14] K. 5,330 and 35,056, *ana* for *a-na*.
[15] 35,056, *mar*.
[16] 35,056, NAḲBU for *E-a*.
[17] K. 5,330, „ ; 35,056, *maš-ma-šu*.
[18] 35,056, *ma-ri*.
[19] 35,056, *tu-u* for *ti-i*.
[20] K. 5,330, *ana* for *a-na*.
[21] K. 3,152, [*a-ši*]-*pu*; 35,056, *a-ši-pu*.
[22] 35,056, *la-at*.

[a] Literally "fox of the city."

[b] *Idul*: *dâlu* is a synonym for *alâku*, *W.A.I.*, ii, 35, 53, and the corresponding root in Syriac is *dâl*, se movit, tremuit. Apparently *dâlu* has the idea of moving *furtively*, and if so, possibly the word *am daialu* means a "scout." See *A.J.S.L.*, xvii, 3, April, 1901, p. 163, note, and cf. l. 67, *mudalla*.

[c] *Šaḳummiš*: from a comparison of the Fifth Tablet, col. v, l. 15 ("They stand in the highway to befoul the path"), with l. 22 ("Ishum, overseer of *suḳi šaḳummi*"), *šaḳummu* has evidently the meaning "foul" or "muddy." Cf. *W.A.I.*, iv, 20, l. 4, *lib âli aḫat âli ṣîru bamâti šaḳummatu ušamlima ušalika namuiš*, "The middle of the city, the side of the city, the plain, the high places I filled with mud and turned to ruins."

A - LA - ḪUL ZI - GA - ZU - KU GAB - ZU ZI - ZI[1] - NE
a-lu-u lim-nu ana[2] *na-sa-ḫi-ka i-rat-ka ni-'-i*
MULU - TIL - LA A - RI - A A - RI - A - KU GIN - [NA]
a - šib na - me - e ana na - me - ka at - lak
EN-GAL DINGIR-EN-KI-GE ID-MU[3]-DA-AN . . .
bêlu[4] *rabu(u)*[5] *ilu E - a u - ma - ' - ir - an - [ni]*[6]
TU - DUG - GA - A[7] - NI KA - MU NE - IN - DUG
„[8] - *šu ana pi - ia u - ṭib*
GAR-NA *VII*-NA ME-EL-LA-GE[9] ŠU-MU NE-IN-MAL
„ *si-bit-ti šu-nu ša par-ṣi el-lu-ti*[10] *ana*
ḳa - ti - ia[11] *u - ma - al*[12] *- la*
UGA-ḪU ḪU LIGIR DINGIR-RI-E-NE-GE ID-ZI-DA
MU-NE-IN-TAB
a-ri-ba iṣ-ṣu-ra na-ri-ir[13] *ilâni*[pl] *ina im-ni-ia*
at-mu-uḫ
SUR-DU-ḪU ḪU KA-ZAL-LA IGI-ḪUL-IK-ZU-KU
ID-KAB-BU MU-NE-IN-UŠ
„ *iṣ-ṣu-ra mu-dal-la ina pa-ni-ka lim-nu-ti*[10]
ina šu - me - li - ia ir[14] *- di - šu*
KU-TIG-E-SA NI-TEMEN-NA-GE TIG-GA NE-IN-KU
na-aḫ-lap-ta sa-an-ta ša pu-luḫ-ti[10] *aḫ-ḫa-lap-ka*
KU-SA-KU NI-GAL-LA-GE BAR-AZAG-GA NE-IN-KU
ṣu-ba-ta sa-a-ma ṣu-bat nam-ri-ir-ri zu-mur elli[15]
u - lab[16] *- biš - ka*

O thou evil demon, turn thee to get hence,
O thou that dwelleth in ruins, get thee to thy ruins,
For the great lord Ea hath sent me;
He hath prepared his spell for my mouth
With a censer for those Seven, for clear decision,
He hath filled my hand.
A raven, the bird that helpeth the gods,
In my right hand I hold;
A hawk, to flutter[a] in thine evil face,
In my left hand I thrust forward;
With the sombre[b] garb of awe I clothe thee,
In sombre dress I robe thee,
A glorious dress for a pure body.

---

[1] K. 3,152 inserts GA.
[2] K. 3,152, *a-na*.
[3] 35,056 inserts UN.
[4] 35,056, *be-lu*.
[5] 35,056, *ra-bu-u*.
[6] 35,056, *na*.
[7] 35,056 omits GA-A.
[8] K. 3,152, TU.
[9] 35,056, EL (?)E (?)NE (?) for EL-LA-GE.
[10] 35,056, *tu*.
[11] 35,056, *ḳatâ* ^{II}-MU.
[12] 35,056, *mal* for *ma-al*.
[13] 35,056, *ri*.
[14] 35,056, *ar*.
[15] 35,056, *el-lu*.
[16] 35,056, *il-la* for *u-lab*.

[a] See note to l. 45.
[b] Or "blue."

(PLATE XXIX.)

KIŠ-ḪUL GIŠ-ZAG-DU KA-NA-GE NE-IN-LAL

ḫu-la-a ina ḫi-it-ti ša ba-a-bi a-lul-[*la*]

GIŠ-ISIMU GIŠ-NIM AŠ-A-AN GIŠ-DU-TA NE-IN-[LAL]

pi-ri-' bal-ti it-ṭi ina sik-ka-tim a-lul-[*la*]

SU - USAN - TA ẠNŠU - KAR - RA - GIM SU - ZU NE - IN - DUB - DUB . .

ina ḳi-na-zi ki-ma i-me-ri mun-nar-bi zu-mur-ka u-zar-ri-[*ib*?]

UTUG-[ḪUL] ZI-GA-AB A-LA-ḪUL ZI-GA-AB

u-tuk-ku lim-nu na-an-si-iḫ a-lu-u lim-nu te-bi

SU MULU-GIŠGAL-LU DU DINGIR-RA-NA A-LA-ḪUL ZI-GA-AB

ina zu-mur ameli mâr ili-šu a-lu-u lim-nu ˙*te*[1]*-bi*

USUG - DINGIR - E - A - TA NAM - BA - GUB - BU - NE NAM - BA - NIGIN - E - NE

ina eš-rit *ilu**E-a la ta-at-ta-nam-za-az la ta-as-sa-na-aḫ-ḫar*

E-A-UB-UB-TA NAM-BA-GUB-BU-NE NAM-BA-NIGIN-E-NE

ina tub-ḳat bîti la ta-at-ta-nam-za-az la ta-as-sa-na-aḫ-ḫar

E - A GA - BA - GUB NAM - BA - AB - BI - EN

ina bîti lu - uz - ziz la ta - ḳab - bi

UB - UB - TA GA - BA - GUB NAM - BA - AB - BI - EN

ina tub - ḳa - a - ti lu - uz - ziz la ta - ḳab - bi

[DA - DA] - TA GA - BA - GUB NAM - BA - AB - BI - EN

[*ina ša - ḫa - a*] *- ti lu - uz - ziz la ta - ḳab - bi*

(PLATE XXIX.)

Fleabane (?)[a] on the lintel of the door I have hung,
St. John's wort (?),[b] caper (?),[c] and wheatears[d]
On the latch I have hung;
With a halter as a roving ass
Thy body I restrain;
O evil Spirit, get thee hence,
Depart, O evil Demon!
From the body of the man, the son of his god,
O evil Demon, depart!
In the Temple of Ea stand not, nor circle around;
In the precincts of the house stand not, nor circle around;
"In the house will I stand," say thou not,
"In the precincts will I stand," say thou not,
"In the neighbourhood will I stand," say thou not,

---

[1] K. 3,152, *ti.*

[a] *Ḫulâ*, possibly the Syriac *ḫla* (Payne Smith, *Thesaurus*, p. 1,273, *a*), which has been identified with the fleabane.

[b] *Piri'*, probably the Syriac *per'a*, hypericum (Brockelmann, p. 291, *a*).

[c] *Balti.* On *W.A.I.*, ii, 23, 31–32, *bala*, *baltu*, and *amumešlu* are given as synonyms. *Bala* is possibly the Syriac *bl* (Payne Smith, *Thesaurus*, p. 527, *a*), *medicamentum quoddam, sc. radix capparis spinosae.*

[d] *Itti.* The Sumerian is AŠ-A-AN, i.e. "wheat." Cf. the Hebrew *ḫiṭṭim* and Syriac *ḫeṭetha* (Brockelmann, p. 109, *a*), √*ḫ-n-ṭ*.

[UTUG - ḪUL] E - BA - RA KI - BÀD - DU - KU
[*u*] - *tuk - ku lim - nu ṣi - i ana ni - sa - a - ti*
[A - LA] - ḪUL GIN - NA A - RI - A - KU
[*a*] - *lu - u lim - nu at - lak ana na - me - e*
[KI] - GUB - BA - ZU KI - SAG KUD - DA
[*man*] - *za - az - ka aš - ru par - su*
[KI] - TUS - A - ZU E - ŠUB - BA A - RI - A
šu - bat - ka bîtu na - du - u ḫar - bu
[?-LA] IGI-MU-TA [ZI AN-NA KAN]-PA ZI KI-[A KAN]-PA
[*dup-pir ultu pani-ia niš šame(e) lu-ta-ma*]-*ta niš* [*irṣitim(tim)*] *lu-ta-ma-ta*

[INIM - INIM - MA UTUG] - ḪUL - A - KAN

[ ] NA - A - AN ZI - GA
[*Ekal* [m ilu] *Aššur-bani-apli šarru rabu šarru dan-nu*] *šar kiššati šar* [mātu ilu] *Aššuri* [KI]
(Etc.)

O evil Spirit, get thee forth to distant places,
O evil Demon, hie thee unto the ruins,
Where thou standest is forbidden ground,
A ruined, desolate house is thy home;
[Be thou removed from before me! By Heaven] be thou exorcised!
By [Earth] be thou exorcised!

PRAYER AGAINST THE EVIL SPIRITS.

[Incantation] " . . . . removeth "

Tablet "C."

COL. I (B)[1] (PLATE XXX).

a.[2] . . . .

b. „ *ša ameli la ra* (?) . . . . .

c. UTUG - ḪUL - IK . . . .

d. „ *ša da - mu u* (?) . . . .

e. UTUG - ḪUL - IK . . . .

42. „ *ša ri - gim* . . . .

UTUG - ḪUL - IK KUR - RA . . . .

„ [3] *ša ina ma-a-tu it-ta-*[*na-aš-rab-bi-ṭu* ?]

45. [4] GA-E SANGU (?)-UḪ (?)-TU GA-TU-[SURRU-MAḪ] . . . . .

a-ši-pu ša-an-gam-ma-ḫu ša ^ilu^ . . . [*a-na-ku*]

[5] EN - ' NA . . . .

[6] *be - lum* . . . .

NUN * ṬUR - RA - GE MU - UN . . . .

50. *ru - bu - u ina ap - si - i* . . . .

EGIR - MU ? NAM - NE - IN - GI

ar - ki - ia la [*ta - šag - gum* ?]

EGIR - MU GU - NU [7] - MU - UN - DA - AB - RA - RA

ar - ki - ia la ta - ša - [*as - si* ?]

55. MULU - ḪUL - IK ŠU - NAM - [BA - ZI - ZI ?]

lim - na[8] *la tu - šaḫ* - [*ḫaz* ?]

UTUG - ḪUL - IK ŠU - NAM - BA - [ZI - ZI ?]

u - tuk - ka[9] *lim - na*[8] *la tu - ša* - [*aḫ - ḫaz* ?]

---

[1] Col. I (A) contains the following ends of lines:—(1) . . . BAD KUR-RA, (2) . . . *šadi*(*i*), (3) . . . KAS-KAS-BU, (4) . . . [*it*]-*ta-na-aš-rab-bi-ṭu*, (5) . . . TU-TU, (6) . . . *i-kam-mu-u*, (7) . . . BIR-RA, (8) . . . *i-ša-as-su-u*, (9) . . . *la še-mu-u*,

Tablet "C."

Col I (B). (Plate XXX.)

a. . . . .
b. O evil Spirit that hath . . . the man,
c. O evil Spirit that . . . blood . . . . . .
42. O evil Spirit whose roar . . . .
O evil Spirit that [roameth] o'er the land,
45. I am the Sorcerer-priest of . . . .
The lord . . . .
50. The prince in the Deep . . . .
Behind me [howl] not!
Behind me shriek not!
55. Unto that which is evil deliver (?) him (?) not!
Unto the evil Spirit deliver (?) him (?) not!

---

(10) . . . *ta la i-šu-u*, (11) . . . DI-A, (12) . . . *-ḫu-u*, (13) . . . [ZI-IR]-ZI-IR, (14) . . . [*aš-ša*]-*šu*, (15) . . . [NIGIN]-E, (16) . . . [*iṣ-ṣa*]-*nun-du*, (17) . . . BI, (18) . . . *-'-u*, (19) . . . PA (?)-RA, (20) . . . *-al-pu*, (21) . . . [NIGIN]-E, (22) . . . [*iṣ-ṣa*]-*nun-du*, (23) . . . LU, (24) . . . [*i-dal*]-*la-ḫu*, (25) . . . I, (26) . . . *-ru*, (27) . . . SU, (28) . . . [*i-šaḫ-ha*]-*la*, (29) . . . DU-DU, (30) . . . *-nam-du-u*, (31) . . . *-ḫu-šu*, and traces of ll. 32–41.

[2] *Cuneiform Texts*, part xvii, pl. 46.

[3] K. 2,470 . . . *lim-nu*.

[4] 60,886 has [GA]-E GAM UḪ (?)-TU GA-DUB . . .

[5] 60,886 has . . . E MU . . .

[6] 60,886 has . . . . *-an-ni* . . . .

[7] K. 8,476 omits; K. 4,917, NAM.

[8] K. 8,476, *nu*.

[9] K. 8,476, *ku*.

MULU - TUR - RA - KU NAM - BA - TE - [MAL - NE]
ana mar - ṣi e ta - a[ṭ - ḫi]
MULU - TUR - RA - KU NAM - BA - GE - [GE - NE]
ana mar - ṣi e ta - [at - bi?]
ZI DINGIR-GAL-GAL-E-NE[1]-GE I-RI-PA ḪA-BA-[RA-DU-UN]
[2] *niš ilâni*^{pl} *rabûti*^{pl} *u-tam-me-[ka lu-ta-at-tal-lak]*

INIM - INIM - MA UTUG - ḪUL - [A - KAN]

EN UTUG - ḪUL - IK NAM - BA - TE - [MAL - NE]
u - tuk - ku lim - nu e ta - aṭ - [ḫi - šu]
A - LA - ḪUL - IK NAM - BA - TE - MAL - NE
a - lu - u lim - [nu] e ta - aṭ - ḫi - šu
GIDIM - ḪUL - IK NAM - BA - TE - MAL - NE
e - kim - [mu lim - nu] e ta - aṭ - ḫi - šu
MULLA - ḪUL - IK NAM - BA - TE - MAL - NE
gal - [lu - u lim - nu] e ta - aṭ - ḫi - šu
DINGIR - ḪUL - IK NAM - BA - TE - MAL - NE
ilu [lim - nu] e ta - aṭ - ḫi - šu
MAŠKIM ḪUL - IK NAM - BA - TE - MAL - NE
ra - [bi - ṣu lim - nu] e ta - aṭ - ḫi - šu
DINGIR - RAB - KAN - ME NAM - BA - TE - MAL - NE
[la - bar - tu e] ta - aṭ - ḫi - šu
DINGIR - RAB - KAN - ME - A [NAM - BA] - TE - MAL - NE
[la - ba - ṣu e ta - aṭ] - ḫi - šu
[DINGIR-RAB KAN-ME-KIL NAM-BA-TE]-MAL-NE
[aḫ - ḫa - zu e ta - aṭ] - ḫi - šu
[MULU - LIL - LA NAM - BA - TE - MAL] - NE
[li - lu - u e ta - aṭ] - ḫi - šu

Unto the sick man draw not nigh,
Unto the sick man come not,
By the Great Gods I exorcise thee that thou mayest depart.

PRAYER AGAINST THE EVIL SPIRITS.

Incantation :—
O evil Spirit, approach him not,
O evil Demon, approach him not,
O evil Ghost, approach him not,
O evil Devil, approach him not,
O evil God, approach him not,
O evil Fiend, approach him not,
O Hag-demon, approach him not,
O Ghoul, approach him not,
[O Robber-sprite], approach him not,
[O Phantom of Night], approach him not,

[1] K. 8,476 omits.
[2] K. 2,470 omits this line.

[KI - EL - LIL - LA NAM - BA - TE - MAL] - NE
[li - li - tu e ta - aṭ - ḫi] - šu
[KI - EL - UD - DA - KAR - RA NAM - BA - TE - MAL] - NE
[ar - da - at li - li - i e ta - aṭ - ḫi] - šu
. . . . [NAM - BA - TE - MAL] - NE
[e ta - aṭ] - ḫi - šu
. . . . [NAM - BA - TE - MAL] - NE
. . . .

[Hiatus.]

. . . .
mur - ṣu . . . .

COL. II (PLATE XXXI).

SAG - GIG KA - GIG ŠA - GIG LIKIR - GIG
mu-ru-uṣ ḳaḳ-ḳa-di „ šin-ni „ libbi ki-iṣ lib-bi
IGI-GIG AZAG : *mu-ru-uṣ i-ni a-šak-ku sa-ma-nu* : SA-MA-NA
UTUG-ḪUL A-LA-ḪUL GIDIM-ḪUL MULLA-ḪUL DINGIR-ḪUL MAŠKIM-ḪUL
DINGIR - RAB[1] - KAN - ME DINGIR - RAB[1] - KAN - ME - A DINGIR-RAB-KAN-ME-KIL
MULU-LIL-LA KI-EL-LIL-LA KI-EL-UD-DA KAR-RA
NAM-TAR-ḪUL-IK AZAG-GIG-GA TUR-RA-NU-DUG-GA
GAR - GIG GAR - ŠA - A GAR - ḪUL - GIM - MA
SUR-AŠ-ŠUB A-ḪA-AN-TUM U-ŠU-UŠ-ŠUB DUB-GIM-MA BAR-GIŠ-RA
SILA-A GIN-GIN AB-BA ŠU-ŠU GIŠ-ŠAGIL TU-TU-E-NE
mut-tal-lik su-ḳi mu-ta-at-bi-ik a-pa-a-ti mu-tir-ru[2]-bu me[3]-di-lu

[O Night Wraith], approach him not,
[O Handmaiden of the Phantom], approach him not,
. . . . approach him not,
. . . . approach him not,

[Hiatus.]

Sickness, ...

COL. II (PLATE XXXI).

Sickness of the head, of the teeth, of the heart, heartache,
Sickness of the eye, fever, poison (?),[a]
Evil Spirit, evil Demon, evil Ghost, evil Devil, evil God, evil Fiend,
Hag-demon, Ghoul, Robber-sprite,
Phantom of Night, Night Wraith, Handmaiden of the Phantom,
Evil pestilence, noisome fever, baneful sickness,
Pain, sorcery, or any evil,
[b] Headache, shivering, (?), terror, (?), (?),
Roaming the streets, dispersed through dwellings, penetrating bolts,

---

[1] K. 4,863, LUGAL. [2] S. 793, *ri*.
[3] S. 793, *mi*.

[a] *Samanu*, possibly connected with the Syriac *sammâ*, pl. *sammânê* (Brockelmann, p. 228, *b*), "poison."

[b] See note to Tablet III, l. 199. For DUB-GIM-MA I do not know any Assyrian equivalent. BAR-GIŠ-RA is translated *'-i-lu* (*W.A.I.*, v, 50, 29–30, *b*), apparently parallel to *ašakku*, but no satisfactory meaning has been suggested for it.

MULU - ḪUL IGI - ḪUL KA - ḪUL EME - ḪUL
lim-nu ša pa-an[1] *lim-nu pu-u lim-nu li-ša-nu* „
[2] UḪ (?)-ḪUL UḪ (?)-ZU UḪ (?)[3] -A-RI-A GAR-ŠA-A GAR-ḪUL
-GIM-MA-TA[4]
ŠA-E-A-TA : *iš - tu ki - rib bîti ṣi - i* : IB - TA - E
[5] MULU-GIŠGAL-LU DU DINGIR-RA-NA BA-RA-AN-TE-MAL
-NE BA-RA-AN-GE-GE-E-NE
GIŠ-GU-ZA-NA : *ina ku-us-si-šu la tu-šab-šu* :
NAM-BA-TUŠ-NE-EN
GIŠ-* NAD-DA-NA : *ina ir-ši-šu la ta-na-al* :
NAM-BA-NA-U-NE-EN
* UR-KU : *ana u-ri-šu la te-el-li-šu* : NAM-BA-GIBIŠ-NE
E-KI-TUŠ-A-NA : *ana bît šub-ti-šu la te-ru-ub-šu* :
NAM-BA-TU-TU-NE
ZI AN-NA-KI-BI-DA-GE I-RI-PA ḪA-BA-RA-DU-UN
niš šame(e) u irṣitim(tim) u - tam - me - ka
lu - u - ta - at - ta - lak

INIM - INIM - MA UTUG - ḪUL - A - KAN

EN UTUG - ḪUL - IK MULU - ŠA - KU - AB - ŠA - ŠA
u - tuk - ku lim - nu ḫab - bi - lu
MAŠKIM - ḪUL - IK UB - DA GUB - GUB - BU
ra - bi - ṣu lim - nu mut - ta - az - ziz tub - ḳi
GIDIM - ḪUL MULLA - ḪUL U - NU - KU - KU - NE
e-kim-mu lim-nu gal-lu-u lim-nu la ṣa-li-lu
[E-NE]-NE-NE ḪUL-A-MEŠ ERI-A NIGIN-NA-A-MEŠ
[*šu-nu lim*]-*nu-ti ša ina ali iṣ-ṣa-nun-du šu-nu*
. . . . IM - MI - IN - GAZ - E - NE
. . . . *i - pa - al - li - lu*

Evil man, he whose face is evil, he whose mouth
is evil, he whose tongue is evil,
Evil spell, witchcraft, sorcery,
Enchantment and all evil,
From the house go forth!
Unto the man, the son of his god, come not nigh,
Get thee hence!
In his seat sit thou not,
On his couch lie thou not,
Over his fence rise thou not,
Into his chamber enter thou not,
By Heaven and Earth I exorcise thee,
That thou mayest depart.

PRAYER AGAINST THE EVIL SPIRITS.

Incantation :—
The evil Spirit that destroyeth,
The evil Fiend that lurketh near,
The evil Ghost and evil Devil that find no rest,
These are they that scour the city,
Scattering[a] . . . .

[1] K. 4,863, *ni.*
[2] K. 4,863 translates [*kiš*]-*pu ru-ḫu-u ru*-[*su-u*] . . .
[3] S. 793 inserts ZU. [4] S. 793 omits.
[5] K. 4,863 translates [*a*]-*na ameli mâr ili*-[*šu*] . . .

[a] *Ipallilu.* Cf. Syriac *pall*, adspersit, fregit (Brockelmann, *Lexicon*, p. 272, *a*).

. . . . IM - MI - IN - ŠUM - E - NE

. . . . *i - ṭa - ab - ba - ḫu*

(PLATE XXXII.)

. . . . [TU - TU] - NE

130. . . . . [*i*] - *kam - mu - u*

. . . . A - MEŠ

. . . . *-ḳu - u*

. . . . GAZ (?) - AK - E - NE

. . . . *i - šag - gi - šu*

135. . . . . IM - MI - IN - SU - SU

. . . . *ki-ma nu-ni ina me-e i-šaḫ-ḫa-lu*

[SIGIŠŠE - SIGIŠŠE NU] - UN - ZU - MEŠ A - RA - ZU NU - UN - ZU - MEŠ

[*ik-ri-bi ul i-du-u*] *tas-li-tu ul i-du-u*

. . . . . MI - IN - DUL IGI - NA BA - AN - MI - MI

140. . . . . [*i - kat - tam*] *- ma i - ni - šu u - ta - aṭ - ṭu - u*

. . . . [NU - UN] - ZU - A

. . . . [*ul*] *u - ta - ad - di*

. . . . NAM - ŠUB BA - AN - SUM

. . . . *šip - tu id - di*

145. ḪI

. . . . *il - pu - tum*

. . . . ḪUL

. . . . *a* (?)

REVERSE.

[Several lines wanting.]

a. [*pi - ti - ik - ti a - a ib - bal*] *- ki - tu -* [*u - ni*] . .

b. [UTUG-ḪUL-IK : *u-tuk-ku lim-nu*] *a-na ṣi-ri-ka* : [EDIN-NA-ZU-KU]

150. [A-LA-ḪUL-IK : *a-lu-u lim-nu*] *a-na ṣi-ri-ka* : [EDIN-NA-ZU-KU]

151. [MU NU - TUK MU - NE AN] - ZAK - [KU]

c. [*šu-ma ul i-šu u šum-šu*]*-nu ana pa-aṭ* [*šame*](*e*)

Slaughtering . . . .

(PLATE XXXII.)

Seizing upon . . . .

. . . .

Rending in pieces . . . .

. . . like fish from the water they draw forth [a]

Knowing neither prayer nor supplication.

They cover his . . . and darken his eyes,

. . . . not known.

He performs the incantation . . . . . .

[Several lines broken or wanting.]

REVERSE.

a. May they not break through [the mud wall].

b. [O evil Spirit], to thy desert!

[O evil Demon], to thy desert!

c. [O they that have no name (their name)], unto the breadth [of heaven!] [b]

[a] *Išaḫḫalu*: cf. the Chald. *š'ḫal* (Levy, *Chald. Wörterb.*, p. 468, *a*) which is the word used in Exod. ii, 10, for drawing Moses forth from the water.

[b] See ll. 185 ff., p. 153.

152. [DINGIR-PA-SAG-GA . . . : ^{ilu}*I-šum*] . . . *-e ni-ši* :
MULU-GIŠGAL-LU-ZU-KU
d. [TU-DUG-GA : *ina* „ *-e a-mat* ^{ilu}]*E-a* : I
DINGIR-EN-[KI-GA-GE]
153. . . . . . . *mar* ^{alu}*Eridi* : DU NUN-KI-GA-GE
154. [TU-TU ZU-AB NUN-KI-GA] NAM-MU-UN-DA-AN-BUR-RA
e. [*ši-pat ap-si-i* ^{alu}]*Eridi a-a ip-pa-aš-ra* . . .

---

155. [INIM - INIM - MA] UTUG - ḪUL - A - KAN

[EN] UTUG-ḪUL-IK GIDIM MAS-TIG-GAR EDIN-NA
u-tuk-ku lim-nu e-kim-mu ša ina ṣi-e-ri šu-pu-u
NAM-TAR MULU ḪUL-IK : *nam-ta-ru ša ameli lim-niš*
tal-pu-tum : TAG-GA-ZU
EME GAR - ḪUL - GIM - MA MULU KEŠDA(DA) - GE
160. *li-ša-nu ša itti*[1] *ameli lim-niš ir-rak-su*
DUG-GIM : [2]*ki-ma kar-pa-ti li-iḫ-*[*tap-pu-u* :
ḪE] - EN - TA - GAZ
A-GIM : [2]*ki-ma me-e lit-*[*tab-ku* :] ḪE-EN-TA-DE
[GIŠ-GAM]-MA GIŠ-ŠA-KA-NA-GE NA-AN-TA-BAL-E
kip-pa-ti . . . . . *a-a ib-bal-ki-tu-ni*
165. . . . . . . [*a-a ib*]*-bal-ki-tu-ni* : NA-AN-TA-BAL-E
[UTUG-ḪUL EDIN-NA-ZU-KU] A-LA-ḪUL EDIN-NA-ZU-KU
UTUG-ḪUL E-A-TIL-LA ŠU-NU-GAR-RA-ZU-KU
DINGIR-MULU-GIŠGAL-LU-GE
u-tuk-ku lim-nu ša ina bîti tuš-bu-[*u*] . . .
ilu u amelu ana la ga-ma li-ka

(PLATE XXXIII.)

UTUG-ḪUL A-LA-ḪUL GIDIM-[ḪUL] MULLA-ḪUL
DINGIR-ḪUL MAŠKIM-ḪUL

152. [Išum] . . . men,
d. [By the magic of the] word of Ea,
153. . . . the son of Eridu,
154. [Let the Incantation of the Deep] of Eridu never be unloosed!

[Prayer against] the Evil Spirits.

[Incantation]:—
The evil Spirit (and) Ghost that appear in the desert,
O Pestilence that hast touched the man for harm,
160. The Tongue that is banefully fastened on the man,
May they be broken in pieces like a goblet,
May they be poured forth like water,
May they not break through the lintel of the door.
165. May they not break through the . . . .
[O evil Spirit, to thy desert!] O evil Demon, to thy desert!
O evil Spirit that dwellest in the house
God and man to spare thee not . . . .

(Plate XXXIII.)

Whether it be evil Spirit or evil Demon,
Or evil Ghost or evil Devil,
Or evil God or evil Fiend,

[1] K. 5,251, *it-ti.*
[2] K. 5,290 omits these translation lines.

LA-DUG-BUR-ZI-DUG-ḲA-BUR-GIM AN-AŠ-A-AN
KAN-NI-IB-GAZ-GAZ
ki-ma ḫaṣ-bi pur-si-it pa-ḫa-ri ina ri-bi-ti liḫ-tap-pu-u

INIM-INIM-MA UTUG-ḪUL-A-KAN

EN UTUG-ḪUL-IK GIDIM MULU EDIN-NA TAG-GA-ZU
u-tuk-ku lim-nu e-kim-mu ša ina ṣi[1]*-ri ameli tal-pu-ut*
NAM-TAR MULU SAG-GA TAG-[GA]-ZU
nam-ta-ru ša ḳaḳ-ḳad ameli tal-pu-ut
KA-ḪUL-IK EME-ḪUL-IK MULU[2]-ERIM-MA-GE
pu-u lim-nu li-ša-nu li-mut-tu mu-ta-[mu]-u
UTUG-ḪUL-IK MULU IGI[3]-MU-UN-ŠI-IN-BAR-RA
u-tuk-ku lim-nu ša ameli ip-pal-la-su
[4]GAR-ŠA-A UḪ(?)-ḪUL-IK MULU-NAM-ERIM-MA-GE
u-pi-[šu kiš]-pi lim-nu-ti[5] *ša ma-mi-ti*
DUG-GIM [:[6] *ki-ma*] *kar-pa-ti li-iḫ-tap-pu-u* :
ḪE-EN-TA-GAZ
A-GIM :[6] [*ki-ma*] *me-e lit-tab-ku* : [ḪE]-EN-TA-DE
IM-RU-A NA-AN-TA-BAL-E
[6]*pi-ti-ik-ti a-[a ib]-bal-kit-u-ni*
UTUG-ḪUL-IK :[6] *u-tuk-ku lim-nu a-na ṣi-ri-ka* :
EDIN-NA-ZU-KU
A-LA-ḪUL-IK :[6] *a-lu-u lim-nu a-na ṣi-ri-ka* :
EDIN-NA-ZU-KU
MU NU-TUK MU-NE AN-ZAK-KU :[6] *šu-ma ul i-šu-u*
šum-šu-nu ana paṭ šame(e)

Like the sherd that is cast aside[a] by the potter
May they be broken in the broad places.

Prayer against the Evil Spirits.

Incantation :—
O evil Spirit (or) Ghost that hath touched the man in the desert,
O Pestilence that hath touched the head of the man,
The evil Mouth (or) evil Tongue that hath uttered a spell,
The evil Spirit that hath looked on the man,
The enchantment or evil sorcery of a ban,
May they be broken in pieces like a goblet,
May they be poured forth like water,
May they not break through the mud wall.
O evil Spirit, to thy desert!
O evil Demon, to thy desert!
O they that have no name (their name),[b] unto the breadth of heaven!

[1] K. 4,955 inserts *e*.
[2] K. 2,470 inserts NAM.
[3] K. 2,470 omits.
[4] S. 69 inserts two lines: (*a*) *A* . . . . . (*b*) *a-* . . . . .
[5] K. 2,470, *tum*.
[6] K. 2,470 omits this line.

[a] *Pursit*, from *parâsu*, "to separate."

[b] Presumably this refers to certain demons whose names are unknown on earth, and the magician here addresses them with the inclusive term "their name," i.e., whatever their name may be.

DINGIR-PA-SAG-GA . . . [MULU-GIŠGAL-LU-ZU-KU]
TU-DUG-GA I DINGIR-EN-KI-GA-[GE :] . . . [DU NUN-KI-GA-GE]
TU-TU ZU-AB NUN-KI-GA [NAM-MU-UN-DA-AN-BUR-RA]

INIM - INIM - MA [UTUG - ḪUL - A - KAN]

EN UTUG-ḪUL-IK EDIN-NA ID BA-AN . . . . .
u-tuk-ku limnûti^{pl} *ša ina ṣi-ri is-su-nu tar* . . . .
UR-SAG DU DAGAL AŠ-A-MEŠ *VII*-NA . . . .
ḳar - ra - du . . . *iš - ta - [at]* . . . . . .
. . . .

[Hiatus.]

(PLATE XXXIV.)

. . . .
GURUŠ E - UR - A - NI - TA BA - RA - [E - NE]
[1] NI-BI-A ṢIR-GIM MU-UN-SUR-SUR-RI-E-[NE]
ina ra-ma-ni-šu-nu ki-ma ṣi-ir[2] *it-ta-na-aš-lal-lu*
AN-NIN-KIŠ-GIM UR-E-GAR-RA-GE IR-SI-NI-IN-NA-AG-E-NE
ki-ma šik-ki-e a-sur-ra-a uṣ-ṣa-nu šu-nu
UR-KU-GIM NIGIN-E ŠI-MU-UN-ŠI-IN-BAR-RI-E-NE
ki-ma kal-bi ṣa-[i]-du it-ta-nab-ra-ar-ru šu-nu
UTUG-ḪUL A-LA-ḪUL GIDIM-ḪUL MULLA-[ḪUL] DINGIR-ḪUL MAŠKIM-ḪUL
ZI AN - NA KAN - PA ZI KI - A KAN - PA

Ishum . . . . [men]
By the magic of the word of Ea,
. . . the son of Eridu
Let the Incantation of the Deep of Eridu [never be unloosed]!

PRAYER AGAINST THE [EVIL SPIRITS].

Incantation :—

The evil Spirits whose hands in the desert . . .
Warriors, sons of one mother, seven [are they].

[Hiatus.]

(PLATE XXXIV.)

They drive forth the man from his home.
Upon themselves like a snake they glide,
Like mice they make the chamber stink,
Like hunting dogs they give tongue.[a]
Be thou evil Spirit or evil Demon,
Or evil Ghost or evil Devil,
Or evil God or evil Fiend,
By Heaven be thou exorcised! By Earth be thou exorcised!

---

1 K. 8,475 translates . . . *-šu u-še-iṣ-[ṣu-u]*.
2 K. 5,079 and K. 8,475, *ri*.

a *Ittanabrarru*: according to *W.A.I.*, v, 28, vii–viii, 62, *bararum* = *ikkillum*, "wailing," and, as Muss-Arnolt suggests, it may be connected with *barbaru*, "jackal."

EN-NA SU MULU-GIŠGAL-LU DU DINGIR-RA-NA [1]

EN-NA BA-RA-AN-TA-RI EN-NA BA-RA-AN-ZI-GA EN-NA-AŠ [2]

U BA-RA-AN-DA-AB-KU-E A BA-RA-AN-DA-AB-NAK-E

GIŠ-BANŠUR A-A MUḪ-ZU-NE DINGIR-EN-LIL-LA-[GE ŠU-ZU BA]-RA-NE-IN-TUM

A A-AB-BA A-DUG-A A-ŠIS-A A ID-[MAS-TIG-GAR] A ID-UD-KIB-NUN-KI

[A PU]-TA A ID-[DA BA-RA-AN]-ŠU-ŠU-NE

[ANA - KU BA - RI - EN PA - NA - A]N - TUK - TUK

[KI - KU BA - GUB - BA TUŠ NAM - BI] - GA - GA

[MULU-GIŠGAL-LU DU DINGIR-RA-NA BA-RA-AN-TE-MAL-DA BA-RA-AN-G]E-GE-NE

[ZI AN-NA-KI-BI-DA-GE I-RI-PA ḪA-BA-R]A-DU-UN

[INIM - INIM - MA UTUG - ḪUL] - A - KAN

. . . . E - SIR - RA ŠU - ŠU

. . . . *um*

. . . .

---

[1] K. 8,475 translates . . . *ili-šu.*

[2] K. 8,475 translates . . . [*ta-as*]-*su-ḫu.*

(Whatever thou be), until thou art removed,
Until thou departest from the body of the man, the son of his god,
Thou shalt have no food to eat,
Thou shalt have no water to drink,
Thou shalt not stretch forth thy hand
Unto the table of my father Bel, thy creator,
Neither with sea water, nor with sweet water,
Nor with bad water, nor with [Tigris] water,
Nor with Euphrates water, nor with [pond water],
Nor with river water shalt thou be covered.
[If thou wouldst fly up to heaven]
Thou shalt have [no wings],
[If thou wouldst lurk in ambush on earth]
Thou shalt secure [no resting-place].
[Unto the man, the son of his god, come not nigh],
Get thee hence!
[By Heaven and Earth I exorcise thee],
That thou mayest depart.

[PRAYER AGAINST THE EVIL SPIRITS.]

[Incantation :—] " . . . . that in the street overwhelmeth."

Tablet "D."

[The Obverse is entirely lost.]

REVERSE.

COL. III (PLATE XXXV).

(1) DINGIR . . . . (2) . . . . (3) . . . . (4) MULU . . . . (5) *amelu* . . . . (6) URUDU-GAR . . . . (7) . . . . . . (8) *ru-uk* . . . . (9) . . . . . . (10) MULU . . . . (11) *ša ameli ik-* . . . . . .

12. MULU - GIŠGAL - LU - BI . . . .
amelu šu - u . . . .
URUDU-GAR-LIG-GA UR-SAG AN-[NA] . . . . . .
15. ^{eru} „ - *u ḳar - rad* ^{ilu}*A - nim* . . . .
KU-U-LI-IN-TAR-A GAR-UR-* ŠIM-[MA] . . . . . .
u-li-in-na bur-ru-un-ta [. . *bûli*] . . . . .
I-NE-GAR-NA ZAG GIŠ-* NAD-DA-NA . . . . . .
ḳut-ri-in-na ša naḳ-ḳa- . . [*ir-ša-šu*] . . . .
20. ŠA DINGIR-SUR TUG-GA AN-NA-GE MULU . . .
ina lib-bi ^{ilu}*Ṣaluli*(*li*) *ša ṣu-ba-ta* [^{ilu}*Anim*] . . .
KU-SUR-RA : *ku-sur-ra-a e-ṣir-*[*ma* : U-ME-NI-ḪAR]
ZAG KU-SUR-RA IM-* DAR-RA : *i-da-at* „ *-e me-e* (?) . . .
KA-BAR-RA ID-ZI-DA ID-KAB-BU [U-ME (?)-NI (?)-ḪAR]
25. . *ba-ab ka-ma-a im-na u šu-*[*me-la*] . . . . .
KA-BI NAM-TIL-LA : *ina ba-bi-šu ba-la-ṭa* . . . .
SAG-BI NAM-ERIM-BUR-RU-DA GAR-ḪUL . . . .
ma-mit la pa-ša-ri mimma(*ma*) *lim-*[*nu*] . . .
U-I-KAM : *ûmu*(*mu*) *ak-kal liš-tab-ri* . . . . .

Tablet "D."

['The Obverse is entirely lost.]

REVERSE.

COL. III (PLATE XXXV).

This man . . . .
[Take] the potent meteorite of heaven . .
[Bind] a two-coloured cord . . . . . .
A smoke offering which . . . his couch . .
Under the shadow of the Robe of Heaven . .
Fasten a bandage and
[a] Wash (?) in water (?) the ends of the bandage,
With the door locked right and left [shut (?) him in],
Within his door life [shall he receive (?)].
A ban that cannot be loosed [on] everything evil . . .
When he[b] eats, may he be satisfied!

---

[a] IM-DARA (*W.A.I.*, v, 27, 13, *e*, which is probably to be restored this way) = [*ḫ*]*a-a-pu*, with which we may compare the Syriac *ḫâph* (Brockelmann, *Lexicon*, p. 106, *b*), lavit. It seems possible that the scribe has here added the word *mê*, "water," but the text is so mutilated that no restorations are trustworthy. The explanatory text K. 246 (Haupt, *Akkad. u. Sum. Keils.*, pp. 92–93, ll. 14 ff.) has: MULU-GIŠGAL-LU-BI KU-SUR-RA U-U-ME-NI-ḪAR KU-SUR-RA-A IM-BABBAR-RA KA-BAR-RA ID-ZI-DA ID-KAB-BU U-BA (?) . . ḪAR, which is translated *a-me-lu šu-a-tu* [*ku-sur-ra-a e-ṣir-ma*] *ku-sur-ra-a ša* . . . [*ga*]*ṣ-ṣi.bâba ka-ma-a* [*im*]*-na u šu-me-la* . . .

[b] First person in the text.

DINGIR-USAN-AN-NA *BIR-ḪUL-DUB-BA SU MULU-GIŠGAL-LU DU DINGIR-RA-[NA] . . . .

. . MU-UN-NA-AN-TE . . .

[*ilu* *Si-me*]*-tan* „ *-e* „ *-*[*e ina*] *zu-mur a-me-li mâr ili-šu ṭu-uḫ-*[*ḫi*] . . .

. . . . [ḪUL]-DUB-BA SAG-GA-NA U-ME-NI-[KEŠDA]

. . . . . *ša* „ *-e ḳaḳ-ḳa-su ru-ku-us-*[*ma*]

[UTUG-ḪUL A]-LA-ḪUL GIDIM-ḪUL MULLA-ḪUL DINGIR-ḪUL MAŠKIM-[ḪUL]

[*u-tuk-ku*] *lim-nu a-lu-u lim-nu e-kim-mu lim-nu gal-lu-u lim-nu ilu lim-nu ra-bi-ṣu* [*lim-nu*]

[DINGIR-RAB-KAN]-ME DINGIR-RAB-KAN-ME-A : *la-bar-tum la-ba-ṣu aḫ-ḫa-zu* : DINGIR-RAB KAN-ME-KIL

UTUG-MULU-DIB-BA : *u-tuk-ku ka-mu-u ša ameli e-kim-mu ša ameli ṣab-tu* : GIDIM-MULU-DIB-BA

MULU-ḪUL IGI-ḪUL KA-ḪUL EME-ḪUL : *lim-nu ša pa-ni lim-nu pu-u lim-nu li-ša-nu lim-nu*

SAG-GIG KA-GIG ŠA-GIG LIKIR-GIG *mu-ru-uṣ ḳaḳ-ḳa-di* „ *šin-ni* „ *lib-bi ki-iṣ lib-bi*

---

[a] *Hulduppû.* This word occurs with the determinative for "wood," but more commonly with the determinative *BIR (= *uriṣu* ?). It is difficult to see what its exact meaning is, but the following additional passages are instructive:—*W.A.I.*, iv, 21, ll. 27–29, *ana mimma lim-ni* . NU-TE-*e* *ilu* „ (= MULU-*LAL) *ilu* „ (= *La-ta-rak*) *ina ba-a-bi ul-ziz, ana mimma lim-ni ṭa-ra-di* „ (= *BIR-ḪUL-DUB-BA) *ina mi-iḫ-rit bâbi ul-ziz*, "To prevent any evil drawing nigh I have set up MULU- *LAL (and) Latarak by the door, to drive away any evil I have set the *ḫulduppû* before the door." Zimmern, *Ritualtafeln*, p. 122, 20 ff., *arki šu ina* *BIR

In the evening place a *ḫulduppû* [a]
Near the body of the man, the son of his god;
Bind on his head the . . . of the *ḫulduppû*;
Whether it be an evil Spirit, or an evil Demon,
Or an evil Ghost, or an evil Devil, or an evil God, or an [evil] Fiend,
Or a Hag-demon, or a Ghoul, or a Robber-sprite,
Or an evil Spirit that holdeth the man in its grip,
Or an evil Ghost that hath seized on the man,
Or an evil man, or one whose face is evil, whose mouth is evil, whose tongue is evil,
Headache, toothache, heart disease, or heartache,

ḫulduppe(e) ina *BIR *gibillē(e) ina* LU-TI-LA(*-e*) *ina* URUDU-ŠA-KAL-GA(*-e*) *ina sugugallē(-e) ina zērē ekalla tu-ḫap*, "Afterwards must thou, with *ḫulduppu*, with the torch, with the 'living sheep,' with 'strong copper,' with the 'skin of the great bull,' with seed corn, purify the palace." *Cun. Texts*, part xvii, pl. 28, ll. 54–55 . . . [*ḫulduppa*]*-a ina ma-a-a-li-šu kut-tim-šu-ma*, "With . . . *ḫulduppû* on his bed cover him and . . . ," and ibid., l. 67, [INIM-INIM-MA] . . . SU *BIR-ḪUL-DUB-BA MULU-TUR-RA DUL LA, "[Prayer] . . . the skin (?) of (?) a *ḫulduppû* cover the sick man." Tablet "F," pl. 38, col. iii, l. 13, GIŠ-MA-NU GIŠ-ḪUL-DUB-BA . . . "[Let him carve] a *ḫulduppû* of tamarisk." Tablet "K," l. 140 ff., *e-ri* iṣu *ḫul-dup-pu-u ša ra-bi-ṣi ša ina lib-bi-šu* ilu *E-a šu-mu zak-ru ina šip-ti ṣir-ti ši-pat E-ri-du ša te-lil-ti ap-pa u iš-di i-ša-a-ti lu-pu-ut-ma*, "A tamarisk *ḫulduppû* of a fiend, whereon is inscribed the name of Ea, with the all-powerful incantation, the Incantation of Eridu of Purification, set alight both in front and behind . . ." From this latter passage the iṣu *ḫulduppû* would appear to mean "figure."

INIM-INIM-MA-NE-E SAG-GA-NA ḪE-IB-TA-AN-ZI-ZI-E-NE
šip-ti an-ni-ti ina ri-ši-šu li-in-na-as-ḫu
. . . . NA ḪE-EN-GUB-BA MAL-LA NA-AN-DAK . . .
. . . . *šu li-iz* . . . . . .
. . . .

COL. IV (PLATE XXXVI).

. . . . . . : *ûmu(mu) ta-šil-ti ša ina* [alu] *Eridi ir-bu-u* : KUR-KUR-GA
. . . . . . TA : *ûmu(mu) dam-ḳu ša ina zir La-gaš šu-pu-u* : E-A
. . . . . . E-A : *ûmu(mu) ša pa-ni ba-nu-u tar-bit Ki-e-ši* : UḪ-KI-GE
. . . [ŠIR] - PUR - LA - KI - GE DIKUD - MAḪ
[[ilu] *A-da-p*]*a da-a-a-nu ṣi-i-ru ša La-ga-aš*
. . . . DUG-GA NAM-TIL-LA SUM-MU AN-SUR * KUR (?)-RU-KI-GE
. . . *-riš-ši ba-la-ṭa i-nam-di-nu ṣu-lul Šu-ru-ub-ba-ak*
. . . NE NIN GAB-NU-GI SAG-GA-NA-A BA-AN-LAḪ-LAḪ-GI-EŠ
. . . *-ti šu-nu ir-šu-tum ša la im-maḫ-ḫa-ru ina ri-ši-šu li-iz-zi-zu*
. . . MULU-BA-GE SIGIŠŠE-SIGIŠŠE ḪE-EN-NA-AB-BI
. . . *amelu šu-a-tum tas-li-tum liḳ-bu-u*
. . . E-NE TU . . . . BAD-GA NAM-TIL-LA SUM-MU
. . . . GAB AN-GA-GA-A
. . . . *šip-ti ba-la-ṭi*
. . . . *ti ni*
. . . . *ga-na-? li-pu-uš*
. . . . *-ti ka-a-a-nu*

[By] this incantation at his head may they be removed

. . . . may it stand . . . .

. . . .

Col. IV (Plate XXXVI).

The Pleasant Day risen forth from Eridu,

The Gentle Day that hath appeared in Lagash,

The Day of shining Presence sprung from Kish,

Adapa (?), puissant judge of Lagash,

The Shadow of Shurubbak, granting life to the suppliant (?),

With their wise [counsel ?] unopposed

May they take their stand at his head:

May they utter a prayer [for ?] this man;

May they perform an incantation of life . . .

May they make . . . .

. . . . firm

. . . . TE-MAL
. . . . *[li]ṭ-ḫu-šu*
. . . . * UR - * UR
. . . . *ru* (?)-*kus-ma*
. . . . SAG-BI . . ḪE-EN-GUB-BU-UŠ
. . . . *la uṣ-ṣu ina ri-ši-šu li-iz-ziz*
. . . . [BAR]-BI-KU ḪA-BA-RA-AN-GUB-[BA]
. . . . *ina a-ḫa-a-ti li-[iz-ziz]*
. . . . AŠ (?) SAR TAB-BA U . . . . .
. . . . . . *-ma* (?)*-ši ki-iṣ-ru-ti šu-[un-nu-ti]* . . .
. . . . LAL INIM-INIM-MA U . . . . .
. . . . . . *[pu] - ru - us šip - tu i* (?) - *[di* ? - *ma]*
[ŠU- * ŠAG]-GA DINGIR-RA-NA-KU ḪE-EN-ŠI-IN-[GE-GE]
[ma ḳa]-at dam-ḳa-a-ti ša [ili-šu-lip-pa-ḳid]
. . . . SAG-GA-NA NAM . . . .
. . . . . . *-tim ina ri-ši-šu a-a* . . . . .
. . . . . . NAM-TIL-LA ḪE-EN-NA . . . . . .
. . . . *-zi-šu ba-la-ṭi lit* . . . . .
. . . . UD (?) E - NUN - NA - TA E - A - NA
. . . . . . *iš - tu ku - um - me ina a - ṣi - šu*
. . . . . SU MULU-GIŠGAL-LU PAP-ḪAL-LA DU DINGIR-RA-NA
. . . . . . *ša ameli mut-tal-li-ki mar ili-šu*
. . . . . . [*ilu*] *Ša-maš liṭ-ḫi* : ḪE-EN-NA-AN-TE-MAL
[DINGIR-SILIG-ELIM-NUN-NA DU-SAG-ZU-AB-GE] ŠAG-GA TAG-TAG-BI ZA-A-KAN
[*ilu Marduk mar riš-tu-u ša ap-si-i bu-u*]*n-nu-u du-um-mu-ḳu ku-um-ma*

[INIM - INIM - MA] UTUG - ḪUL - A - KAN

. . . .

May they draw nigh unto him . . . .

. . . .

May . . . that goeth not forth, stand at his head,

May . . . . stand away from him

[Tie] double (?) knots . . . . . .

Make a decision . . . , perform the incantation,

[Into the] kindly [hands] of his god let him be [commended]

. . . . . at his head let them not . . . .

. . . . . . life may they grant [him],

. . . . . when he goeth forth from the dwelling

[Unto the body] of the wanderer, the son of his god,

. . . . . may Shamash draw nigh,

O Marduk, eldest son of the Ocean Deep!

Thine is the power to brighten and bless.

PRAYER AGAINST THE EVIL SPIRITS.

Tablet "E."

(Plate XXXVII.)

. . . . *ir-ši-šu e-ṣir-ma* . . . .
. . . MULLA-ḪUL MULU-RA NAM-BA-TE-[MAL] . . .
. . . [*gal-lu-u lim-nu a-na*] *ameli a-a iṭ-ḫu-u-*[*ni*]
. . . . SAG - BI U - ME - NI - [GAR]
. . . . . . *ina ri - ši - šu šu - kun -* [*ma*]
. . . . BAR - KU ḪE - IM - TA - [GUB]
. . . . *šu-ti-iḳ-ma ina a-ḫa-a-ti li-iz-ziz* . .
. . . . GAR - ŠA - A NAM - BA - TE - MAL - E - NE
. . . . - *tum* (?) *u - pi - šu a - a iṭ - ḫu - šu*
[ŠU] - LAḪ - LAḪ - GA - A - NI - TA ḪE - IM - MA - AN - ŠED - DE
[*ina ḳa*] *- ti - šu el - li - ti li - pa - aš - ši - iḫ*
[ŠU]-* ŠAG-GA DINGIR-RA-NA-KU ḪE-EN-ŠI-IN-GE-GE

[INIM - INIM - MA] UTUG - ḪUL - A - KAN

[EN UTUG-ḪUL] . . . DINGIR-EDIN-NA GIN-A
[*u*]*-tuk-ku lim-nu ša ina ṣi-e-ri il-la-ku*
. . . . DINGIR - EDIN - NA DUL - LA
. . . . [*lim*]*-nu ša ina ṣi-e*[1] *- ri i-kat-ta*[2] *- mu*
. . . . DINGIR - EDIN - NA LA - A
. . . . [*lim-nu ša ina*] *ṣi-e-ri it-te-ni-'-lu-u*
. . . . . . DINGIR - EN - LIL - LA ŠE - IR - ZI - DA
. . . . *ilu* „ *nam - ru*
. : . . . . : DINGIR - EN DU ŠA - BI[1]
. . . . [3] : URUGAL A[1] - RI - A

Tablet "E."

(Plate XXXVII.)

[With] . . . surround his bed and . . . .
That . . . no evil devil may draw nigh unto the man,
Put . . . . . at his head,
Let pass by . . . . and let it stand aside,
That . . . . no sorcery may draw nigh unto him.
That by his pure hand he may be assuaged,
That unto the kindly [hands][a] of his god he may be commended.

[Prayer against] the Evil Spirits.

Incantation :—
The evil Spirit that stalketh in the desert,
The evil [Demon ?] that shroudeth (man) in the desert,
The evil [Ghost ?] that lieth in the desert,
. . . . Bel radiant,
. . . . Bel . . .
[Evil Spirits] . . . spawned in the tomb,

---

[1] Rm. 314 omits. [2] K. 2,337, *mu*.
[3] Rm. 314 . . . *-mu-u*.
[a] For this line see *Cun. Texts*, part xvii, pl. 22, l. 145.

. . . . [1]*-ti* : BI

. . . . *ra-ma-ni-šu-nu* : IM-TE-MAL-DA-BI

. . . . [2]MU - UN - TAR - RI - EŠ - A - AN

. . . . NI - IN - UŠ

. . . . - *nim* - *mi* - *du*

. . . . GIN DU - MU

. . . . ŠU - U - ME - TI

. . . . *li - ḳi - e - ma*

. . . . SU - BI U - ME - NI - TAG - TAG

. . . . *zumri - šu* *lu - up - pi - it - ma*

. . . : *ab-kal-lu* *ab-riḳ-ḳu* *ka-la-šu-nu* : KAL-A-BI

. . . . SA - AZAG - GA ḪU - MU - RA - AB - SAR - RA

. . . . . . *ri - ik - sa* *el - la* *li - ir - ku - su - ka*

. . . . ID-DAR *BIR ḪAR-SAG-GA-GE DUBBIN AM-GUL DAR-A

. . . *u-ri-iṣ* *šadi*(*i*) *ša* *ṣu-pur* *ri-me* *bu-un-nu-u*

. . . . . . TA NA NE ḪAR-SAG-GA-TA GIN-A

. . . *-ri-ni-šu-nu* *ḳut-ri-in-nu* *ša* *ul-tu* *šadi*(*i*) *ib-bab-la*

. . . MU-UN-E DA-BI-TA . . *bi*(?)-' *ša-ḫa-tu*[3] *ri-di-ma* : GIN-A

. . . SAR DINGIR-PA-TE-SI-MAḪ U-ME-NI-IB-TE-SUM

. . . . . - *kil - ti* *ši - pat* *ilu* „ *i - di - šum - ma*

. . . . E . . . BA - NI - IB - E

. . . . [*a*] - *ṣi* - *šu*

. . . .

. . . .

. . . . . . themselves,

. . . . . . they have ordained,

. . . . . . they take their stand,

[[a] Marduk hath seen: What I:] "Go, my son, (Marduk),

"Take . . . .

"[And with it] . . . . touch his body.

"Ruler (and) chieftain of all of them,

"With a clean bandage let them bind thee,

". . . of a kid of the mountains which hath polished a bull's hoof,

"With their . . . as a smoke offering brought from the mountains,

". . . unto the neighbourhood go down and

"Perform for him the Incantation of the God Patesi-maḫ [b] . . . .

. . . . at his going forth

. . . .

---

[1] Rm. 314 . . . *-ti-šu-nu ṣir-tum.*

[2] Rm. 314 for this line has . . . *i-šim-mu.*

[3] K. 5,100, *ta.*

[a] See Tablet "A," l. 17 ff.

[b] "Supreme Ruler."

[Reverse of K. 5,100.]

. . . .

BAR . . . . SIG - GA - A . . . . . .

ina . . . [*ma*]-*ḫi-iṣ* . . . *ku* (?) *ma-ḫi-iṣ* . . .

GAR - [ḪUL - GIM - MA] ? - LAL . . . .

mimma[(*ma*) *lim*] - *nu* *dup* - *pir* . . . .

UTUG-ḪUL A-[LA-ḪUL GI]DIM-ḪUL MULLA-ḪUL
E-TA ḪA-BA-R[A-E]

u-tuk-ku lim-[*nu a-lu-u lim*]-*nu e-kim-mu*
lim-nu gal-lu-u lim-nu iš-[*tu bîti ṣi-i*]

U-NE-Z[I (?)] . . . ZI AN-NA KAN-PA [ZI KI-A KAN-PA]

na-an-si-[*iḫ*] . . . [*niš*] *šame*(*e*) *lu-u-ta-*[*mat*
niš irṣitim(*tim*) *lu-u-ta-mat*]

EN ḲU . . . .

[Reverse of K. 5,100.]

. . . . . smiting . . . . . smiting . . . .

50. Whatever is evil, be thou removed . . . . . !

O evil Spirit, ev[il Demon], evil Ghost, evil Devil,

Go forth from the house (and) depart!

By Heaven be thou exorcised! [By Earth be thou exorcised!]

---

55. Incantation :— . . . .

Tablet "F."

Col. III (Plate XXXVIII).

. . . .

*BIR UTUG . . . .

u-ri-ṣu [*u-tuk-ku*] . . . .

U-GIG-A ŠU-ŠU-BI . . . .

mu-u-ša u ur-ra ina . . . .

MULU-GIŠGAL-LU-BI BARA-*ŠIG-GA . . . .

amelu šu-u ina „-e . . . .

E-NUN-AZAG-GA KI NAM-TIL-[LA] . . . . . .

ku-um-mu el-lu aš-ru ša [*balaṭi*]

URUDU-*SIG-TAK-ALAM AZAG-ZU . . . .

TAG-GAM-ME KUBABBAR GIŠ-TIR AZAG . . .

gur-gur-ru en-ḳu mu-di . . . .

ša-aš-ša-ru ša ṣar-pi ana kiš-ti [*elli?*] . . .

GIŠ-MA-NU GIŠ-ḪUL-DUB-BA . . . .

ṬUN U-ME-NI-TAG : *ina pa-a-ši* . . . .

ALAM NAM-TIL-LA : *uš* . . . .

MU-MUD-NA-A-BI : . . . .

. . . .

Col. IV.

. . . .

. . *ša niš ar* . . . .

*BIR(?)-GIG LU ID . . . .

. . MU BI TAG-GA : *na* . . . .

*BIR-AZAG DUG-GA . . . .

u-ri-ṣa el-la . . . .

Tablet "F."

Col. III (Plate XXXVIII).

. . . .
A kid . . . .
Night and day in . . . .
That man at a lucky shrine . . . . .
A pure dwelling, the abode of life . . .
Let a wise (and) cunning coppersmith
[Take an axe of gold (?)[a] and] a silver pruning-knife[b]
Unto a grove undefiled,
[Let him carve] a *ḫulduppû* of tamarisk
Touch it with the axe . . .
An image (?) of life . . . .
[Inscribe thereon] the name of his . . . .
. . . .

Col. IV.

. . . .
A dark-coloured kid . . . .
Touch its . . . .
An undefiled kid . . . .

---

[a] On this restoration see Zimmern, *Ritueltafeln*, p. 140, Nos. 31–37, l. 45, and p. 156, Nos. 46–47, l. 12.

[b] This restores the word *ša-aš*-[*ša-ru*] in *W.A.I.*, iv, 18, 3, col. ii, l. 2, which evidently means some small tool. Cf. the Syriac *tâthwârâ*, subula (Payne Smith; *Thesaurus*, col. 4,516).

. . DINGIR-NIN-ḪAR-SAG-GA-GE * BIR-GIG . . .
ina ṭe-im ^{ilu}Be-lit-ili u-ri-ṣa ṣal-[ma] . . .
KA-AZAG MAḪ-DI NAM-ŠUB NUN-KI-GA-GE . . .
ina pi-i el-li ti-iz-ḳa-ri ši-pat ^{alu}Eridi i
MULU - GIŠGAL - LU DU - DINGIR - [RA] - NA
ANA - GIM ḪE - [EN - AZAG] - GA
KI - GIM ḪE - [EN - EL] - LA
ŠA - ANA - GIM ḪE - [EN - LAḪ - LAḪ] - GA
EME - ḪUL - IK BAR - KU ḪE - [IM - TA] - GUB

[INIM - INIM] - MA UTUG - [ḪUL] - A - KAN

. . . . ḪA-LA BA-AN-UŠ . . . BI(?) NU* ŠAG[1]
[*Duppu-* $^{KAM-MA}$] UTUG-ḪUL-A-KAN . . . . *Akkadi* ^{KI}
gab-ri Bab ^{KI}
. . . *tu*(?) *mâr* ^{m}*Mu-kal-lim* ^{am}A-[BA] ^{ilu}*Marduk*
. . . . [$^{m\ ilu}$*Sulma*] *- nu - ešir šar* ^{mātu}*Aššur u*
$^{m\ ilu}$*Nabu-apli-*[*iddina*] *šar Babili* ^{KI}
. . . . *iš-ṭu-ru ša-ṭir-ma sa-niḳ . . . ka tig*
sum up-pu-uš
. . . . ^{am}*rab-dupšarri* ^{pl} *ša* $^{m\ ilu}$*Aššur-*[*bani*]*-apli*
šar ^{mātu}*Aššuri*
. . . . [^{am}]*rab-dupšarri* ^{pl} . . *dup-šarri . . .* ^{pl} *ša*
ki-rib ^{alu}*Arba-ili*

. . . .

---

[1] The colophon mentions Shalmaneser (II), King of Assyria, and Nabû-apli-iddina, King of Babylon, both living in the ninth century B.C.

At the command of the Lady of the Gods
The dark-coloured kid . . . . . .
With a clear (and) loud voice
[Perform] the Incantation of Eridu,
May the man, the son of his god,
Become pure as Heaven,
Clean as Earth,
Bright as the middle of the Heavens,
May the Evil Tongue be absent from him!

PRAYER AGAINST THE [EVIL] SPIRITS.

Tablet "G."

OBVERSE.

COL. I (PLATE XXXIX).

. . . .

[aṣi-šu su]-ḳu ṣi-it ^{ilu}Šamši ni-rib-šu su-ḳu e-rib ^{ilu}Šamši(ši)

[UTUG-ḪUL A-LA]-ḪUL GIDIM-ḪUL MULLA-ḪUL DINGIR-ḪUL MAŠKIM-ḪUL

[u-tuk-ku lim-nu] a-lu-u lim-nu e-kim-mu lim-nu gal-lu-u lim-nu ilu lim-nu ra-bi-ṣu [lim-nu]

. . . . . . ŠU GIR-GIN-GIN-A-TA : *ina bi-e-ti ana li-mut-ti ina i-tal-lu-ki-šu*

. . . . E-A IM-MA-AN-DA-AN-TI-EŠ : *il bi-ti ^{ilu}Iš-tar bi-tim lu-ṭar-du-[šu]*

. . . . BA-AN- . . . . : *la-mas-si bît pu-uz-ra i ta-ḫal*

. . A (?) . . . E-A-GE UR-BI IM-MA-AN-DA-AN-UR-GI-EŠ

. . . . *ana ši (?)-ip (?)-ta ṣi-ḫir ra-bi ša bîti mit-ḫa-riš i tar-ru*

. . . A DINGIR-SILIG-MULU-ŠAR ME-EN MAŠ-MAŠ ANA-KI-A DIB-DIB-BI ḪUL-E-NE

. . . *^{ilu}Marduk maš-maš šamê(e) u irṣitim(tim) tu-mu-[uḫ] lim-nu-ti-[šu ?]*

. . . IGI-IGI E-TA E-IB-TA GAB-ZU GI-BI-IB . . .

. . . *-nu ina bîti i ta-aṣ-ṣi i-rat-ka ni-'-i* . . .

Tablet "G."

OBVERSE.

COL. I (PLATE XXXIX).

. . . .

[It hath its exit] at the Street of Dawn[a]
(And) its entrance at the Street of Sunset.
Be it [evil Spirit] or evil Demon
Or evil Ghost or evil Devil
Or evil God or evil Fiend,
When it cometh to the house for evil
May the God (and) Goddess of the house drive [it] forth.
O thou Guardian Spirit of the inner chamber, tremble not!
O ye [spirits] . . . , great and small of the house alike, quake not!
O . . . . Marduk, magician of heaven and earth, seize upon its iniquity!
O . . . ,[b] go not forth from the house, turn back!

---

[a] Or "Street of the East" and "Street of the West."

[b] IGI-IGI = *ḫarranu*; possibly here we may restore "O wayfarer."

GIDIM UB . . . BU . . A GU-MU-TA UB-TA SILA-A-KU UD-[DU] . .

še-e-du [ša ina tub-ḳi iz]-za-zu ina rig-mi-ia ul-tu tub-ḳi ana su-[u-ḳi ṣi-i]

GIDIM DA . . . GAR(?) GU-MU-TA [DA-TA SILA-A-KU] E . .

še-e-du ša ina [šaḫati] . . . ša ina rig-mi-ia [ul-tu šaḫati ana su-u-ḳi ṣi-i]

. . . . TA SILA - A - [KU E] . . .

. . . . *ḫu te lu . . . [ana] su-u-[ḳi ṣi-i]*

. . . . UN(?) IB(?) ANA TU . . . SILA-A KU [E] . .

. . . . . *ti te sur . . . [ana su-u-ḳi ṣi-i]* . .

. . . .

REVERSE.

COL. IV.

. . . .

. . . ṢI . . . A E . . . SAR . . . . . .

. . . . *ša bîti la taḫ-ta-na-ab*(?)-*[ba-tu]*

. . MA(?) DIR-TA NAM-BA-ZA-LA-AḪ-ḪI-EN : *it-ti ša-a-ri ḳip . . . [la ta-ziḳ-ḳu]*

. . E-NA-TA NAM-BA-TU-TU-E-NE : *it-ti a-ṣi-i la tir-[ru-bu]*

. . TUR-RA-TA NAM-BA-TU-TU-NE : *it-ti e-ri-bi la [tir-ru-bu]*

. . . EN NA-AN-TUŠ-EN : *la ta-az-za-zi la tu-[šab]*

. . . GE-GE-E-NE NAM-BA-GUR-GUR-E-[NE]

[la ta-at]-ta-an-nu-ur-ra la ta-as-sa-na-ḫu-[ur]

[ZI] ANA-KI-BI-DA-GE KAN-RI-PA ḪA-BA-RA-DU-[UN]

[niš šame](e) u irṣitim(tim) u-tam-me-ka lu-ta-at-ta-lak [TU EN]

. . . SI PA(?) U-TU-UD-DA BA . . . . . .

[Duppi] . . . *KAM-MA* UTUG - [ḪUL - A - MEŠ]

O Spirit that standest close at hand,
At my cry go forth therefrom unto the street!
O Spirit that standeth near,
At my cry go forth [therefrom unto the street]!
. . . . go forth unto the street!
. . . . go forth unto the street!
. . . .

REVERSE.

COL. IV.

. . . .
. . . . plunder not the . . . of the house,
With the . . . wind blow not,
With one that goeth forth come not in,
With one that cometh in, come not in,
Stand not, sit not,
Return not, turn not round!
By Heaven and Earth I exorcise thee,
That thou mayest depart!

. . . . begotten . . . .

[ ]TH TABLET OF THE SERIES "THE EVIL SPIRITS."

Tablet "H."

OBVERSE.

(PLATE XL.)

. . . .

. . . . . . GU - BA (?) - DE . . . .

. . . . *is - su* . . . .

. . . . GA MU RA . . . .

. . . . . [*u*] - *ṣu - rat* ^{ilu}*E - a* (?) . . . . . .

. . . . . AK-DA DINGIR-SILIG-MULU-ŠAR . . . .

. . . *ana* (?) *še* (?) *- e - ti ša* ^{ilu}*Marduk* . . .

. . . . MULU - TU - TU . . . .

. . . . *ma* (?) *a - ši - pu* . . . . .

. . . . LI DINGIR - EDIN - NA SAR - A . . . .

. . . . *lu-u ša ina ṣi-ir ib-ba-na-a ul* . . .

. . . . . . LA ZU . . . .

. . . .

REVERSE.

. . . .

. . . . E KA . . A . . . . . .

. . . . BA - RA - AN - DA . . . . . .

. . . . . . E - A - A - KU . . . .

. . . . [*ana*] *bîti a* - [*a i - ru - ub*]

[UTUG-ḪUL DIB-BA]-A-[NI] BAR-KU [ḪE-IM-TA-GUB]
[UTUG - * ŠIG - GA ALAD] - * ŠIG - GA ḪE - EN - DA -
[LAḪ - LAḪ - GI - EŠ]

[INIM - INIM - M]A UTUG - ḪUL - [A - KAN]

. . . .

𝔗𝔞𝔟𝔩𝔢𝔱 "J."

REVERSE.

(PLATE XL.)

. . . .

. . . . LUGAL-GE . . .

. . . . LUGAL-GE . . .

. . . . LUGAL-GE-MAḪ . . .

. . . . LUGAL-GE . . .

. . . KA-A-NI SU-NI-TA KAN-NI-IB-TA-E . . . .

. . . *zu-um-ri-šu lit-ta-aṣ-ṣi-ma ina a-ḫa-a-ti [li-iz-ziz]*

. . . . BAR - KU ḪE - IM - [TA - GUB]

. . . . *[lim] - nu ina a - ḫa - a - ti li - iz - zi - [iz]*

[UTUG- * ŠIG-GA ALAD]- * ŠIG-GA ḪE-EN-DA-LAḪ-LAḪ-[GI-EŠ]

[u-tuk-ku dum-ḳi še-e-du dum]-ḳi i-da-a-šu lu-u-ka-a-a-an . . .

[INIM - INIM - MA] UTUG - ḪUL - A - [KAN]

. . . . AN-NA MU-UN-NIGIN-E-[NE]

. . . . I - A - AN MU - BI - IM

. . . . [UTUG] - ḪUL - MEŠ NU - AL - BAD

. . . . *ri ša*

. . . . *ir dup - šar ṣiḫru*

. . . . *ib ri* (?) *ki* (?)

. . . .

Tablet "J."

OBVERSE.

(PLATE XLI.)

. . . .

. . . . DA

. . . . GE - GE - E - NE

[INIM - INIM] - MA UTUG - ḪUL - A - KAN

[EN UT]UG - ḪUL - IK AZAG EDIN - NA

[u - tuk] - ku lim - nu a - šak - ku ša ṣi - ri

[NAM] - TAR MULU ḪUL - IK TAG - GA - ZU

[nam] - ta - ru ša ameli lim - niš tal - pu - tum

[UTUG] - ḪUL - IK MULU MU - UN - ŠI - IN - BAR - RA

[u - tuk] - ku lim - nu ša ameli ip - pal - la - su

. . . [ḪUL] - IK MULU MU - UN - ŠI - IN - DUL - LA

. . . . . *lim - nu ša ameli i - kat - ta - mu*

. . . . ḪUL - IK MULU MULU ŠA

. . . . NA ŠA - A

. . . . *- pi lim - nu - tum*

. . . . *li - šak - nu*

. . . . [ḪE] - EN - TA - GAZ

. . . . *[li - iḫ] - tap - pu - u*

. . . .

Tablet "J."

OBVERSE.

(PLATE XLI.)

. . . .

[PRAYER] AGAINST THE EVIL SPIRITS.[a]

The evil Spirit (and) Fever of the desert,[b]
O Pestilence that hast touched the man for harm,
The evil Spirit which hath cast its glance on the man,
The evil [Demon] which hath enshrouded the man,

. . . .

[a] The ending of the reverse of Tablet "H" is the same as that of the Fifth Tablet, p. 80, but unless the text of the obverse fills the hiatus of ll. 47–55, which does not, as far as can be judged at present, seem probable, Tablet "H" must be regarded as part of a separate Tablet.

[b] This line and the similar lines in Tablet "C" (156 and 173) have been translated thus in preference to "The evil Spirit (is) the Fever of the desert," for the reason that the verb *talput* in Tablet "C," l. 174, is in the second person.

Tablet "K."

(Plate XLII.)

. . . .

. . . . - MEŠ

. . . . - *u*

. . . . - MEŠ

. . . . *ki - na* *saḫ - pu* (?) *šu - nu*

. . . . LA ḪUL * SIG - * SIG - GA A - MEŠ

. . . . . [*ma*]-*a-ti* *lim-niš* *i-sap-pa-nu* *šu-nu*

. . . . MEŠ KI - A KIN - KIN - NA A - MEŠ [1]

. . . [*ša*]-*ḳu-miš* *aš-bu* *šap-liš* *it-ta-ab-ra-ru* *šu-nu*

. . . . RA KUR - KU - GAR - RA MEŠ

. . . *e* (?) - *ti* - *ḳu* *la* *i - nam* (?) - *du - u* *šu - nu*

U - RI - IN - MA - NE - ḪA - A U - GIG - GIG - GA MEŠ

u-ri-in-nu sa-aḫ-pu-tum ša na-ma-ru uṭ-ṭu-u [*šu*]-*nu*

(Plate XLIII.)

IM-ḪUL-BI-TA MU-UN-DA-RU-UŠ ID-NU-UN-UŠ (?) MEŠ

it-ti im-ḫul-li i-ziḳ-ḳu ul im-[*maḫ-ha-ru šu*]-*nu*

· IM-SU-ZI GIŠGAL-LU-GIM MU-UN-DA-RI-EŠ MELAM
. . . MEŠ

pu-luḫ-ti ša-lum-ma-ta ki-ma a-li-e ra-mu-u
me-lam-mu . . . *šu-nu*

Tablet "K."

(Plate XLII.)

. . . .

. . . . they overwhelm

. . . balefully they cover the land,

They dwell in gloom [on high], below they howl,

(Nor) are they ready (?) to pass by . . . .

They are the widespreading clouds[a] which darken the day,

(Plate XLIII.)

With the storm wind they blow, and cannot be withstood.

Haloed with awful brilliance like a demon,

They carry terror far and wide;

---

[1] K. 5,183, MEŠ.

[a] *Urinnu* occurs also in *W.A.I.*, i, 15, 57 (Tiglath-Pileser), *ša nubalušu kima urinni eli mâtišu šuparruru*, "whose net like a cloud is spread over his land."

AŠTE KI-NA UD-ZAL-LI-DA-GE MELAM ŠU-ŠU A-MEŠ
pu-uz-ra ma-a-a-la ki-ma ûmi(mi) u-nam-ma-ru me-lam-mu saḫ-pu šu-nu

E-NE-NE-NE SILA-A-TA . . . BA-AN-LAḪ-GI-EŠ GIR KUR-RA-GE BA-AN-SIG-GA-EŠ
šu-nu ina ri-bi-ʾti iz-za-zu-ma tal-lak-ti ma-a-ti u-saḫ-ḫa-ri

E-DINGIR-E-NE-GE BA-AN-RI-RI A-MEŠ
bi-ta-at ilâni^{pl} *ir-ta-nab-bu-[u šu-nu]*

KU-KUR-MAL-LA BA-AN-DUB-DUB-BU-[MEŠ]
maš (?)-ḫa-ti ul is-sar-rak šu-[nu]

SIGIŠŠE [NU]-BAL UB-GUB-BI ḪUL BA-AN . . .
[niḳî] ul i-naḳ-ḳi šu-nu-ti a-lak-ta-šu-nu lim-ni . . .

. . . NIN-BI-TA AB-BA GURUŠ (?)-RA AN-NU-BI ID . .
. . . nim-ti a-ḫa a-ḫa-ti id-lu ši-i-bi ša la ili

. . . [A-A] DU-A-NI-TA RI [. . . BA]-AN-KAR-KAR-EŠ KI-A BA-AN-LAḪ-GI-EŠ
. . . a-bi it-ti [mari-šu mit (?)-ḫa (?)]-riš im-šu-ʾ-u-ma ana irṣitim(tim) uš-te-ri-du[1]

. . . . IB-LAḪ-EŠ ZIR-BI BA-AN-KAL-KAL-EŠ
. . . [ṭe?]-e-mu iš-lu-lu-ma zi-ri[2] *u-tak-ki-ru*

. . . . BA-AN-SIG-GA[3]-EŠ
. . . . pa su-un-ti[4] *iš-ḫu-ṭu*[5]

. . . . UMMEDA-BI BA-AN-GABA-EŠ
. . . . [mu-še]-niḳ-ti ta-ri-ti ip-ṭu-ru

They make the secrets of the couch as clear as the day,
Spreading terror afar.
They stand in the broad places
And circle round the highways of the land,
(In) the temples of the gods they exalt themselves (?)
They pour no libations of oil (?) [a]
Nor offer sacrifices ;
Evil is their way.
. . . brother, sister, hero, old man, (all) without a god,
. . the father together with his son they rob
And fell them to the earth.
They steal away desire (?) and bring to nought the seed,
They tear out the . . . . . of the loins,[b]
They rend the [womb ? [c]] of the nursing mother,
And of the woman in travail.

---

[1] K. 5,133 . . . *ru*.
[2] K. 4,905, *ru*.
[3] K. 4,905, GI.
[4] K. 4,905, *tu*.
[5] K. 4,905, *uṭ*.

[a] *Mašḫati*; if the reading *maš* be correct, we may compare the Syriac *mešḫa*, "oil" (Brockelmann, p. 195, *b*).

[b] *Sunti*, possibly a feminine form of *sunu*, "side" or "loins," a synonym of *utlu*. For an analogous case of a feminine bye-form compare *šupilu ša sinništi* and *šupiltu*, *W.A.I.*, ii, 28, 43, *d* and 45, *e*.

[c] For this restoration cf. *W.A.I.*, ii, 17, ii, 41 : *taritu ša kirimmaša paṭru*.

. . . [BA]-AN-GAZ ŠA-ḪA-LAM-MA BA-AN-GAR-RI-EŠ

. . . *i - du - ku - ma šaḫ - lu - uḳ - ti*[1] *iš - ku - nu*

. . . MU - UN - SIR - RI - EŠ KALAM - KUR - RA - GE BA - AN - SIG - GI - EŠ

. . . *[šame](e) u irṣitim(tim) is-su-ḫu-ma niši*[pl] *mâti u-sip-pu*

. . . . KIŠADU-NE-RA BA-AN-DIB-BI-EŠ DINGIR-BI LA BA-RA-E

šamû(u) ir-ṣi-ti[2] *ki-ša-da-nu-uš-šu-nu*[3] *iṣ-ṣab-tu-ma ilu-šu*[4] *ul ip-du-u*

KI - BI - TA LA BA - RA - E GIŠ - ḪAR - BI BA - ḪUL

ir-ṣi-ti[1] *ul ip-du-u u-ṣur*[5] *-ta-šu-nu lim-ni-it*

AN-NA AN-NI-BI[6]-NE IM-MA-AN-BU-I[4]-EŠ ANA[7] NU-E-A BA-AN-BAD-DA-EŠ[8]

ana šamê(e) ša-ḳiš[9] *iš-du-du-u*[4] *-ma a-na*[10] *šamê(e) ša la a-a*[11] *-ri is-su-u*

MUL-AN-NA ŠI-DUB-BI LA BA-RA-AN[4]-DU-DU-EŠ EN-NUN EŠ-ŠA[12]-BI-TA[13]

ina kak-kab ša-ma-mi[14] *ul u-ta-ad-du-u ina ma-aṣ-ṣa-ra*[15] *- a*[16] *- ti še-lal-ti ši-na*

NUN SAG-MAḪ AN-NA IM-MA-AN-BU-I[4]-EŠ A-A-NI[17] LA BA-AN-ZU-UŠ

ru-bu-u a-ša-ri-du ṣi-i-ri[18] *a-na*[10] *šamê(e) ir*[19] *-du-du*[20] *-ma a-ba*[21] *-šu ul i-di*

DINGIR-BIL-GI AN-TA MAḪ ŠI-GIN GAL GU AŠ-BAR-MAḪ AN-NA

[ilu] „ *ša-ḳu-u ṣi-i-ri*[18] *a-ša-ri-du ra-bu*[22] *-u pa-ri-is purussi ṣi-i-ri*[23] *ša* [ilu] *A-nim*

They slay the [offspring ?] and spread destruction ;
They carry off the . . . of heaven and earth,
And cut off[a] the people of the land.
They fasten their hold on heaven and earth and spare not their gods.[b]
On earth they are ruthless,
Evil is their ban ;
Unto heaven on high they betake themselves,
And unto the impenetrable heaven hie them far away,
Unknown amid the celestial stars
In their three watches.
The prince, the mighty chieftain, unto heaven had betaken himself,
And his father knew it not ;
The Fire God, high and powerful,
Great chieftain who giveth the awful decisions of Heaven,

[1] K. 4,905, *tu*.
[2] K. 4,905, *irṣitim*(*tim*).
[3] K. 4,905 omits (?) *šu-nu*.
[4] K. 4,905 omits.
[5] K. 4,905, *ṣu-ur*.
[6] K. 4,905 inserts E.
[7] K. 4,867 and K. 4,905 insert NA.
[8] K. 4,867 and K. 4,905, DU-UŠ for DA-EŠ.
[9] K. 4,905, *ḳi-eš*.
[10] K. 4,905, *ana*.
[11] K. 4,867 and K. 4,905 omit.
[12] K. 4,867, III-A-AN ; K. 4,905, NA III-A-AN for EŠ-ŠA.
[13] K. 4,867, KU.
[14] K. 4,905, *šame*(*e*).
[15] K. 4,905, *ṣar* for *aṣ-ṣa-ra*.
[16] K. 4,867 omits.
[17] K. 4,905, NA.
[18] K. 4,905, *ru* for *i-ri*.
[19] K. 4,905, *iš*.
[20] K. 4,867 and K. 4,905, *ud*.
[21] K. 4867, *bu*.
[22] K. 4,905, *rabû*.
[23] K. 4,905, *rim* for *i-ri*.

[a] *Usippu* : cf. Syriac *sâph*, periit (Brockelmann, p. 222, *a*), and *W.A.I.*, iv, 19, 3, 46 : *nakru dannu kima ḳanê idi usip*[ ]*ni* (MU-UN-SIG-SIG-GI).

[b] Literally "of heaven and earth the necks thereof they seize upon."

(PLATE XLIV.)

[DINGIR]-BIL-GI TUKUL-LI KI-* AG-GA-A-NI DA-BI DA-AB-GUB

^{ilu} „ *ib-ri na-ram-šu it-ti-šu ’-ram-ma*

[ḪUL]-IK *VII*-BI ŠI-MI-IN-ZU-UŠ

[lim]-nu-ti ṣi-bit-ti-šu-nu um-ta-ad-di

. . . U-BI-KU-KI-GAR-RA-BI ŠA-BI MU-UN-DA-AB-SIG-SIG

ši-tul-ti ina a-ša-bi-šu im-tal-lik

[DINGIR]-BIL-GI *VII*-BI ME-A-BI U-TU-UD-DA-A-MEŠ ME-A-BI KUL-GA-A-MEŠ

^{ilu} „ *si-bit-ti-šu-nu e-ka-a-ma al-du e-ka-a-ma ir-bu-u*

VII-BI ḪAR-SAG GIG-GA BA-U-TU-UD-DA-A-MEŠ

si-bit-ti-šu-nu ina ša-ad e-rib ^{ilu} *Šamši(ši) ’-al-du*

VII-BI ḪAR-SAG BABBAR-RA BA-KUL-A-MEŠ

si-bit-ti-šu-nu ina ša-ad ṣi-it ^{ilu} *Šamši(ši) ir-bu-u*

KI-IN-TAR KUR[1]-RA-GE DURUN (?)-NA-A-MEŠ

ina ni-gi-iṣ-ṣi ir-ṣi-ti it-ta-na-aš-ša-bu

KISLAḪ KUR-RA-GE AB-TA-ḪA-A-A-MEŠ

ina ni-du-ti[2] *ir-ti*[3] (sic) *it-te-ni-en-bu-u*

E-NE-NE-NE ANA KI-A NU-UN-ZU-MEŠ MELAM DUL-LA-A-MEŠ

šu-nu ina šame(e) u irṣitim(tim) ul il-lam-ma-du me-lam-mu kat-mu šu-nu

DINGIR-GAL-AN-ZU-BI NU-UN-ZU-MEŠ

ina[4] *ilâni*^{pl} *ir-šu-ti ul u-ta-ad-du-u*

MU-BI ANA KI-A LA BA-AN-GAL-LA-A-MEŠ

šum-šu-nu ina šame(e) ir-ṣi-ti[5] *ul ib*[6]*-ba-aš-ši*

VII-BI KUR-GIG-GA-TA ḪU-UB[7]-MU-UN-SIR-SIR-E-NE

si-bit-ti-šu-nu ina ša-ad e-rib ^{ilu} *Šamši(ši) il-ta-na-as-su-mu*

(Plate XLIV.)

The Fire God, his beloved comrade,
With him started forth and
The evil of those seven became known.
While he sate himself down he pondered;
"O Fire God, those seven,
"Where were they born, where were they reared?
"Those seven were born in the Mountain of Sunset,
"And were reared in the Mountain of Dawn,
"They dwell within the caverns of the earth,
"And amid the desolate places of the earth they live,
"Unknown in heaven and earth
"They are arrayed with terror,
"Among the Wise Gods there is no knowledge of them,
"They have no name in heaven or earth;
"Those seven gallop over the Mountain of Sunset,

[1] 36,690, E.
[2] 36,690, *tu*.
[3] 36,690, *irṣitim*(*tim*).
[4] 36,690 omits.
[5] K. 4,886, *u irṣitim*(*tim*).
[6] K. 4,886, *i*.
[7] K. 4,886 . . . ḪUB for ḪU-UB.

VII-BI KUR-UT-TA-E-NE IM-MA-NI-IN-DI-EŠ
si-bit-ti-šu-nu ina ša-ad ṣi-it [ilu] *Šamši(ši)* *im-ma*[1] *-lil-lu*

KI-IN-TAR KUR-RA-GE GIR-MU-UN-GA-GA-A-MES
ina ni-gi-ṣi[2] *ir-ṣi-ti*[3] *it-ta-na-aḫ-lal-lu*

KISLAḪ KUR-RA-GE GU-MU-UN-LAL-EŠ
ina ni-du-ti ir-ṣi-ti[3] *it-te-ni-'-lu-u*

E-NE-NE-NE GAR NU-UN-ZU-MES ANA KI-A NU-UN[4]-ZU-MES
šu-nu ina mimma šum-šu ul u-ta-ad-du-u ina šame(e) u irṣitim(tim) ul il-lam-ma-du

DINGIR-ASARU BA-AN-NA-TE I-BI ḪU-MU-RA-AB-BI
[a-n]a [ilu] *Marduk ṭi*[5] *-ḫi-e*[6] *-ma a-mat*[7] *šu-a-ti*[8] *liḳ-bi-ka*

ḪUL-IK *VII*-BI IGI-ZU[9]-NA BA-AN-SUM[10] ID-* AG-GA-BI ḪU-MU-RA-AB-SUM-MU
ša lim-nu-ti[11] *si-bit-ti-šu-nu ma-la a-na*[12] *pa-ni-ka i-ši-ru ur-ta-šu-nu lid-din-ka*

DUG-BI DUG-GA ŠUG(?)GA DIKUD-MAḪ AN-NA
· *ša ḳi-bit*[13] *pi-i-šu ma-ag-ra-tu*[14] *da-a-a-nu ṣi-i-ru*[15] *ša*[16] [ilu] *A-nim*

DINGIR-BIL-GI DINGIR-ASARU BA-AN-NA-TE I-BI BA-AN-NA-AB-BI
[ilu] „ *a-na*[17] [ilu] *Marduk iṭ-ḫi-e-ma a-mat*[7] *šu-a-ti*[8] *iḳ-bi-iš*

(Plate XLV.)

GIŠ-LAL KI-NAD-DA-NA GIG-A-BI-KU[18] I-BI GIŠ-NE-IN-TUK-A
ina kul-ti ma-a-a-al mu-ši a-mat šu-a-ti iš-mi-e-ma

"And on the Mountain of Dawn they cry;[a]
"Through the caverns of the earth they creep,
"(And) amid the desolate places of the earth they lie.
"Nowhere are they known,
"In heaven nor earth are they discovered.
"Draw nigh, (then), unto Marduk,
"That he may explain this matter to thee,
"That he may vouchsafe unto thee an explanation
"Of the evil of these seven
"That are arrayed against thee.
"For kindly is the instruction of his mouth,
"The puissant judge of Heaven."
So the Fire God drew nigh unto Marduk,
And told him of this matter;

(PLATE XLV.)

He under the canopy[b] of his couch of night
Gave ear to this matter,

[1] K. 4,886, *me*.
[2] K. 4,886, *iṣ*.
[3] K. 4,886, *irṣitim*(*tim*).
[4] K. 5,133 omits.
[5] K. 11,543, *ṭe*.
[6] K. 11,543 omits.
[7] K. 5,133, *ma-tu*; K. 11,543, *ma-ta*.
[8] K. 5,133, *tu*.
[9] K. 11,543 inserts A.
[10] K. 5,133 and K. 11,543, SI-EŠ.
[11] K. 11,543, *tu*.
[12] K. 5,133 and K. 11,543, *ana*.
[13] K. 11,543, [*b*]*i-it*.
[14] K. 5,133 and K. 11,543, *rat* for *ra-tu*.
[15] K. 5,133, *ri* for *i-ru*.
[16] K. 5,133 omits.
[17] K. 5,133 omits *a-na*.
[18] K. 5,133, TA.

[a] *Immallilu*: Syr. *mallel*, "utter a sound, speak."

[b] *Kulti*, the Chaldee *kiltha* (Levy, *Chald. Wörterb.*, p. 364, *a*), a canopy or bedchamber. This word was apparently recognized by Sayce (Hibbert Lectures, p. 470), who translates it thus.

A - A - NI DINGIR - EN - KI - RA E - A BA - ŠI - IN - TU
GU - MU - UN - NA - AN - DE - E
a-na a-bi-šu *ilu* *E-a a-na bîti i-ru-um-ma i-ša-as-si*

. . . : A-A-MU DINGIR-BIL-GI DINGIR-BABBAR-E-TA
GUL-GA DUG-BI MU-UN-NA-AB-BI
a-bi *ilu* *Gibil a-na ṣi-it* *ilu* *Šamši(ši) is-nik-ma*
pu-uz-rat-si-na iṭ-ṭi-ḫa-a

VII - BI A - DU BA - AN - ZU KI - BI IN - ḲI - ḲI - GA
SAG - NA - AN - GI - U - MU - UN - NA - AN - SUM
al-ka-ka-a[1] *-ti si-bit-ti-šu-nu la-ma-du aš-ra-ti-šu-nu*
ši-te-'-a ḫi-šam-ma

DINGIR (?) - BUR - SIL - SA - A DU NUN - KI - GA - GE
rap - ša uz - ni[2] *mar* [3]*E - ri - [di]*
DINGIR-EN-KI DU-NA DINGIR-SILIG-MULU-ŠAR
MU-UN-NA-NI-IB-GE-GE
ilu *E - a ma - ra - šu*[4] *ilu* *Marduk ip - pal*

DU - MU *VII* - BI KUR - TA DUR - RU - NA - MEŠ
ma[5] *- ri si - bit - ti - šu - nu ina ir - ṣi - ti*[6] *aš - bu*
VII-BI KUR-TA : *si-bit-ti-šu-nu iš*[7] *- tu irṣitim(tim)*
u[8] *- ṣu - ni* : E - A[1] - MEŠ
VII - BI KUR - TA BA - U - TU - UD - DA - A[1] - MEŠ
si - bit - ti - šu - nu ina ir - ṣi - ti[9] *' - al - du*
. *VII* - BI KUR - TA BA - GUL - GA[10] - A - MEŠ
si - bit - ti - šu - nu ina ir - ṣi - ti[11] *ir - bu - u*

DA-DA E[12] - * ṬUR-RA-GE UMUN-E BA-AN-NA-TE-EŠ
i-da-at ap-si-i a-na ka-ba-su[13] *iṭ-ḫu-u*[1]*-ni*
GIN-NA DU-MU : *a-lik ma*[14] *-ri* *ilu* *Marduk* : DINGIR-
SILIK-MULU-ŠAR

And entered the house,
And spake unto his father Ea :
"O my father, the Fire God hath arrived at the Place of Dawn,
"And hath penetrated its secrets ;
"Speed thee to learn the ways of those seven,
"(And) to seek out their places."
Then the sage son of Eridu, Ea,
Gave answer to his son Marduk :
"O my son, those seven dwell in the earth,
"Those seven have come forth from the earth ;
"Those seven in the earth were born,
"Those seven in the earth were reared ;
"They have come nigh to tread the Bounds of Ocean.
"Go, O my son Marduk,

---

[1] K. 5,133 omits.
[2] K. 4,905, *nu*.
[3] K. 4,905 and K. 5,133, [alu] [*Eridi*].
[4] K. 4,905, *mâri-šu*.
[5] K. 4,905 inserts *a*.
[6] K. 4,905 and K. 5,133, *irṣitim*(*tim*).
[7] K. 4,905, *ul*.
[8] K. 4,905 and K. 5,133, *it-ta*.
[9] K. 4,905, *irṣitim*(*tim*).
[10] K. 4,905 and K. 5,133, KUR-KUR-GA for GUL-GA.
[11] K. 4,905, *irṣitim*(*tim*); K. 12,000, BB, *irṣitim*[*tim*].
[12] K. 4,905 and K. 12,000, BB omit.
[13] K. 4,905 and K. 5,133, *si*.
[14] K. 4,905 inserts *a*.

GIŠ-MA-NU GIŠ-ḪUL-DUB-BA UTUG-E-NE-GE

e-ri[1] *isu ḫul-dup-pu-u*[2] *ša ra-bi-ṣi*

ŠA-BI DINGIR-EN-KI-GE MU PA-DA

ša ina lib-bi-šu ilu E-a šu-mu zak-ru

INIM-INIM-MA TU-MAḪ NUN-KI-GA NA-RI-GA[3]

ina šip-ti ṣir-ti ši-pat E-ri-du[4] *ša te-lil-ti*

UR-PA-BI BIL U-NE-TAG MULU-TUR-RA *VII*-BI IM-TE-MAL-E-NE-GE[5]

ap-pa u iš-di[6] *i-ša-a-ti*[7] *lu-pu-ut-ma ana marṣi*[8] *si-bit-ti-šu-nu a-a iṭ-hu-u*

SA-PAR-DAGAL-LA KI-DAGAL-LA NA-A U-ME-NI-ŠUB[9]

ki-ma[10] *sa-pa-ri rap-ši ina aš-ri rap-ši šu-ni-'*[11]*-il i-di-ma*

AN-BIL U-GIG-BI SAG-GA-NA ḪE-EN-GUB-BA

ina ka-ra-ri-e mu-ši[12] *u ur-ra ina ri-ši-šu lu-u*[13] *-ka-a-a-an*

GIG-A SILA E-SIR-RA U-NI-E-NE[14]-GE ŠU-NA[15] ḪE-EN-DA-AN[16]-GAL

mu-ši[12] *su-u*[17]*-ḳu su-la-a u na-ma-ri*[18] *ina ḳa-ti-šu lu-u-na-ši*

GIG-BAR-A-AN U-DI-DUG-GA-GE[19] KI-NA SAG MULU-GIŠGAL-LU PAP-ḪAL-LA-GE ḪE-EN-GUB-BU-UŠ[20]

ina mu-ši ma-šal[21] *ina šit-ti ṭa-ab-ti ina ma-a-a-lu*[22] *ina ri-eš a-me-lu*[23] *mut-tal-li-ka*[24] *lu-u*[25]*-ka-a-a-an*

"A tamarisk *ḫulduppû* of a fiend
"Whereon is inscribed the name of Ea,
"With the all-powerful incantation,
"The Incantation of Eridu of Purification,
"Set it alight both in front and behind,
"That these seven may not draw nigh unto the sick man.
"As a wide net spread in a wide place set it,
"And smouldering[a] by night and day
"At his head let it stand.
"By night (it is) a highway, a path,
"And at dawn let him hold it in his hand.
"At midnight in a gentle sleep in bed
"At the head of the wanderer let it stand."

---

[1] K. 4,905, *ra*.
[2] K. 4,905 ,, -*a*; K. 4,626 ,, -*e*.
[3] K. 4,626 . . . GA-A-AN.
[4] K. 4,626, ^{alu}[*Eridu*].
[5] K. 4,626, NU-TE-MAL-DA-GE.
[6] K. 4,905, *ap-pu u il-du*.
[7] K. 4,905, *tu* for *a-ti*.
[8] K. 4,626, *mar-ṣi*.
[9] K. 4,626, NE-IN-ŠUB for ME-NI-ŠUB.
[10] K. 4,905, *kima*.
[11] K. 12,000, BB omits '.
[12] K. 4,905, *šu*.
[13] K. 4,905, K. 4,626, and K. 5,133 omit.
[14] K. 4,905, LI-DI; K. 4,626, [L]I-DA for E-NE.
[15] K. 4,905 and K. 4,626, BI.
[16] K. 4,626, K. 5,133, and K. 12,000, BB omit.
[17] K. 4,905 omits.
[18] K. 4,905 and K. 4,626, *ru*.
[19] K. 4,905, BI.
[20] K. 4,905, BA-NI-IN-GAR-RI-EŠ.
[21] K. 4,905, *aš-li*.
[22] K. 4,905 and K. 4,626, *li*.
[23] K. 4,626 and K. 4,905, *amelu*.
[24] K. 4,626 and K. 4,905, *ki*.
[25] K. 4,626 and K. 5,133 omit.

[a] Literally "on fire."

(Plate XLVI.)

UR - SAG KU - LI - E - NE[1] KIN - GA - A - MEŠ
ḳar - ra - du a - na ib - ri - šu i - šap - par

DINGIR-BIL-GI MAŠKIM-BI-KU ḪA-BA-RA-AN-GUB-BA
ilu „ a - na[2] ra - bi - ṣu - ti - šu li - iz - ziz

ḪUL - IK *VII* - BI ḪE - IB - TA - AN - ZI - ZI SU - BI ḪE-IB-TA-SIR-RI-EŠ
lim-nu-ti si-bit-ti-šu li-is-suḫ-ma ina zumri-šu liṭ-ru-ud

U - ŠA - DUG - GA UTUG GIŠ - BAR - RA
ûmu(mu) da - ' - i - ku ra - bi - ṣi la kak - ku

DINGIR-BIL-GI ID-DAN MAḪ GABA-BI ḪE-EN-GE-GE
ilu „ e-mu-ḳan ṣi-i (?)-[*ir*]-*ti i-rat-su li-tır*

DINGIR-NIN-KI-GAL DAM DINGIR-NIN-[A-ZU]-GE IGI-BI KI KUR-KU ḪA-BA-RA-AN-GA-GA
ilu „ al-ti ilu „ pa-ni-[*ša a-na aš*]*-ri ša-nam-ma liš-kun*

SAG-GIG ŠA-GIG U-ŠU[ŠUB . . . .]-LU ŠEḌ-DE
ṭi-' šu-ru-ub-bu-u [*ḫar-ba-šu* . . .]*-ti ku-uṣ-ṣu*

DINGIR-NIN-A-ḪA-KUD-DU SU-BI ḪA-BA-AN-ZI-ZI SAG-BI ḪA-BA-AN-GUB-BA
ilu „ ina zumri-šu li-is-suḫ-ma ina ri-šu-šu lu-u-ka-a-a-an

TU - DUG - GA DINGIR - NIN - A - ḪA - KUD - DU - GE
ina „ - e[3] *ša ilu „*

NAM - ŠUB NUN - KI - GA - GE
ina šip - ti ša E - ri - du

ZU-AB NUN-KI-GA TU-MAḪ NA-AN-GE-GE KAN-PA
ina [*ši*]*-pat ap-si-i u E-ri-du ṣir-ti*[4] *la tar-šu* (?) *liḳ-ḳa-bi*

(PLATE XLVI.)

The hero sent unto his comrade,
"Let the Fire God stand up against his demons,
"That he may remove the evil of those seven, and drive them forth from his body,
"(For) a fiend unarmed (?) is a raging tempest.
"May the Fire God, supreme of power, turn it back;
"May Ereshkigal, the wife of Ninazu, turn her face elsewhere.
"Headache, shivering, heartache, ? . . . , cold,
"May Nin-akha-kuddu remove them from his body,
"And stand continually at the sick man's head.
"With the spell of Nin-aḫa-kuddu,
"And the Incantation of Eridu,
"With the Incantation of the Ocean Deep and Eridu
"Mighty (and) unconquerable let it be uttered;

---

1 K. 4,626 and 4,905, NA for E-NE.

2 K. 4,626 and 4,905, GIŠ-BAR *ana* for ,, *a-na*.

3 K. 5,120, TU *du ki* . . . for ,,-*e*.

4 K. 5,120, *šip-ti ṣir-tim ša ap-si-i u* ^{alu}[*Eridi*].

DINGIR-PA-SAG-GA LIGIR-GAL MAŠKIM-MAḪ DINGIR-RI-E-NE-GE SAG-GA-NA GUB-BA GIG EN-NUN-MU-ḪE-A [1]

[ilu] I-šum na-gir [2] ra-bu-u ra-bi-ṣi ṣi-i-ri ša ilâni [pl] ina ri-ši-šu li-iz-zi-iz [3] -ma ina mu-ši lu-u-na-ṣir-šu

GIG-UD-DA AN-BABBAR-RA ŠU-* ŠIG-GA ḪA-BA-RA-AN-GA-GA

mu-ši [4] u [5] ur-ra a-na [6] ḳatâ [II] [ilu] Šamši dam-ḳa-a-ti lu-pa-ḳid TU EN

[7] ———————————————

EN NUN-KI GIŠ-KIN-GIG-E [8] KI-EL-TA SIR-A

ina E-ri-du [9] kiš-ka-nu-u ṣal-mu ir-bi ina aš-ri [10] el-lu ib-ba-ni

SUḪ - ME - BI ṢI - ZAGIN - A ZU - AB - TA [11] LAL - E

zi-mu-šu uk-nu-u ib-bi ša a-na ap-si-i tar-ṣu

DINGIR-KI-GE [12] GIN-GIN-A-TA NUN-KI-GA ḪE-GAL * SIG-GA-A-AN [13]

ša [ilu] E-a [14] tal-lak-ta-šu ina E-ri-du [15] ḫegalli ma-la-a-ti

---

[1] K. 5,120, ḪE-EN-GUB-BA after NA.

[2] K. 5,120, *gi-ru*.

[3] K. 5,120, *ziz* for *zi-iz*.

[4] K. 5,120, *šu*.

[5] K. 5,120 omits.

[6] K. 5,120, *ana*.

[7] This line is replaced by INIM-INIM-MA GIŠ-MA-NU SAG . . . on K. 5,120.

[8] 55,479, E-A.

[9] K. 5,120 and 55,479, *[alu] Eridu*.

[10] 55,608 . . . *ba a-šar* for *ina aš-ri*.

[11] 55,608 inserts NI.

[12] 55,479 inserts KI.

[13] 55,608 . . . SU-SU-GA-A.

[14] 55,479, NAḲBU.

[15] 55,479, *[alu] [Eridu]*.

[a] *Kiškanû.* From the description of the *kiškanû ṣalmu* in these lines it may be inferred that it grew wild (it "springeth forth in a place undefiled"), it was of thick or dense growth ("bountiful in luxuriance," "like a forest grove"), its locality was the river bank ("where earth is, there is its place, and the Couch of the Goddess Id (the River Goddess) its home"). It occurs in the grammatical lists

"May Ishum, the great overseer,
"The potent sprite of the Gods,
"Stand at his head and guard him through the night.
"Unto the kindly hands of Shamash
"Night and day may he commend him."
Exorcism, incantation.

Incantation :—
In Eridu groweth the dark *kiškanû* [a]
That springeth forth in a place undefiled,
Whereof the brilliance is shining lapis
Which reacheth unto Ocean ;
From Ea its way in Eridu
Is bountiful in luxuriance,

(*W.A.I.*, ii, 45, 4, l. 52 ff.), where three kinds are mentioned, *piṣû* ("white"), *ṣalmi* ("dark"), and *sâmi* ("brown" ?), and a few lines below several kinds of vine are explained. The determinative in Sumerian is GIŠ, "wood," and not U, "plant," or SAR (postpositive), and it does not occur in the plant lists still extant (see *Cun. Texts*, part xiv), or in the list of vegetables, etc., in Merodach Baladan's Garden (ibid., pl. 50) ; and since three varieties are known (white, blue (?), and brown), *kiškanû* must therefore be the name of several species of tree or shrub bearing different coloured flowers, berries, or fruit. From the first line of this incantation we know that it grew in Eridu (i.e. Southern Babylonia). Everything points to its being a real shrub or tree and not a mythical one, and Mr. H. H. W. Pearson, of the Royal Gardens at Kew, has kindly suggested to me that the *astragalus*, of which there are more than thirty varieties (v. also Mr. Pearson's article on Palestinian Flora in Encyclopædia Biblica, under Palestine), agrees with the description given above. On the possibility of its being one of the tragacanth-bearing varieties, and the various explanations of this text, see Introduction.

KI - TUŠ - A - NA KI - ŠI - KUR - A - AN
šu - bat - su a - šar ir - ṣi - tim ma
KI - NA - A ? DINGIR - ID - A - AN
ki-iṣ-ṣu-šu ma-a-a-lu[1] *ša* *ilu* „
E-AZAG-GA-A-NI-TA GIŠ-TIR GIŠ-MI LAL-E ŠA-BI
MULU NU-M̃U-UN-DU-TU-TU-NE
[i]-na[2] *bîti el-lu ša ki-ma kiš-ti*[3] *ṣil-la-šu*
tar-ṣu ana lib-bi-šu man-ma la ir-ru-bu
ŠA DINGIR - BABBAR [DINGIR] - DAGAL - GAL - BUR - AN - NA - GE
ina ki - ri - bi - šu *ilu Šamšu* *ilu Dumu - zi*

(Plate XLVII.)

RI - BA - AN - NA ID KA - *II* - A - TA
ina bi - rit[4] *pi - i na - ra - [a - ti] ki - lal - la - an*
DINGIR-KA-ḪE-GAL DINGIR-IGI-DU-GAL DINGIR . . . .
GIŠ-KIN-BI ŠU-IM-MA-AN-ḪU MUḪ-[MULU] . . . . .
ilu „ *ilu* „ *ilu* „ *ša* *alu Eridi kiš-ka-nu-u šu-[a-tu*
iš-bu-šu-ma eli ameli]
ši-pat ap-si-i id-[du-u] . . .
SAG MULU - GIŠGAL - LU - PAP - ḪAL - LA - GE
BA - NI - IN - GAR - [RA]
ina ri - eš ameli mut - tal - li - ku iš - ku - [nu]
MULU-GIŠGAL-LU DU DINGIR-RA-NA UTUG-*ŠIG-GA
ALAD-*ŠIG-GA ḪE-EN-LAḪ-LAḪ-[GI-EŠ]
ša ameli mar ili-šu še-id dum-ḳi la-mas-si
du-un-ḳu[5] *i-da-a-šu lu-ka-a-[a]-an*
. . . LAL - GE ŠU[6] - DIB - BA IGI - BI ŠA - BI
NU - MU[7] - UN - TAR - RA
. . . *-lu (?)-ti-i ṣa-bit ḳa-ti ša pa-ni-šu a-na*
kir-bi[8] *-šu la šum-mu*

Where earth is, there is its place,
And the Couch of the Goddess Id its home.
In an undefiled dwelling like a forest grove
Its shade spreadeth abroad, and none may enter in.
In its depths (are) Shamash and Tammuz.

(Plate XLVII.)

At the confluence of two [a] streams
The gods Ka-Hegal, Shi-Dugal, (and) . . . of Eridu
[Have gathered] this *kiškanû*, [and over the man]
Have performed the Incantation of the Deep,
(And) at the head of the wanderer have set (it).
That a kindly Guardian, a kindly Spirit
May stand at the side of the man, the son of his god.
The . . . which seizeth on the hand
Of him whose face hath not been turned towards it

---

[1] 55,479, *-al-tum* (?).
[2] 55,479, *ina*.
[3] 55,479, *tum*.
[4] K. 5,183, *ri-ta*.
[5] K. 5,183, *dum-ḳi*.
[6] Thus, and not BA as in the text.
[7] K. 5,183 omits.
[8] K 5,183, *ana ki-rib*.

[a] Literally "between the mouths of two (or both) streams." On the meaning of *šabâšu*, see Introduction.

. . . LAL - E GIR - BI[1] ḪA - BA - AN - KUD

. . . *it - te - ni - ' - lu - u še - ip - šu li - ip - ru - us*

. . . . . . ḪUL BAR - KU ḪE - IM - TA - GUB

. . . . . . *-ḫa* (?) *li-mut-ti ina a-ḫa-a-ti li-iz-ziz*

. . . . . AN-NA KA (?) LUGAL-LA-GE GIR-A-AN ḪU-MU-UN-DA-AN-GUB

. . . *-e* (?)*-ri* (?) *ša pi šar-ri ina ur-ḫu lik-liš*

[NIN - GAL] ZU AZAG DINGIR - NINNI - GE E - A ḪU - MU[2] - DA - AN - KUD

[be-el]-ti rabî-ti mu-du-ti el-lit[3] *ilu Iš-tar ina bîti lip-ru-us-su*

[4] [UTUG-ḪUL] A-LA-ḪUL GIDIM-ḪUL MULLA-ḪUL DINGIR-ḪUL MAŠKIM-ḪUL

[5] ZI [AN] - NA KAN - PA ZI KI - A KAN - PA

MULU - GIŠGAL - [LU] *a - me - lu mar ili - šu* : DU DINGIR - RA - NA

UTUG-ḪUL DIB-BA-A-NI BAR-KU ḪE-IM-TA-GUB

u-tuk-ku lim-nu ka-mu-šu ina a-ḫa-a-ti li-iz-ziz

UTUG - [* ŠIG] - GA SAG - GA - NA ḪE - EN - GUB - BA

[še - e - du da]m - ḳu ina ri - ši - šu li - iz - ziz

ALAD - [* ŠIG - GA ID - BI] ḪU - MU - UN - DA - AN - GUB

la-mas-[si dam-ḳu i-d]a-a-šu lu-u-ka-a-a-an

DINGIR - RA . . . . ḪE - EN - GUB - BA[6]

ilu . . . . *li - iz - ziz*

DINGIR - EN - [KI - GA ?] . . . . ḪE - I - I

ilu [E - a ?] . . . . *lit - ta - ' - id*

MULU - [GIŠGAL - LU - BI] . . . ME UR ḪE - I - I

[amelu šu - u] . . . . *lit - ta - ' - id*

[From where] he lieth, may it retard its foot.
May an evil . . . stand aside therefrom,
May . . . from the mouth of the king restrain it on the way.
May Ishtar, [the Lady] mighty, wise, and pure,
From the dwelling-place cut it off.
[O evil Spirit], evil Demon, evil Ghost, evil Devil, evil God, evil Fiend!
By Heaven be ye exorcised! By Earth be ye exorcised!
The man, the son of his god,
May the evil Spirit that hath seized him stand aside!
May a kindly Guardian stand at his head,
May a kindly Spirit stand continually at his side,
May . . . . stand,
Let [this man?] praise Ea (?)
Let [this man?] praise . . .

---

[1] K. 5,183, NI.

[2] K. 3,235 inserts UN.

[3] K. 3,235, *li-ti*.

[4] K. 3,235 translates (a) . . . *e-kim-mu lim-nu*, (b) . . . *ra-bi ṣu lim-nu*.

[5] K. 3,235 translates . . . *irṣitim(tim) lu-u-ta-mat*; K. 4,626 translates *niš* . . . .

[6] K. 3,235 inserts the ends of two lines, (a) . . . DA-AN-GÚB-BA, (b) . . . *-šu li-iz-ziz* after l. 225.

I [DINGIR - EN - KI - GE PA] - ḪE - E - A - GE
[*a* - *mat* *iluE* - *a*] *liš* - *te* - *pi*
[DINGIR - DAM - GAL - NUN - NA ḪE - EN] - SI - DI - E
[*iluDam* - *ki* - *na*] *liš* - *te* - *šir*
[DINGIR-SILIG-ELIM-NUN-NA DU-SAG ZU-AB-GE ŠAG-G]A TAG-TAG-BI ZA-A-KAN

(PLATE XLVIII.)

. . . . GA - GA - DA - GE

Ends of lines 238–251 :—(238) . . . SAR-TA GAR-RA, (239) . . . [*rik-sa* ?]-*a-ti šak-nu*, (240) . . . GIŠ-BANŠUR-GE, (241) . . . *pa-aš-šu-ri*, (242) . . . NAM-LUGAL-LA-GE, (243) . . . -*mat šar-ru-ti*, (244) . . ZI (?) UR-SAG-GA-GE, (245) . . . *ḳar-da-a-ti*, (246) . . . GUB-BA, (247) . . . *iz za-az*, (248) . . . UŠ-SA, (249) . . . *en-da*, (250) . . . NA-GE, (251) . . . -*te*.

[Hiatus of about nine lines.]

. . . . *kiš*
. . . . SAG - GA - NA BA - NI - IN - GAR
. . . . *ša* *iluA-nim* *ina* *ri-ši-šu* *iš-ku-un-ma*
[UTUG-*ŠIG-GA] ALAD-*ŠIG-GA DINGIR-SAG-GAG-GA-GIM [SAG]-GA-NA ḪE-EN-LAḪ-LAḪ-GI-EŠ
„ „ *kima ili ba-ni-šu ina ri-ši-šu lu-u-ka-a-a-an*
SAG GAR-*ŠIG-GA-A-NI ḪE-EN-TUK-TUK-E-NE
ri - is - su ana da - me - iḳ - ti li - kil - lu
UṬUG-ḪUL A-LA-ḪUL GIDIM-ḪUL MULLA-ḪUL DINGIR-ḪUL MAŠKIM-ḪUL
DINGIR-RAB-KAN-ME DINGIR-RAB-KAN-ME-A DINGIR-RAB-KAN-ME-KIL

May [the word of Ea] make clear!
May [Damkina] direct aright!
[O Marduk, eldest son of the Ocean Deep!]
Thine is the power [to brighten] and bless.[a]

(PLATE XLVIII.)

[Incantation] . . . .

[Ends of ll. 238–251 remaining.]

[Hiatus of about five lines.]

He hath put the [potent meteorite?] of heaven at his head,
That a kindly Spirit (and) a kindly Guardian,
Like the God that created him,
May stand at his head continually,
To exalt his head to favour,
Whether it be an evil Spirit or an evil Demon,
Or an evil Ghost or an evil Devil,
Or an evil God or an evil Fiend,
Or a Hag-demon,
Or a Ghoul,

---

[a] These lines are restored from *Cun. Texts*, part xvii, pl. i, ll. 30 ff., and pl. 26, ll. 80 ff.

MULU-LIL-LA KI-EL-LIL-LA KI-EL-UD-DA KAR-RA
UḪ (?)-ḪUL UḪ (?)-ZU UḪ (?)-RI-A GAR-ŠA-A GAR-ḪUL-GIM-MA
BAR - KU ḪE - IM - TA - GUB
UTUG-*ŠIG-GA [ALAD]-*ŠIG-GA ḪE-EN-DA-LAḪ-LAḪ-GI-EŠ

INIM-INIM-MA . . . MULU-TUR-RA IN . . .
GIŠ-KIR . . . .

EN . . . .
. . KU SAL - *ŠIG - GA BUR - ŠU - MA - TA . . .
[ID]-ZI-DA-KU MU-UN-KEŠDA ID-KAB-BU . . .
. . . *sin-niš-tu da-me-iḳ-tu pur-šu-[um-tu]* . . .
. . . *- tu ru - ' - tu ša* ^{ilu}*Iš - tar [ana im - ni]*
[li - ir - ku - u]s - ma ana šu - me - li . . . . . .
. . . . BI ID - ŠU - GIR - BI U - ME - [NI - KEŠDA]
[NAM - ŠUB] NUN - KI - GA U - ME - [NI - SUM]
. . . . BI - A U - ME - [NI] . . .

(PLATE XLIX.)

. . . . *- tu me - e* . . . .
[GAR - NA GI] - BIL - LA . . . .
. . . . . [GI] - BIL - LA . . . .

[Small hiatus.]

. . . .

. . . . UTUG - ḪUL SIG (?) . . . .
. . . . . . ZU MULU - TUR - RA ID . . . . . .

. . . . GIG - GA KI - A . . . .
. . . *-ru-ru-tu mur - ṣa ana ma-a-ti id-ku* . .

Or a Robber-sprite,
Or a Phantom of Night,
Or a Wraith of Night,
Or the Handmaid of the Phantom,
Or evil spell, witchcraft, sorcery,
Enchantment or any evil,
May it stand aside!
May a kindly Spirit (and) a kindly Guardian
Be present.

Incantation . . . . the sick man . . .
. . . .

Incantation . . . .
. . . .
Let a woman pure and aged
Bind on his right the . . . spittle of Ishtar,
And on his left . . . . .
[Of that man] do thou [bind] his limbs,
[Perform the Incantation] of Eridu,
. . . . . water . . . . . .

(PLATE XLIX.)

[Bring unto him a censer] and a torch,
. . . a censer . . . .

[Small hiatus.]

[Incantation]:—
. . . [casteth ?] disease upon the land,

. . . . [G]I - NA NAM - MULU - GIŠGAL - LU - GE
. . . . *ša a - me - lu - ti*
. . . . . GIG-GA MULU-RA MU-UN-NA-AN-GAR
. . . . *i̥ - ša - ti i - ḫa - am - ma - ṭu*
. . . . *it - taš - kin*
. . . . E SAG - GA - NA GUB - BA
. . . . . . [*ina ri - ši*] *ameli ka - a̩ - a - nu*
. . . . [SAG] - GA - NA GUB - BA
. . . . . . *ša ina ri - eš ameli iz - za - zu*
. . . DINGIR-BABBAR-GE UḪ (?) MULU-RA SU-SU
[*ša*] *ilu Sin u ilu Šamši im-tum amelu iṣ-ṣa-an*
[DINGIR]-DINGIR-NINNI-GE UḪ (?) MULU-RA SU-SU
ša ilu Iš - tar im - tum amelu iṣ - ṣa - an
UTUG DINGIR-RAB-KAN-ME UḪ (?) MULU-RA SU-SU
ša še - e - di u la - bar - ti im - tum iṣ - ṣa - an
DINGIR-NIN-A-ZU LUGAL GIŠ-KU-GE UḪ (?) MULU-RA SU-SU
ša ilu „ *šar kak-ki im-tum amelu iṣ-ṣa-an*
DINGIR-LUGAL DINGIR SILA-A-* SIG-GA-GE UḪ (?) MULU-RA-SU-SU
ša ilu „ *il su-ḳi ša-ḳu-um-me im-tum amelu iṣ-*[*ṣa-an*]
DINGIR-PA-SAG-GA LIGIR GIG U NA . . . . .
[*ša ilu I*]*-šum na-gir mu-ši* . . . .

[Hiatus.]

U-ZAG-ḪI-LI-SAR . . . .
lil-lu-u . . . .
. . . . EL . . . .
. . . *el* . . . .
. . . .

. . . . of mankind,
. . . that burneth [like] fire
. . sick . . hath settled on the man,
. . . at the head of the man standeth continually,
The . . . which at the head of the man standeth,
From Sin and Shamash hath filled the man with venom,
From Ishtar hath filled the man with venom,
From Spirit and Hag-demon hath filled the man with venom,
From Ninazu, king of the sword, hath filled the man with venom,
From Sharru, the god of foul streets, hath filled the man with venom,
From Ishum, overseer of night . . [hath filled the man with venom].
. . . .